The Language of the
English Street Sign

Full details of all our publications can be found on http://www.multilingual-matters. com, or by writing to Multilingual Matters, St Nicholas House, 31–34 High Street, Bristol BS1 2AW, UK.

The Language of the English Street Sign

Vivian Cook

MULTILINGUAL MATTERS
Bristol • Jackson

DOI https://doi.org/10.21832/COOK4563
Library of Congress Cataloging in Publication Data
A catalog record for this book is available from the Library of Congress.
Names: Cook, Vivian, author.
Title: The Language of the English Street Sign/Vivian Cook.
Description: Bristol; Blue Ridge Summit: Multilingual Matters, [2022] | Includes bibliographical
    references and index. | Summary: "This book opens readers' eyes to something they see all the
    time but take for granted: street signs. It is a portrait of the signs on modern English streets:
    what they look like, who and what they are for, how they link to English history and how they
    form part of life in multilingual England today"—Provided by publisher.
Identifiers: LCCN 2021042667 (print) | LCCN 2021042668 (ebook) | ISBN 9781800414556
    (paperback) | ISBN 9781800414563 (hardback) | ISBN 9781800414570 (pdf) | ISBN
    9781800414587 (epub)
Subjects: LCSH: Signs and signboards—Semiotics—England.
Classification: LCC GT3911.44.A2 C66 2022 (print) | LCC GT3911.44.A2 (ebook) | DDC
    302.23—dc23/eng/20211028
LC record available at https://lccn.loc.gov/2021042667
LC ebook record available at https://lccn.loc.gov/2021042668

British Library Cataloguing in Publication Data
A catalogue entry for this book is available from the British Library.

ISBN-13: 978-1-80041-456-3 (hbk)
ISBN-13: 978-1-80041-455-6 (pbk)

Multilingual Matters
UK: St Nicholas House, 31–34 High Street, Bristol BS1 2AW, UK.
USA: Ingram, Jackson, TN, USA.

Website: www.multilingual-matters.com
Twitter: Multi_Ling_Mat
Facebook: https://www.facebook.com/multilingualmatters
Blog: www.channelviewpublications.wordpress.com

The policy of Multilingual Matters/Channel View Publications is to use papers that are natural,
renewable and recyclable products, made from wood grown in sustainable forests. In the
manufacturing process of our books, and to further support our policy, preference is given to
printers that have FSC and PEFC Chain of Custody certification. The FSC and/or PEFC logos will
appear on those books where full certification has been granted to the printer concerned.

Typeset by Nova Techset Private Limited, Bengaluru and Chennai, India.

Contents

Preface

This book emerged out of the courses on the English writing system I taught at Newcastle University and I am very grateful to all the students for their ideas and lively discussion. I would like to thank Adam Trigg, Debbie Chaplin and Scott Windeatt for contributing some photos I couldn't take myself and Li Wei, Mei Lin and two anonymous reviewers for commenting on drafts. And of course I am grateful to the creators of the street signs without which this book would not exist. The music that kept me going was mostly Miles Davis, Tuba Skinny and Sidney Bechet. My constant keyboard companion, Topaz, would also like to add 'yg69kkmjkuhjjsaw\ zaza8iiwfodyujdwfodfujyUgg?gvg@fv]'.

1 Describing Street Signs

The streets of our cities, towns and villages are where people live and meet, flock to as workers, shoppers, protesters and patients, and move through as pedestrians, cyclists and drivers. They are alive with the names of restaurants, the numbers of houses, for sale signs, no parking notices, fire hydrant signs, posters, graffiti and much more. Without signs, we do not know where places are or what they are; we cannot tell how to get from one place to another; we do not know when shops are open or buses depart. This chapter describes the background and methodology for looking at street signs and introduces the issues that are developed throughout the book.

What is a street sign? One answer is 'any piece of written text within a spatially definable frame' (Backhaus, 2007: 55), that is to say, a piece of language that stands out from its physical environment in the street; another answer is 'place names and street names on officially mandated signboards' (Raos, 2018). But street signs have meaningful features that go beyond writing. The red-coloured border of a traffic sign means prohibition; the stone of an inscription shows permanence; serif capital letters suggest respectability; the location of a Wet Paint sign defines its scope. For this book, the defining aspect of street signs is that they have meaning, not that they have writing.

There are many aspects to studying street signs: their efficiency for communicating directions; their commercial power to attract customers to shops and restaurants; how their location asserts ownership; how the choice of one language rather than another reveals bilingual communities; the aesthetics of their forms; how street addressing systems serve the needs of the individual and the state; the psychological processes through which people perceive them; and much else. For example, understanding how the typeface Times New Roman contributes to a street sign involves an awareness of its origin in classical inscriptions, the conventional ways in which capital letters are used in modern street signs, its legibility in the street, and its overtones of formality and stability for present-day readers.

A country landscape is viewed quite differently by a farmer, a hiker, a geologist, an artist, a soldier or a pilot. Similarly, typographers do not see a traffic sign in the same way as psychologists, linguists get something different from a building name sign from calligraphers, and so on. This book does not restrict itself to a single approach but utilises ideas from writing system research, linguistics, typography, psychology, linguistic landscapes research and other disciplines, which have had little previous contact. It borrows selectively from these disciplines, to focus on the unique area of street signs: 'no single discipline can lay claim to the city' (Tonkiss, 2005: 2).

The book emerged from a sequence of papers on street signs from Cook (2013a) onwards, listed in the references. Partly, it is a portrait of two places, Newcastle and Colchester, seen through their signs, reflecting their current life as well as their local history. It uses historical and contemporary background information to provide a fuller picture and to humanise street signs within the context of life in England. Since many readers will not live in England, it spells out some details that may not be needed by residents.

The book does not have an invisible author. Like most linguistics books, much of it relies on the author's interpretation of signs, not on data from street users, similar to the approach to street signs by, for example, Scollon and Scollon (2003), Baines and Dixon (2002) or Gray (1960) in their different disciplines, backed by the photos of the signs themselves for the reader to check (please note that the electronic edition of this book has all the figures in full colour). The book is in a sense also participant research in that I was a full-time or part-time resident of both areas for many years and so a user of many of these signs and of the cafés, dentists and shops they identify, as, say, was Jan Blommaert a resident in the part of Antwerp he described (Blommaert, 2013).

The Framework of Streets

The reasons for having cities and towns change over time and vary in different parts of the world. In England, many cities are post-industrial in that industry is no longer their main rationale, having moved out or become smaller units. Their centres are chiefly non-residential with comparatively few people actually living there – the area called the City of London at the core of London, for example, has only 8000 residents (City of London, 2021). Many English cities are now primarily attractors that suck in people to visit for leisure, eating out and shopping, to commute to for work or to utilise centralised services such as hospitals and courts, being only secondarily places to live (Kotkin, 2016) – 513,000 people work in the City (City of London, 2021). The street is a meeting point where different cultures interact daily, through globalisation and immigration, and through gentrification, attested by the increasing presence of art galleries, boutiques and cafés (ABC) (Zukin *et al.*, 2016).

Street signs are anchored in the physical reality of the street and serve the functions of the street users. Town planners too have to take the multiple functions of the streets into account in concrete physical terms. A practical starting point for this chapter is then official guides to street design such as *Complete Streets Design Guide* (City of Los Angeles, 2014) and *UK Manual for Streets* (Department for Transport, 2007), which enumerate the practical rationale for streets.

Streets as movement

A goal of many planners has been to make urban travel swift and unimpeded:

to ensure that the safety, accessibility, and convenience of all transportation users – pedestrians, bicyclists, transit riders, and motorists – is accommodated. (City of Los Angeles, 2014: 3)

In the mid-20th century, the movement of motor vehicles was emphasised at the cost of other street users. From Los Angeles to Newcastle upon Tyne, city centres were seen as complex movements of traffic. New cities like Brasilia were designed to ease their flow. Pedestrians and cyclists were either ignored or segregated from traffic, say in the grid road system of the 'new towns' like Milton Keynes interwoven with pedestrian and cyclist routes or in the car-free campuses of 1960s universities like Essex or Lancaster. The separation of pedestrians from vehicles has been extended vertically by skyways and tunnels in cities such as Hong Kong and Houston, where the outdoor ground-level street is often reserved for vehicle movement and for people who are socially excluded from the interior pathways (Graham, 2016).

Streets are then one means of getting people to the places where they want to be. Street signs aid this movement by telling street users where they are, where to go and where *not* to go.

Streets as social interaction

But, for planners, streets are also:

... lively gathering places that foster community building and neighborhood identity. (City of Los Angeles, 2014: 3)

To Jane Jacobs (1961), urban streets thrive on the people who live, work and visit there; they enable a bustling communal life. City streets are safe because they are watched by many eyes, they foster cooperation between their users and they develop physical skills and moral behaviour in the children who play there. Street signs contribute to the social life of visitors and residents by informing, attracting and warning, and in many other ways.

... local life on a city street is a primary platform through which people are known and come to know others; street signs promote and identify the resources for living, whether cafés, dentists or dry cleaners. (Hall, 2012: 12)

Other planned purposes of streets

The official *UK Manual for Streets* (Department for Transport, 2007) accepts that a street is 'a highway that has important public realm functions beyond the movement of traffic'. One is access: people need to get in and out of the buildings. Signs for pedestrian access include instructions on doors and markers of emergency rendezvous points. Access goes with parking, controlled by parking signs, both private or public. The design of the street is crucial in promoting the well-being of the city's inhabitants through provision of greenery, walkability and control of the height and density of its buildings (Boys Smith, 2016). But it is also how the state tracks its citizens to particular addresses for electoral, legal and taxation purposes.

Other practical uses for streets lurk beneath their surfaces or on poles above them. Beneath the streets are service conduits for sewage, electricity and gas, and for electronic signals such as telephones and broadband, for which modern streets provide a convenient thoroughfare. The provision of power lines and telephone wires above the street is now less visible in England, more common in countries where the dangers of earthquake give it some advantages. Manhole covers and hydrant signs are directed at those who provide and maintain these services; other signs warn the public of the dangers of interfering with them.

Street Space

If we imagine ourselves reading, it probably involves sitting facing a book or a laptop. The reading surface is around 18 inches from our eyes and offset at an angle from the vertical; it has a constant, even illumination. The size and layout of pages, letters and computer screens are designed for this virtually standard situation.

The reading distance for street signs, however, varies from a few inches to hundreds of yards; we look down at them beneath our feet or wheels and peer up at them on the sides of buildings, usually while we are moving about. How well we see them depends on the fickle sun or artificial lighting, what they are made of and how often they are cleaned and repainted. Street sign users have to cope flexibly with a range of factors and situations, unlike the uniformity of reading from book or screen.

As well as the two-dimensional location systems that locate street signs within the specific urban space of their area, outlined in, say, Soukup (2020), street signs research needs to place the signs systematically within the three-dimensional geometry of the street – street space. The simple model of street space presented in Figure 1.1 is based on planning manuals such as *NY Design* (2013). It is intended as a working framework rather than a rigid classification system, and may well not work for countries other than England, such as the street space of Hong Kong or Tokyo. It complements the schemes that locate street signs on maps with a general locational scheme, recognising the verticality of most street signs and the common framework for their positioning.

The street has **horizontal and vertical planes**. Horizontally, there are two main components: the roadway and the pavement, alias sidewalk in North America, footpath in Australasia. The roadway is for vehicles to move along and pedestrians to move across. Signs appear horizontally on its surface, and so are read from above, and mostly belong to local councils.

The pavement has three main horizontal zones. The **frontage zone** is closest to the buildings, used inter alia for sandwich A-boards and sitting-out areas; next comes the **movement zone** along which pedestrians, wheelchairs and prams manoeuvre; closest to the road is the **amenity zone** occupied by bollards, trees, bus shelters, poles and further sitting-out areas, defined by an outside kerb or line. The pavement is thus both for movement and for social living. Movement zones are usually owned by local authorities and so are subject to tight regulation.

Vertically, the street space consists of the fronts of buildings, walls and vertical poles. The **eye-level zone** often displays building numbers, brass plates and door instructions; the **fascia zone** shows shop names, etc.; the **high zone** contains street or building names and advertising hoardings; and the **low zone** displays service signs and warnings.

Signs on vertical poles planted in the amenity zone are typically official instructions about movement or parking.

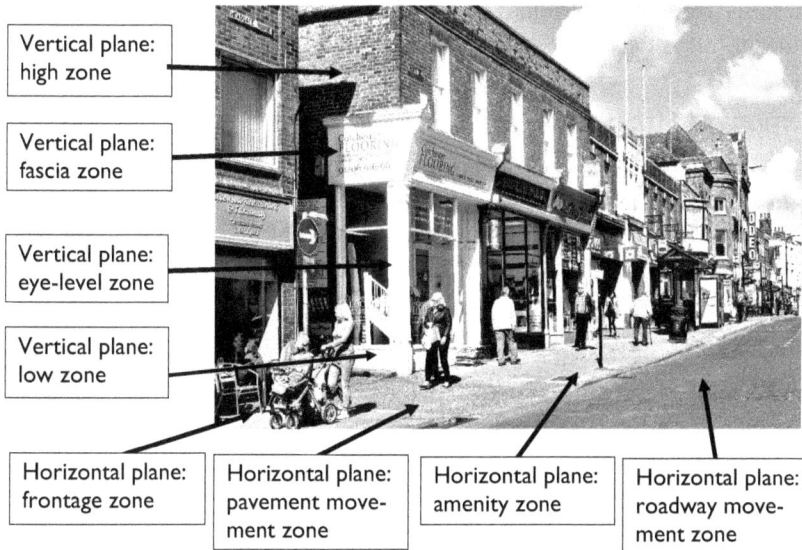

Figure 1.1 Planes and zones of street space (*Head Street,* Colchester)

Figure 1.1 applies this scheme to Head Street, a main street in Colchester. Horizontally, the roadway has painted no parking lines and lane markings. The pavement has a narrow frontage zone with café seating and movable A-boards, a movement zone with differences of surface texture, and an amenity zone cluttered with litter bins, poles and bus shelters. On narrower streets, frontage and amenity zones may barely exist; on wider streets, they may include planting and sitting areas. In Leazes Park Road (LPR) (Figure 1.9, left) the pavement movement zone is narrow; the extended frontage zone in Figure 1.9 (right) is largely given up to car parking.

Vertically, the eye-level zone in Head Street shows various notices and names; the fascia zone has assorted restaurant and shop names on fascia boards and a traditional red and white barber's pole; the high zone has the street name sign and a vertical sign for the Odeon cinema. The Stowell Street signs in Figure 1.10 are dominated by restaurant names on fascias.

Location within the street space largely determines the appropriacy of particular street signs. A painted horizontal roadway sign needs elongated, hard-wearing letters for road users and can only consist of one or two words. An A-board in the frontage zone needs a smaller scale to attract people on foot and can be covered in words. A name sign in the fascia zone needs letters that can be seen from many angles, typically from below at 15 feet or so away, projecting an individual identity for a café or a shop as strikingly as possible above the heads and umbrellas of passers-by. Building names project their respectability and permanence from vertical walls through large formal capital letters, often coloured gold or silver. Parking signs on poles convey authority through their standard colours and letter styles. The zones largely dictate which street users the signs are aimed at. Head Street also reminds us that streets are not empty; street signs do not come to life without people to use them.

The Functions of Street Signs

The overall street functions of movement and social life are broadly reflected in street signs: a high proportion directly control movement, such as traffic signs; other groups facilitate social life, like restaurant signs; still more help service workers maintain the services, like manhole covers. A more detailed account of their functions is then needed to do them better justice.

The linguistic landscapes researchers Ziegler *et al.* (2019) categorise signs as infrastructural, regulatory, commercial, transgressive and commemorative, while Dray (2010) uses Selling, Controlling, Informing and Advocating. The typographers Baines and Dixon (2002: 8) divide street signs into those that are 'signing the way' and those that are 'naming places and defining spaces', while the typographic designer Jock Kinneir (1980) lists 11 functions ranging from regulation to mystification.

These lists were taken into account in drawing up the set of functions seen in Box 1.1, expanded from Cook (2013a) by the inclusion of commemorating signs. The main variable is the functional relationship between the producers and users of the sign, whether controlling, naming, informing and selling, servicing or commemorating.

Box 1.1 Functions of street signs

- *controlling* signs control the behaviour of drivers and passers-by
- *naming* signs label buildings, streets, businesses, etc.
- *informing* and *selling* signs provide information and often try to appeal to passers-by
- *servicing* signs provide information for street service workers
- *commemorating* signs commemorate memorable people and places

Controlling signs

Controlling signs like *No pedestrians* and *One way* (Figure 1.2) control the behaviour of street users by stating regulations, giving advice and so on, and are thus mostly to do with movement. Controlling signs for directing movement and parking are painted horizontally on the roadway or pavement and suspended vertically from poles in the amenity zone as in *One way*. They prohibit or direct the movement of vehicles, or give directions to particular places. Pedestrian movements are typically controlled by eye-level notices on convenient vertical surfaces, like *No pedestrians*, particularly for crossing roads, or by direction signs on fingerposts. More details and examples are found in Chapter 6.

Figure 1.2 Controlling signs (*No pedestrians*, SS; *One way*, LPR)

Naming signs

Naming signs label the structures to which they are attached. Street name signs like *Leazes Park Road* form one variety, with signs minimally at both ends of the street in a vertical plane, sometimes on short posts in the frontage, sometimes on walls; restaurant signs at fascia level like *Great Grub* (Figure 1.3) are another familiar variety. Name signs identify buildings to provide a location for postal and emergency services and reference points for directions, useful for both movement and social life. Naming signs are discussed in Chapter 5.

Informing and selling signs

The prime purpose of many signs is to inform people about times or facilities, i.e. to contribute to their social activities, like the *Pillar box* sign in Figure 1.4, or to the buying and renting of property, like *Percy House*. These are usually in the eye-level zone or on boards in the frontage zone. Informing shades into selling, as in the display of restaurant menus as ancillary notices to the main signs. In one sense, such signs provide factual information to street users; in another they serve to attract custom – the perpetual dual face of advertising.

Figure 1.3 Naming signs (*Leazes Park Road, Great Grub,* LPR)

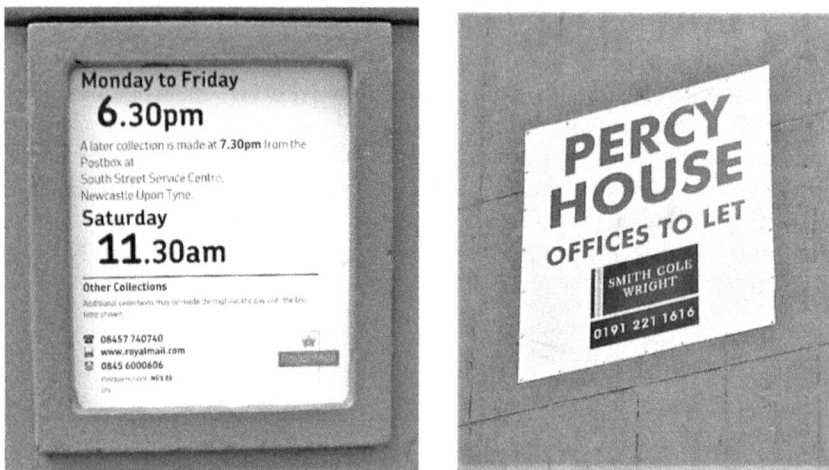

Figure 1.4 Informing and selling signs (*Pillar box,* SS; *Percy House,* LPR)

Commemorating signs

Figure 1.5 Commemorating signs (*Town Wall*, SS; *Remember*, Colchester)

Commemorating signs remind passers-by of historical sites and notable events, such as the *Town Wall* plaque and the war memorial *Remember*; they are then mostly to do with social life. They are made of enduring material, whether metal or stone, and are at eye-level or in the pavement movement zone, usually the property of councils and appropriate historical bodies. The characteristics of commemorating signs are discussed in Chapter 7.

Servicing signs

Figure 1.6 Servicing signs (*CATV*, LPR; *Hydrant*, SS)

The signs for infrastructure services inform relevant workers about access points, like the *CATV* manhole or the fire *Hydrant*. Their meaning is opaque to the average passer-by as they primarily supply information about a particular location to a select audience. They tend to be placed unobtrusively under foot or under wheel in the movement zones or low in the frontage zone. Servicing signs also include the temporary coded chalk marks made by various street inspectors showing where repairs need to be made, etc. In some ways, these signs are distinct from other street signs, partly in the specific audience they are intended for, and partly as providing practical information for the functioning of services that utilise the street.

Table 1.1 Sign functions in the Newcastle (NCL) sample

Controlling signs	20.5%
Naming signs	41.5%
Informing and selling signs	29.4%
Servicing signs	4.6%
Commemorating signs	0.9%
Unclassifiable	3.1%

These five categories broadly cover the main functions of street signs. The controlling and naming functions are different aspects of movement in that, among other features: they label space and how to travel through it; informing/selling and commemorating are aspects of the social function; and servicing is orthogonal in that it concerns the maintenance of the street itself, a kind of meta-language of the street. Other functions of street signs such as text art will be outlined briefly but will not be dealt with in depth as they extend far beyond the limits of the street.

Table 1.1 gives a rough indication of the proportion of different types of signs based on the Newcastle (NCL) sample described below. Naming, informing and controlling signs make up most street signs in this locality, and commemorating the rarest. Street signs thus have many functions, often at the same time. What is true of naming signs, say, is not necessarily true of controlling signs, whether in terms of their form, their location, their audience, the regulations that govern them, and so on. A discussion of restaurant and shop name signs like *Great Grub* (Figure 1.3), for instance, needs to take in their specific characteristics, rather than assuming they are typical of all signs.

Discourse Roles in Street Signs

Speech is usually produced by a known individual: we can identify who is speaking because we can see them as well as hear them. The written language of a newspaper or book also usually has a by-line author. The producers of signs are, however, invisible and anonymous. A street sign rarely states directly who originated it; no individual takes responsibility for movement signs like *One way* (Figure 1.2). To Augé (1995: 96), a characteristic of supermodernity is indeed 'spaces in which individuals are supposed to interact only with texts, whose proponents are not individuals but "moral entities" or institutions'.

Goffman (1963: 144) distinguished four main roles in spoken language: the *recipient* who receives the message; the *animator* who produces speech sounds; the *author* who selects what to say; and the *principal* who acts in other than a personal role, such as a judge pronouncing sentence. The roles of animator and author are distinct in actors, newsreaders and simultaneous translators conveying the words of others. For street signs, Scollon and Scollon (2003: 3) separated the person who utters from the person who views, while Spolsky (2009: 31) distinguished 'the initiator or owner of the sign, the sign-maker and the reader'.

Street signs put up by councils and governments and by other bodies or individuals often imply power and authority. With differing emphases, these have been called 'public' versus 'private' (Landry & Bourhis, 1997), 'top-down' versus 'bottom-up' (Ben-Rafael *et al.*, 2006), 'official' versus 'non-official' (Backhaus, 2007), and 'civic frame' versus 'the marketplace' (Kallen, 2010). Signs like *No Smoking* (Figure 3.2) embody official top-down control by authority, while notices like *Wet Paint* (Figure 3.10) reflect individuals informing people from the bottom up. Coupland and Garrett (2010) argue that most street signs are top-down whether addressed to citizens or consumers. It is hard to imagine a sign in which the public address the government at the top, except for the placards of demonstrators. This power dimension is absorbed here into the roles outlined below (see Box 1.2).

Roles in the production of signs

Licensor

The licensor permits a street sign to exist. In England, signs are licensed by national government regulations as interpreted by the local council. Many signs have 'deemed consent'. That is to say, they need no specific permission provided they conform to certain requirements, mostly to do with size, usually less than 0.3 of a square metre in area and 0.75 of a metre in height (DCLG, 2007: 14). Signs that do not conform need 'expressed consent', that is to say, specific approval from the local council. A sign may have to be removed if it breaks the licensing requirements without expressed consent. There is no official regulation that specifies the English language for signs in England, apart from *No Smoking* signs.

Box 1.2 Roles of makers of street signs

- the licensor, the overall controller of street signs via national and local government
- the owner, the animateur of the sign who owns the rights to the sign location
- the author, who creates the message content
- the writer, who constructs the physical message

Owner

The owner is the entity, whether an individual or an organisation, who owns where the sign appears and decides what it should be, but does not necessarily own the site itself. Signs in the horizontal plane on the roadway or the pavement are largely owned by the local council, who provide signs to control movement and who decide what can appear in the amenity and frontage zones. In Colchester, the location and number of advertising A-boards is particularly controversial, as can be gauged from the crowded pavement zone in Head Street (Figure 1.1). The owner is the animateur who decides on the content and form of the sign, subject to the supervising eye of the licensor. Graffiti and posters put up by billstickers are not necessarily unlicensed by deemed consent, although penalised in other ways.

Author

The author decides the overall form and wording of the sign on the instructions of the owner and is often the same person as the owner or may indeed be effectively a group of people. On billboards, however, the owner rents the space to others to display their posters. The owners of many poster sites are large international letting agents such as JCDecaux, while the authors are advertising copywriters.

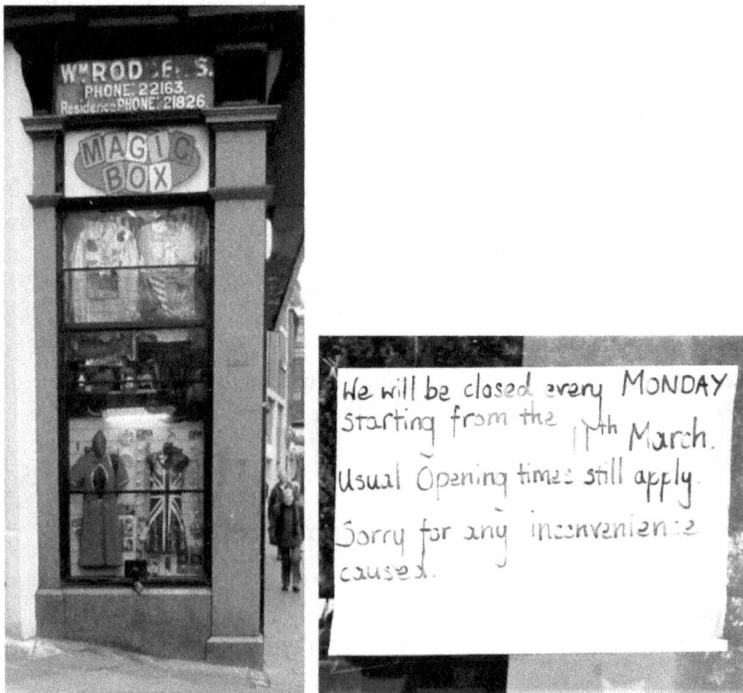

Figure 1.7 Writers (*Wm Rodgers/Magic Box*, LPR; *We will be closed*, Colchester)

Writer

Sometimes the responsibility for designing and executing the sign is handed over by the author to someone else for painting and lettering, such as the signwriter who painted *Wm Rodgers* (Figure 1.7). The profession of signwriting has had its own lettering traditions for centuries (Bartram, 1976, 1978a; Gregory, 2020; Wrights of Lymm, 2020). Below the *Wm Rodgers* sign comes a multi-coloured *Magic Box* sign, which the writer doubtless printed from a computer design. The letters of the *Town Wall* plaque (Figure 1.5) are raised in metal against a light grey background, the product of the sign maker's specialised, and expensive, skill. At the opposite extreme is *We will be closed*, handwritten with a felt-tip in clear individual letters with a line-break and right alignment highlighting <11th March> by a writer with no apparent signwriting skill other than legibility.

None of these signs is produced by an identifiable individual so much as by anonymous, genderless writers and authors on behalf of impersonal entities like businesses and local government. Few signs can be ascribed to a named person, except for graffiti and text art.

Roles of street sign users

Box 1.3 **Roles of users of street signs**

- addressed versus unaddressed users
- drivers and other people on wheels versus pedestrians on foot
- visitors versus workers versus service workers versus residents

---

People who use street signs receptively are not necessarily included in the term *reader* in the usual sense of the word. Street signs are used by those who are unable to read, whether illiterates, children or those who know another writing system: recognition may be all that is needed rather than reading skill. Signs such as the McDonald's Golden Arches or the Coca-Cola logo are recognised by children before they can read or write (Frith, 1985). The barber's pole glimpsed in Figure 1.1 and seen better in Figure 2.21 harks back to non-verbal icons in mediaeval streets when literacy was low. Many traffic signs, emergency exit signs and toilet signs utilise international conventions for image, shape and colour that do not require a knowledge of the local writing system, a potent sign of globalisation. People looking at street signs will be referred to here collectively as street sign users, to include non-readers.

Street sign users are potentially as diverse as the people on the streets (see Box 1.3). Some users are directly addressed by a sign, others unaddressed but nevertheless exposed to it – 'civil inattention' (Goffman, 1963). Passers-by pay little or no attention to signs that are not addressed to them. You do not check restaurant menus if you are not looking for somewhere to eat or pay much attention to parking signs if you are not trying to park. Servicing signs also may be minimally visible, as with the grey manhole cover *CATV* (Figure 1.6), or small but striking, as in *Hydrant* (Figure 1.6). Servicing signs cater for their own specialist service users, such as fire brigades.

Figure 1.8 Signs for drivers and pedestrians (*No Entry*, LPR; *Press to Open*, SS)

Street signs are also divided between those broadly addressed to people on wheels versus those addressed to people on foot. Controlling signs for people moving in vehicles or on cycles are seen in the *No Entry* (Figure 1.8) and *One way* (Figure 1.2) signs, whereas pedestrians are the audience for signs like *Press to Open*. Signs addressed to drivers or pedestrians differ in the distance and angle from which they are viewed; signs for people in vehicles are more like shouting in scale, signs for people on foot more like talking, or even whispering.

The *No Entry* and *One way* signs are in zones confined to traffic signs, namely the roadway movement and amenity zones, and are written in appropriate sizes and shapes for viewing from vehicles. The *No Entry* road marking uses a letter style with elongated letters designed for drivers to view from a low angle, applied in skid-proof paint. *Press to Open* is readable to those on foot in a plain modern letter style. Each sign in the street has an appropriate physical location, on which its meaning depends, and users are selected by their physical positions in relation to it.

It is useful to distinguish at least between signs for visitors, residents, workers and service workers. Visitors need to identify buildings and streets as customers, clients, patients and tourists; they are addressed by parking signs, door signs and signs that lure them into shops and pubs. The residents and workers of the street, however, need comparatively few signs; the shopkeepers, dentists and office workers seldom live in the street where they work, unlike streets of old. Users vary too by time of day (Hall, 2015); morning visitors are different from evening visitors, impacting on the signs addressed to them. Neon signs addressed to the night economy are, for instance, barely legible by day (Chapter 4).

Can these diverse street users be thought of as a community? Sociolinguistic definitions of the speech community in Patrick (2001) include: people living in an area such as Bergen (Kerswill, 1994); people united by a uniform style of speech (Bloomfield, 1926) or by a set of evaluative norms (Labov, 1966); and people who belong to a social network (Levinson, 1996). Most street users come there to visit or to work but they go home at the end of the day, leaving behind a handful of residents. English street users do not usually live in the buildings of the street, have a uniform speech style or belong to the same social network; they are not a community in any of these senses. The cosy street community found in 1960s New York (Jacobs, 1961), the interacting superdiverse communities found in the Walworth Road (Hall, 2012) or even the street life planned for Los Angeles (City of Los Angeles, 2014) do not seem typical of contemporary English streets.

Some signs do not need to be read. Businesses have to display their names near their registered office, hence the many brass plates in streets with offices, as in *McCowie & Co* (Figure 4.6). Buildings assert their legal identity by displaying their names or numbers like *Great Grub* (Figure 1.3). Community signs may be written in languages that few street users understand and none speak, like *Via Urbis Romanae* (Figure 5.3). The main purpose of such signs is to be seen to exist at particular places.

Distinctive and Non-distinctive Features of Street Signs

As seen in later chapters, street signs often show unusual letter forms and language features. But it is dangerous to assume automatically that these are unique to street signs as they are often part of broader trends in written language, not confined solely to the street. The novel spellings of signs like *Kwik-Fit* (Figure 7.14) or *Fresh Fish 4 Sale* (Figure 2.25), for example, might seem typical of street signs. Yet they reflect the same creative processes of novel spelling used in coining names for pop groups, the *Beatles*, and for drugs, *Vioxx*, and in having numbers correspond to words or syllables as in early text messaging, like *gr8 2 c u* (Cook, 2004b). English has exploited alternative sound/spelling correspondences as a source of novel spellings for centuries. The inappropriate choice of the letter < k > rather than < c > to correspond to the phoneme / k / can be traced from 19th century *Ku Klux Klan* to contemporary *Krusty the Clown*.

Street signs exploit the same potential for novel spelling that is available for much informal writing.

Street signs also vary in their degree of uniformity. Street name signs like *Leazes Park Road* (Figure 1.3) have their forms, background colours and letter styles dictated by central government. Traffic signs for movement and direction like *One way* (Figure 1.2) are governed by regulations that lay down precise requirements for their wording and visual form, as seen in Chapter 6. Commemorative blue plaques like *Town Wall* (Figure 1.5) are produced in the same format nationally. These general signs look the same wherever they are in England.

Many street signs for shop and restaurant chains are also spread across different locations and media. Some are designed by large businesses to project their identity in all their business locations and in all their documents from letterheads to webpages to TV commercials, not just on the street, including the design of corporate typefaces such as BBC Reith for all BBC platforms (Dalton Maag, 2020). The signs for *Odeon* (Figure 1.1) and *Greggs* (Figure 3.15) are carefully designed elements of most high streets in England and act as the faces of large businesses on their advertising, their carrier bags, their webpages and everything else involved with the company. The novel spellings *Häagen-Dazs*, *Quiksilver* and *Lands' End* reflect business decisions that are only partially to do with their presentation in street signs. The choice of a German name *Schuh* (Figure 8.2) for a chain of English-based shoe shops, for example, has nothing to with any German speaking visitors or residents, but all to do with the appeal of a foreign name to customers. *Kwik-Fit* (Figure 7.14) is not an inventive piece of graffiti but a cross-media sign of a large garage chain owned by a Japanese company.

In contrast, individual signs like *Great Grub* (Figure 1.3) or *We will be closed* (Figure 1.7) are specific to one location in one street. These can be idiosyncratic or conventional according to the wishes of the owner and may vary even across the signs displayed at one shop. They are the signs of the local area, produced out of traditions of signwriting, whether handwritten notices like *We will be closed* (Figure 1.7) or shop signs like *Wm Rodgers* (Figure 1.7).

So the apparent characteristics of street signs may reflect a general aspect of language or a calculated business image. It is misleading to attribute these general properties of signs to the individual choices of particular owners, writers or communities. We need to know whether a street sign is a general sign used nationally, a carefully designed cross-media sign available for many uses and at many locations, or a unique individual sign tailored for a single place.

Letter Forms and Styles

The basis for the discussion of the forms of street signs has to be typography. In the broadest sense, typography is 'the craft of endowing human language with a durable visible form' (Bringhurst, 2005: 11), which encompasses everything from the Hollywood sign to a postage stamp, as well as street signs. In a narrower sense, typography is often seen as the forms visible in printed books, newspapers, etc., i.e. texts produced by printers or printing presses of one kind or another, rather than handwritten letters or computer monitors.

Street signs, nevertheless, have different characteristics from printed texts. Their appearance is dictated by the distance at which they are read, ranging from a few feet to hundreds of yards, not the standard reading distance of printed texts, and by the materials they are made of, such as stone and neon lights, rarely the paper used in print. Nor do signs typically conform to the standard-sized pages of print, but vary in shape from tall, thin banners to circular plaques, and in size from a few inches to tens of feet.

Some of the letter forms in street signs come from the tradition of public inscriptions, others from the centuries-old tradition of signwriting. Still others hark back to the calligraphic tradition from which early typefaces borrowed. Even now, the typeface Gotham used in the Obama election campaigns was based on New York street signs (Dawson, 2013). Other aspects of street sign letters also need to be described in handwriting terms such as *cursive* and *ductus*, 'used of all aspects of the actual writing of letter forms' (Roberts, 2005: 7).

Typeface, font and letter styles

It is difficult to settle on a suitable overall term for the letter forms of street signs. A *typeface* is defined in typography as 'A set of standardised letters designed for mechanical or digital reproduction', a *font* as a 'A full set of characters of one particular typeface in one style'; typographical definitions in this book are taken from Hill (2010: 184–186). That is to say, a typeface such as Garamond seen in <We will be closed every Monday> includes fonts for italics <*We will be closed every Monday*>, capitals <WE WILL BE CLOSED EVERY MONDAY>, and so on. On personal computers, however, font has come to be the overall term; my Windows laptop tells me of the 'theme fonts' that are available, stored in a folder labelled 'fonts'.

But street signs have comparatively short texts that use only a few different letters rather than a complete typeface or font. The letters are often unique creations, not standardised, and they are produced for a single sign rather than reproduced in quantity, like the painted letters in *Wm Rodgers* (Figure 1.7). Signs seldom call on the variation of fonts within a typeface; italics are comparatively rare on street signs, for instance. Handwritten signs like *We will be closed* (Figure 1.7) probably reflect the style of script the writer learnt in school more than any typeface. Hence the terms *typeface* and *font* do not adequately cover many of the letters in signs, even if some books such as *The Field Guide to Typography* (Dawson, 2013) nonetheless heavily rely on them.

Letters for print are designed to appear together harmoniously on a page of text dense with other letters, often for hundreds of pages; street signs use short texts with only a few letters, altering their whole effect (Uebele, 2007). Large naming signs like *Odeon* (Figure 1.1) exploit three-dimensional letters and their relationship to light, of little relevance to printed letters. The demands on the letters of street signs are thus greater; while printed texts are read in fairly uniform conditions, street signs have to be readable at a variety of distances and angles under different lighting conditions.

In reading a book, the reader soon tunes in to the characteristics of a typeface (Walker, 2008) and finds changes of typeface disturbing (Sanocki, 1992). But there is little need to tune in to the typeface in a sign since the amount of reading is short – indeed it is largely recognition rather than reading, as argued in Chapter 2. A particular street sign may have neighbours with widely divergent letter forms and displays, as is evident on any street scene like Head Street (Figure 1.1).

Using *typeface* or *font* to refer to letters in a sign misleads or annoys different sets of readers. This book therefore prefers the more neutral term *letter style* from Kinneir (1980), except when talking specifically about print, as in the discussion in Chapter 7 on the connotations of typefaces.

Methodology

The focus in this book is on urban streets with plentiful signs rather than on rural or suburban roads. It restricts itself to signs displayed in the street itself rather than those inside buildings accessed from the street or inside public buildings like shopping malls. It concerns stationary signs addressed specifically to street users, whether temporary or permanent, rather than those on passing buses, T-shirts or discarded fast-food containers, and to visible signs rather than the smells of the market strikingly described in Rhys-Taylor (2013). This rules out: interior signs inside the buildings of the street, like the cafés and shops of Walworth Road (Hall, 2012); ephemera that are not restricted to streets, like banknotes (Sebba, 2010), called 'noise' by Blommaert (2013: 53); the 'portals', like stations and airports (Kallen, 2010); and the social encounters between people on the street (Scollon & Scollon, 2003). While there are arguments for extending street signs to these, the conventional view of street signs as static makes them finite rather than infinitely extendable, and so a starting point for street sign research.

The repertoire of signs visible to all street users includes bus stop signs on poles, service signs on manholes, sandwich boards, litter bins, street name signs, and many more. Any act of selection tends to overlook those that do not stand out from the background and those that are difficult to record, whether through the lighting available or the dangers of photographing manhole covers in mid-street. Further selection takes place when photos are chosen for their appearance on the printed page.

Most discussion of street signs has concentrated on a single type, say shopfront signs (Trinch & Snajdr, 2017) or those with 'non-standard language forms' (Dray, 2010), rather than the wide range visible on any street. In contrast, research like Amos (2016) has dealt with 'Every visible piece of written information'.

The aim here was to balance a small exhaustive sample of two streets in one neighbourhood against a large selected sample from many streets in different areas. A detailed sample of a small area can act as a check on selectivity; a large selected sample can confirm how widespread characteristics from particular signs may be. This permits on the one hand micro discussion of a defined area, and on the other, macro discussion of English street signs in general.

The signs in this book come from two complementary sources: one is the totality of signs in two city streets over a short period of time, called **the Newcastle (NCL) sample**; the other is a collection of signs from different towns, called **the general sample**, mainly from Newcastle and Colchester. Both are old post-industrial English cities now functioning as attractors for business and leisure. Like most English cities, they preserve much of the plan of the historic cities from which they grew: in Newcastle particularly the 19th century development areas of grand Victorian buildings; in Colchester the grid layout of the 2nd century Roman colonia built on the ashes of the town sacked by Boudica.

Inevitably, any sample of street signs is a time capsule stored at a particular moment, just as a spoken sample is time stamped with its date of recording. Restaurants change names, florists close, offices change hands, not to mention the tides of temporary signs advertising bargains, warnings of wet paint and posters for circuses; the periods of lockdown of 2020–2021 have taken their toll on businesses. The signs fossilise different eras of history in their forms and their names. Mid-19th century *Percy Terrace* (Figure 5.1), 1900s *Law Covrts* (Figure 2.23), 1930s *Dex Garage* (Figure 2.2) and 1980s *Leazes Arcade* (Figure 4.4) are reminders of particular ages and styles, some still meaningful, some now decorative or forgotten.

The convention used here is that examples of written forms are enclosed in angle brackets < >, <No pedestrians>, and spoken forms in phonetic script are within slants / /, /nəʊ pedestriːənz/; italic letters are used for citing linguistic examples, *No pedestrians*. When individual characters such as < & > or < B > would be difficult to read in angle brackets, they have been padded with spaces. A single slant is used to show a line break when necessary, for example <No / pedestrians> (Figure 1.2) and <Percy / House / offices to let> (Figure 1.4). Signs are usually referred to by labels derived from the first word or phrase of any text they contain.

The Newcastle (NCL) sample

The aim of the NCL micro sample was to collect all the signs in one city centre over a short period of time, i.e. to be non-selective within a defined area. This was originally inspired by the classic study of the Las Vegas Strip by the architects Venturi, Brown and Izenour (1972/1977) over 10 days. The NCL sample extends to all meaningful street signs rather than only those with writing, as in, say, Amos (2016).

The NCL sample was collected in Newcastle upon Tyne in the north of England, where 292,800 people live within the boundaries of the city, 25,535 having languages other than English as their main language (Newcastle City Council, 2017): the catchment area for commuters and leisure is in the region of 616,000. The spelling uses word spaces <Newcastle upon Tyne>, not hyphens – a neat example of how the writing system can be used to assert identity. Many of its inhabitants proudly speak a dialect of English called Geordie, occasionally encountered in this book, such as the words *slippy*, *stottie* and *canny*.

The NCL sample consisted of all the signs visible in two streets in the city centre during March to June of 2012, Leazes Park Road (LPR) and Stowell Street (SS), amounting to 202 for LPR and 197 for SS. These two inner-city streets consist largely of shops, restaurants, offices, pubs and clubs. While both streets have some flats above the ground floor, they are primarily non-residential. Leazes Park Road was chosen as typical of inner city streets in Newcastle in density of businesses and footfall of pedestrians.

Leazes Park Road is seen in Figure 1.9 and is about 250 yards long in a roughly north-south direction on a slight downward slope. Its eastern side is within the designated Leazes Conservation Area (Newcastle City Council, 2000), which affects its appearance; its buildings are three- or four-storey 19th century brick townhouses, some set back from the street; the remainder are various modern brick and concrete buildings up to about three storeys tall. Nos 18–26 of the properties are 'listed' as Grade II, that is to say it would be an offence to alter them without approval (Heritage England, 2019). Leazes Park Road has a single junction controlled by traffic lights (Cook, 2018).

Figure 1.9 Leazes Park Road (LPR), Newcastle upon Tyne, eastern side

Stowell Street, seen in Figure 1.10, is some 300 yards away, about 200 yards long with a roughly north-south direction, a one-way street with no road junctions. The samples from both streets are then close to the optimum sample size of about 200 metres of a two-sided street (Soukup, 2020). Stowell Street is a mixed street of restaurants, clubs, shops and a casino. It was included in the NCL sample to represent Newcastle's Chinatown, with a large Chinese ceremonial arch spanning the roadway that leads to it. The western side of the street and parts of the eastern side are conversions of early 19th century three-storey brick terrace houses and warehouses; the remainder is modern.

The general sample

A detailed study of one neighbourhood cannot, however, do full justice to the range of signs in English streets. Leazes Park Road and Stowell Street happen not to include: official buildings such as stations, churches and government offices;

commemorative signs such as war memorials, apart from some historical plaques; street uses such as pedestrian zones; or traffic control measures such as roundabouts and zebra crossings, etc., each with their own distinctive signs. Nor do they cover the wide range of materials found in signs, for example stone-cut signs, which are common elsewhere in the city centre.

Figure 1.10 Stowell Street (SS), Newcastle upon Tyne, western side

The micro NCL sample was therefore extended through the macro general sample with signs from other urban streets over a period up to the present time. The general sample includes:

- signs from the rest of Newcastle, particularly from the Leazes conservation zone that encloses Leazes Park Road (these are indicated by LPZ in the figure captions), and signs from LPR and SS photographed after the collection period;
- signs from Colchester in Essex, a garrison town 50 miles east of London with 200,000 population but 463,000 catchment area, proud of its Roman origins;
- a few signs from other parts of Essex;
- signs from Blakeney, a coastal town in Norfolk.

These amount to some 3000 in total. The sample has been checked against official regulations and previous street sign books such as Gray (1960) and Bartram (1978b) to ensure that no major type of sign has been omitted.

The samples are restricted to England as the other three countries of the UK have certain differences, for instance over bilingual signs. Wherever they are, signs need to conform to the standards set by the national government in *UK Manual For Streets* (Department for Transport, 2007), with local councils choosing how to interpret the framework, as described in Chapter 3.

The photos

Since their appearance as a whole makes up much of their meaning, the street signs themselves have to be shown rather than described. The photographs were cropped and edited to enhance visibility and legibility; when more intrusive editing was necessary, it is mentioned in the caption. Some surrounding background for the signs is included to show material and scale when relevant. A useful discussion of how to photograph street signs can be found in Schmitt (2018).

The aim here is to convey how the signs actually appear to the street user. The signs have to be taken as they are, warts and all. Gorter (2019: 50) treats this from the perspective of 'what is there to see when a reader looks at the picture in the publication? How does a reader look at the image? How can it be read?' It is doubtless important to reproduce the signs adequately in academic publications, some of which have failed lamentably. But the crucial person is the actual street user, not the academic reader: How do drivers and pedestrians see the signs? Accurate representations of street sign data in print need to start from the street user's perspective. Many signs are far from legible *in situ*, due to dirt and decay, faded paint or intrinsic lack of contrast. Many are hard to see across the range of lighting conditions in which we encounter them over night and day or storm and sun. Presenting them as glossy, brightly coloured, totally legible works of art distorts the data. While photos of signs taken under optimum conditions and visibility or with flash look impressive, signs need to be read by the street users, whatever state they are in.

Figure 1.11 Some difficult to capture signs (*Newcastle Companions*, LPR; *War Memorial*, Colchester)

An example noted by Gorter (2019: 48) is the reflections in signs shown on glass windows or polished surfaces. The reflections of the other side of Leazes Park Road on the brass plate *Newcastle Companions* (Figure 1.11) are clearer than the text, either *in situ* or in reproduction. Most brass plates display the names of registered premises of businesses for legal reasons, as discussed in Chapter 5; it does not really matter whether passers-by can read them.

Doubtless, reflections in photographs could be prevented by using a polarising lens on the camera. Reflections are, however, often part of the deliberate impact of the signs for the street user, for example the metallic letters in *Barker & Stonehouse* (Figure 7.8). Eliminating them would misrepresent how the street user actually encounters the sign. Similarly, the metal signs on war memorials like *War Memorial* (Figure 1.11) proved intractable because of the lack of contrast; their virtual unreadability for the street user has to be conveyed, not Photoshopped away.

One insoluble issue is the parallax problem involved in shooting high zone signs from below and then showing the images on the flat surface of a book, as in, for instance, the large letters of *Offices to Let* way up on a brick wall (Figure 1.4) or *Grand Theatre* (Figure 5.4) high up on the roofline. Since Ancient Greece, writers have compensated for this feature of human vision by making letters and columns taper slightly towards the bottom. Some signs appear odd on the page because the camera does not see perspective like the human eye does.

What cannot be readily captured on the page is the extent to which street signs vary in size, ranging from the two-storey high *Odeon* sign glimpsed in Figure 1.1 through the 4-foot wide street name *Leazes Park Road* (Figure 1.3) down to the 4-inch wide *Hydrant* sign (Figure 1.6). Sheer size is one aspect of a sign's meaning, conveying importance and legibility. The sizes of the images were chosen here to make them equally legible on the page rather than to be in proportion with the actual sign. It is impossible not to juxtapose signs with very different dimensions on the same page, giving a potentially misleading impression of what the signs look like *in situ*.

Conclusion

The language of the street is a rich area for research in its own right as well as having implications for the study of written language in general. The basis for the discussion of street signs is the actual data – the visual, linguistic and functional properties of the signs themselves. This book constructs a foundation for this discussion, drawing on a variety of disciplines, starting with the basic dimensions outlined in this chapter. Street signs research requires an analytical framework for the letters, language and materials from which the signs are made (Chapters 2–4), for their unique functions of naming and control (Chapters 5–6), for their overtones of meaning that go beyond the texts themselves (Chapter 7), and for the place of multiple languages in the life of the city (Chapter 8). Chapter 9 draws out some conclusions, revisiting some of the issues presented in this chapter.

The book then attempts to treat the street sign as an independent field of study. The other disciplines that it draws on have been interested in the street sign more for the use they can make of its elements for their own ends than for the street sign itself. This book starts from the signs, their location, their material, their letters and icons. Only after the properties of the signs themselves have been thoroughly described can they be used for other purposes.

Street signs have an important role in our everyday lives and we could barely manage without them. Being lost in a city where you are completely unable to decipher the signs is frightening, as any English traveller to Hungary or Japan will attest. The aim here is to raise awareness of these signs and how they function to make our lives easier, controlled and regulated by governments and businesses. The data are all around us; it is barely possible to walk or drive a few yards in any urban street without encountering them. While some are repetitive and bland, most are unique, idiosyncratic creations. They work within a set of conventions, some of which have not changed for centuries or millennia, some imposed by their very physical nature in terms of visibility and forms of construction.

Few aspects of language allow one to see interesting and novel examples as soon as one opens one's front door. This book tries to open the readers' eyes to something they see every day and take for granted – the signs of the street.

2 The Writing System of the Street

Just as research into spoken language starts from the sounds themselves, street signs research starts from their physical appearance and how they are produced. This chapter provides some tools for describing the form of street signs, drawn from writing system research, typography and lettering. It discusses on the one hand the direction in which elements flow on the sign, and on the other the visual forms of the letters. It is concerned primarily with the English writing system; systems for other languages are mentioned in Chapter 8. The next chapter deals with how these elements are used within the language system of the street.

The English Writing System

A writing system 'determines in a general way how written units connect with units of language' (Perfetti, 1999: 168). The units in sound-based systems correspond to spoken syllables as in Japanese kana, to phonemes as in English or to consonants alone as in Arabic: a written letter < b > corresponds to a spoken phoneme / b /. The units in meaning-based systems correspond to morphemes, the smallest unit of meaning: < 人 > corresponds to the morpheme 'person' in Chinese, for instance, rather than its spoken forms in Chinese. Although largely based on sound correspondences, English nevertheless has some meaning-based elements, such as < & £ = 3 > etc., which provide no clues to their spoken forms.

A writing system is a way of representing the language, not the language itself. A language may effectively have two alternative writing systems, like Serbian and Croatian, or three simultaneous writing systems, like Japanese. Historically, a language may switch writing system, as in the early 20th century change from Arabic script to the Roman alphabet for Turkish. In reverse, a single overall system may be used for many languages, like the Devanagari script used for Hindi, Gujarati and many others.

Scripts are 'the graphic form of a writing system' (Coulmas, 2003: 35); that is to say, they consist of the actual forms that are used – letters, characters, or whatever. The same script may be used in many writing systems; the Roman alphabet is used for German, Bahasa Malaysia and Turkish, inter alia, with minor variations.

Orthography, on the other hand, concerns how to use a script in a particular writing system, how the symbols spell out words, etc. Modern English, for example, has a hidden invariance principle that each word should always be spelled in the same way, unlike earlier periods of English where spellings could correspond to different accents or personal choice (Cook, 2016a). Shakespeare's contemporaries, for instance, spelled his name in at least a dozen different ways. But the modern norm allows each word only one spelling and it is considered wrong to spell it differently; before the days of spelling correctors, the editors of my first book complained that I had spelled *omelette* in three different ways, none of which was correct. Proper names are a minor exception as their owners have the privilege of claiming unique spellings such as *Caius College* /ki:z/, *Cholmondeley* /tʃʌmlɪ/ and *Psmith* (a P.G. Wodehouse character – 'the p is silent'). Owners of shops seem particularly keen to assert their right to spell their names in unusual ways.

The main features of English orthography are

- **Correspondence rules** that link letters to sounds and vice versa. That is to say, the letter < c > corresponds to the phoneme / k / in <cat> /kæt/ and the phoneme /ɒ/ to the letter < o > in <dog> /dɒg/. English is notorious for the complexity of its correspondence rules, summarised in Ryan (2016). Carney (1994), for example, describes 13 correspondence rules for the letter < g >, with /g/ *guide*, /ʤ/ *contagious*, etc., and 41 correspondence rules for the letter < o >, with /əʊ/ *goat*, /ɔ:/ *floor*, etc.
- **Lexical rules** that link particular words to their spoken forms as wholes and vice versa, like <yacht> /jɒt/, <Leicester> /lestə/ and <great> /greit/. These have to be treated as one-off 'exceptions' to the usual letter-sound correspondence rules, particularly high-frequency words like <of> /ɒv/, <says> /sez/ or <was> /wɒz/. Such direct lexical links are used for the most frequent English words like *the, where* and *for* (Seidenberg, 1992), so that reading involves constantly skipping between sound-based rules and the set of idiosyncratic words. Most common spelling mistakes involve either the wrong sound-letter correspondence or ignorance of the spelling of one-off words.
- **Orthographic regularities** that dictate where particular letters can occur within the written syllable. Alternative correspondences for some letters are limited by where they can appear. For example, < wh > can correspond to / w / at the beginning of a word, such as *what*, but not at the end, *nowh*; < k > and <ck> may both correspond to the sound / k / yet only < ck > occurs at the end of syllables as in *back* and *tick*, not at the beginning, and < k > without < c > rarely occurs at the end, apart from *trek* and *Shrek*; there are no English words *ckab* or *ckit*, although these are perfectly pronounceable as /kæb/ *cab* and /kɪt/ *kit*. People invent novel spellings in English by deliberately using alternative correspondences for particular sounds in the unpermitted position in the word, say putting < k > finally rather than <ck >, <quik >, or substituting < k > for an expected < c >, <Amerika>. Oddly, people seem to make few mistakes with these.

Linguists are by and large interested in how often *receive* or *recieve* are used by English speaking people (Cook, 2004b), not in condemning *recieve*; neither *receive* nor *recieve* is intrinsically better or worse than the other. They take rules of spelling to be neutral observations of what occurs in written English, not regulations that must be obeyed. To the educated non-linguist, however, 'i before e except after c' is a shibboleth that is broken at your peril; using the non-standard form is far worse than, say, pronouncing a word in a non-standard way.

Spelling and punctuation 'mistakes' are relevant to street signs research, not because they breach sacrosanct rules, but because they reflect the attitudes of street users. Accidental mistakes are common enough on street signs, such as *inconenience* (Figure 4.7). Shibboleth mistakes are more dangerous to the status of the author, like the greengrocer's apostrophe in *New's* (Figure 2.22). Deliberate choice of 'incorrect' or unusual spelling can confer identity, as in *The Beatles*. Alternative spellings in street signs are largely associated with brand names like *Kwik-Fit* (Figure 7.14) and appear on blackboards like *Wotz On* (Figure 7.15).

The English writing system then combines elements of several different approaches, not only letter-sound correspondence rules but also lexical one-offs and orthographic regularities. Any skilled user is employing several processes when reading even the simplest looking sign. This eclecticism has been a source of irritation or despair for many, who argue that it should be reformed into something closer to a completely sound-based system (Yule & Yasuko, 2016), usually referred to by non-linguists as a 'phonetic' writing system.

Horizontal and Vertical Direction of Writing

All writing goes in a particular direction, whether along lines from left-to-right, as in English, or from right-to-left, as in Arabic, or in columns from top-to-bottom of the page, as in some Japanese books. The standard English of printed texts is read left-to-right in lines from top-to-bottom of the page. Vertical columns are common in street signs, but are rare otherwise apart from a few book spines.

Since street signs with vertical direction are mostly in the fascia or high zones, they have to be read from a distance at an angle, demanding large letters and short unpunctuated texts. Vertical signs tend to be names, as seen in Figure 2.1. In the NCL sample, all the signs in vertical columns are restaurant names, in Stowell Street (SS) mostly in Chinese.

Figure 2.1 shows a mixture of high-level signs with horizontal and vertical direction in Northumberland Street, the main shopping street in Newcastle city centre. Some go from left-to-right in the fascia zone, like the eye-level *H&M* and *WHSmith* signs; others are vertical, like the banner style high-level *WH S* and *H&M*; and others form vertical columns in the high zone with the text rotated sideways, like *clas ohlson*.

Top-to-bottom in a column

Vertical columns in signs tend to be name signs in the high-zone.

Figure 2.1 Vertical signs on a city street (*Northumberland Street,* Newcastle)

The vertical signs in Figure 2.2 display names in sans serif capital letters. These are true vertical columns reading downward letter by letter, called 'stacked letters' (Lupton, 2004: 90).

— *Dex Garage* extends over three storeys of a semi-derelict car park in Newcastle; its raised art deco letters are 'architectural', i.e. part of the building itself.
— *Fish Shop* has painted letters on a projecting sign at high-level.

Stacked letters are invariably capitals, as the more irregular sizes and shapes of lower case letters are harder to align vertically. Stacked street signs also have single columns for readability. Vertical columns tend to have architectural and hand-painted lettering as these can be adjusted more flexibly for vertical presentation than letters not designed to be read in columns.

Top-to-bottom, letters rotated sideways

While *Dex Garage* and *Fish Shop* (Figure 2.2) are true columns to be read downward letter by letter, vertical signs can also have the text aligned at right angles to the wall, as in Figure 2.3.

Figure 2.2 Street signs in stacked vertical columns (*Dex Garage,* Newcastle; *Fish Shop,* Blakeney)

In *Barker and Stonehouse, tea sutra, Landmark* and *clas ohlson* (Figure 2.1), the tops of the letters are towards the building, but are rotated to suit the reader's angle of approach, so that *Barker and Stonehouse* and *tea sutra* are read from bottom-to-top, *Landmark* and *Cinema* from top-to-bottom. The sideways layout thus allows more than one column of text, as in *Barker and Stonehouse. Cinema* has the reverse orientation where the tops of the letters are away from the building. Since it is unlikely that street users actually turn their heads sideways to read these signs, they function more as wholes for recognition than as texts for reading. While the signs are mostly in capital letters, this is not crucial with rotated signs, as seen in *tea sutra* (Figure 2.3) and *clas ohlson* (Figure 2.1).

English streets nevertheless include a few signs with other than left-to-right writing direction. Primarily these are vertical columns in Arabic with right-to-left direction (Figure 8.4) and Chinese vertical columns (Figure 8.10). Scollon and Scollon (2003) describe more complicated systems in Chinese signs.

Mixed direction

Figure 2.4 shows signs that combine different reading directions.

Figure 2.3 Vertical signs with rotated text (*Barker and Stonehouse, tea sutra,* LPR; Landmark, SS; *Cinema,* Newcastle)

Figure 2.4 Signs with mixed directions (*Mandarin,* SS; *Lisas Coffee Shop,* LPR; *Ke Co,* Newcastle)

In the high-level *Mandarin* restaurant sign, the left-to-right <The> and the Chinese text top and tail the vertical column <MANDARIN>. In *Lisa's Coffee Shop* the two parts of the name <Lisas / COFFEE SHOP> change direction, with sideways-facing text. In both, the change in direction is accompanied by different scripts or letter styles. The restaurant sign *Ke Co* combines rotated text <Restaurant> with left-to-right <Ke Co >, in a visually disturbing way.

Other aspects of writing direction

Direction applies to other aspects of writing. English letters face in a particular direction (Treiman & Kessler, 2014): < d > is not < b > (left-right inversion), a problem for some dyslexics, and < b > is not < p > (top-bottom inversion). English books are read by turning pages from right-to-left, but some Japanese books from left-to-right. Speech balloons are read in a left-to-right sequence in English comics, from right-to-left in Japanese manga.

The concept of direction is not, however, important for street signs that consist of a word or two of text on a single line or of non-verbal icons that represent things concretely (Peirce, 1906). Many street signs are not so much read as recognised: the signs are assimilated as wholes rather than letter by letter with little need for eye movement.

Letters

While the terms *phoneme* and *feature* have proved useful for the discussion of phonetics and phonology across a wide range of linguistic approaches, there has been little agreement about the units for analysing English writing. Perhaps the most common term used by English spelling authorities is *grapheme*, defined as a synonym for letter (Venezky, 1970) and as an orthographic symbol (Albrow, 1972). The dominant view treats it as 'any minimal letter string used in correspondences' (Carney, 1994: xxvii). In English, a grapheme may consist of: one letter corresponding to one phoneme, *car* < c > /k/; two letters to one phoneme, *shirt* <sh> /ʃ/; three letters to one phoneme, *match* <tch> /tʃ/; one letter to two phonemes, *box* < x > /ks/, with problems over counting so-called 'silent' letters that engage in more complex correspondence rules, such as < e > *fine* or < u > *guest*. Many researchers produce exhaustive lists of English graphemes, Brooks (2015) having 89 in his main system, plus 195 others.

The definition in Carney (1994) in effect treats written letters in terms of spoken sounds, summed up in the OED (2015) definition of *grapheme* as 'The class of letters and other visual symbols that represent a phoneme or cluster of phonemes'. This is called by Meletis (2019) the 'referential view' in which a grapheme refers to a phoneme, which he distinguishes from the 'analogical' view in which there is a parallelism between the grapheme and the phoneme rather than a dependency.

As the spoken forms of the words are barely relevant to street signs, the most appropriate term here is *letter*, which is shared across the writing disciplines with *grapheme* used when needed for discussing sound-letter correspondences. Chapter 3 has further discussion. Meaningful elements of the street sign that go outside the letters of the alphabet, such as punctuation, numerals, characters and icons, will be dealt with as they come up.

The distinction made by linguists between spoken *phonemes* and written *letters* is at variance with everyday usage, in which speech sounds are often referred to as *letters*. Ironically this popular usage is more in tune with the traditional meaning of *letter* than its restricted use for written forms by linguists (Abercrombie, 1949).

Letters often feature in current neurolinguistic research into word recognition. The neuronal recycling model of reading, for example, claims:

> We did not invent most of our letter shapes: they lay dormant in our brains for millions of years and were merely rediscovered when our species invented writing and the alphabet. (Dehaene, 2009: 139)

This 'cortical alphabet' recycles a built-in brain capacity, demonstrated by the similarities of shape among human scripts. Given the uproar about Chomsky's proposals for the innateness of language principles, it is ironic to find that it is now written language that is claimed to be innate!

Alternatively, Changizi and Shimojo (2005) declare:

> … visual signs have been culturally selected to match the kinds of conglomeration of contours found in natural scenes because that is what we have evolved to be good at visually processing. (Changizi & Shimojo, 2005: 1160)

They believe, for example, that the configurations < L T X > that correlate with shapes found in natural scenes are prominent, not only in alphabetic and non-alphabetic writing systems, but also in non-linguistic symbols. Letters are also used to support claims that handwriting suits 'our biological architecture' (Pagliarini *et al.*, 2017, reviewed in Cook, 2017). Clearly, while several lines of psycholinguistic research are claiming that reading letters depends on built-in features of human beings, there is no consensus about what these are.

Just as speech sounds reflect the physical properties of the human articulatory apparatus and of air as a transmitting medium, so do letters reflect the physical materials of which they are made and the tools that are used to make them. The physical locations of street signs also mean that they have to be read from different angles and distances with variable lighting, unlike the fairly standard reading distance, angle and level of illumination for reading a book or a newspaper.

Many of the features of modern letters only make sense in terms of how they were once produced. Street sign letters show the effects of the brush, the chisel, the quill, the printing press and the ballpoint pen. A letter < B > displayed on a computer screen differs from the same letter inscribed on stone or written on paper in felt-tip. The material of signs is explored in Chapter 4. Stone signs, for instance, come at a high cost in material and in the skill of the stonemason; paper signs involve little expenditure or skill; in between come signs written on glass, tiles, wood, metal, plastic and other materials.

Printed texts are produced by machine in whatever numbers are needed: they are reproducible. Lettering, however, is produced by the hand of an individual, usually as a single copy. Writing produced by a brush or pen is individually done by hand and is effectively unique; signwriters pride themselves on their work being readily identifiable (Lewery, 1989). Written and drawn letters are not necessarily created in standardised forms but can be specially made for a unique occasion, as in stone monuments, hand-written letters, doctors' prescriptions and a thousand more examples. The sheer adapt-ability of computers has, however, widened the choice of print letter forms.

Variation in letter forms

Figure 2.5 Forms of < e > in street signs (taken from signs in Chapters 1–3, but edited for clarity)

Figure 2.5 shows variations in the letter < e >, taken from signs in Chapters 1–3, slightly edited to isolate them from adjacent letters; their size on the page here does not correspond to their actual size in the street. No-one has any difficulty in seeing all of these as versions of < e >, despite their many differences; any book of typefaces or cal-ligraphy will show hundreds of other variations. The CAPTCHA security system for computers indeed exploits this ability of the human eye to see the ideal prototype letter in many different disguises.

The elements of letters

The discussion of letter forms requires a minimal vocabulary of descriptive terms, mostly taken from print typography, glossed in Box 2.1. The description of print letters is based on the stave framework of four lines given in Figure 2.6, although Primus (2004) prefers a 5-line stave for feature analysis. This diagram underpins the discussion of letters, rather like the Cardinal Vowel diagram in phonetics. More elaborated ver-sions can be found in Haslam (2011: 8) and Beier (2012: 8).

Serif capital letters

For English speakers, capitals seem to be the prototypical style of letter. Official forms need to be completed in block capitals; helpers at preschools write the names of infants on their pictures in capitals; messages on T-shirts are in capitals, as are comic strips, graffiti, stone memorials, crossword puzzles, eye tests, letters on keyboards, alphabets on Sesame Street, demonstrators' placards, traditional architects' drawings, and so on. A message has to be in capital letters to be notable. When the Guardian newspaper was redesigned in 2018, the editor wanted 'a masthead with capital letters to signify a serious intent. I felt the lower case T and G didn't quite fit the mood of these serious times' (Chadwick, 2018).

Box 2.1 Terms for describing letters

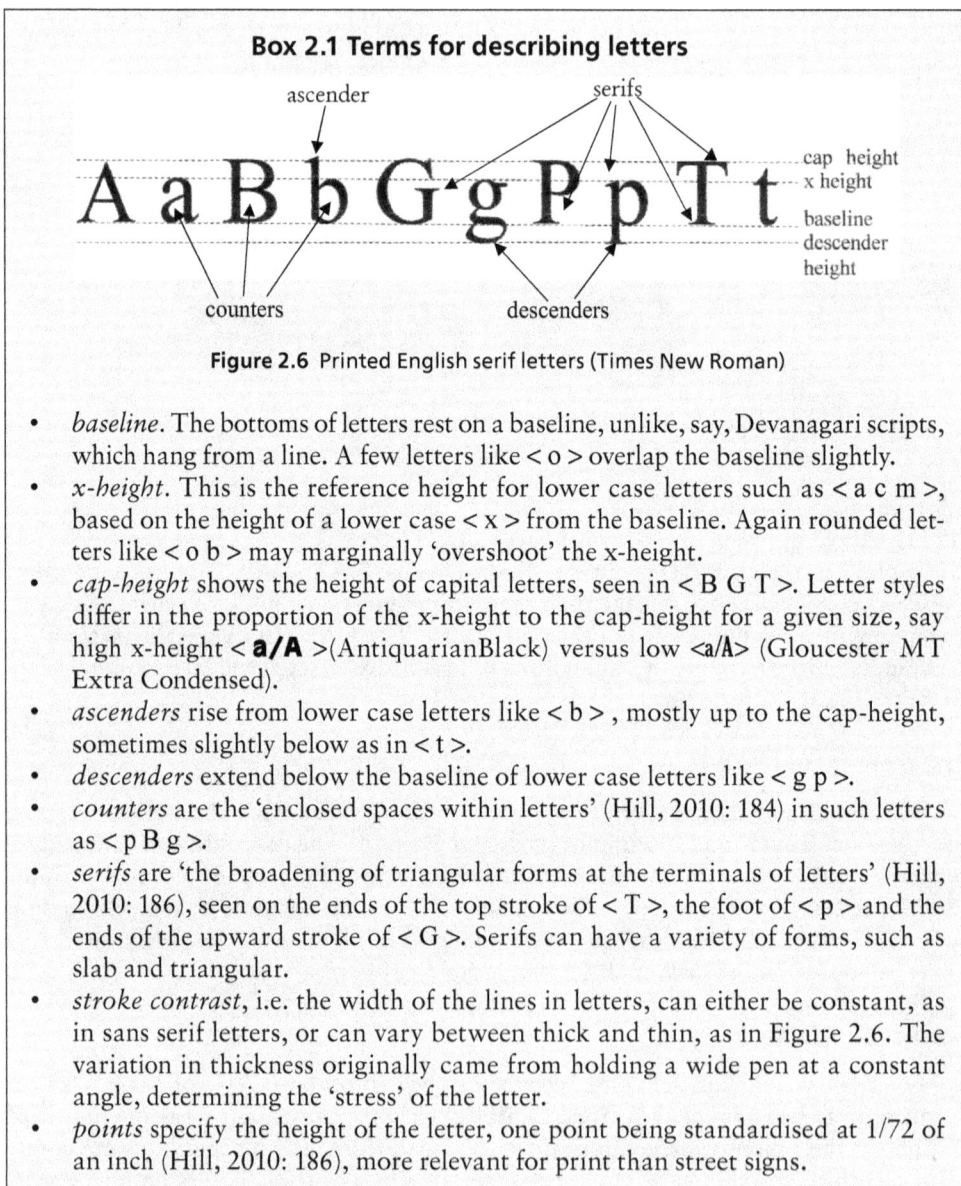

Figure 2.6 Printed English serif letters (Times New Roman)

- *baseline*. The bottoms of letters rest on a baseline, unlike, say, Devanagari scripts, which hang from a line. A few letters like < o > overlap the baseline slightly.
- *x-height*. This is the reference height for lower case letters such as < a c m >, based on the height of a lower case < x > from the baseline. Again rounded letters like < o b > may marginally 'overshoot' the x-height.
- *cap-height* shows the height of capital letters, seen in < B G T >. Letter styles differ in the proportion of the x-height to the cap-height for a given size, say high x-height < a/A >(AntiquarianBlack) versus low <a/A> (Gloucester MT Extra Condensed).
- *ascenders* rise from lower case letters like < b > , mostly up to the cap-height, sometimes slightly below as in < t >.
- *descenders* extend below the baseline of lower case letters like < g p >.
- *counters* are the 'enclosed spaces within letters' (Hill, 2010: 184) in such letters as < p B g >.
- *serifs* are 'the broadening of triangular forms at the terminals of letters' (Hill, 2010: 186), seen on the ends of the top stroke of < T >, the foot of < p > and the ends of the upward stroke of < G >. Serifs can have a variety of forms, such as slab and triangular.
- *stroke contrast*, i.e. the width of the lines in letters, can either be constant, as in sans serif letters, or can vary between thick and thin, as in Figure 2.6. The variation in thickness originally came from holding a wide pen at a constant angle, determining the 'stress' of the letter.
- *points* specify the height of the letter, one point being standardised at 1/72 of an inch (Hill, 2010: 186), more relevant for print than street signs.

A B E G L M O P R T   Times New Roman

Figure 2.7 Serif capital letters sample

The capitals in Modern English street signs derive in part from the alphabet used in classical Roman inscriptions, named after Trajan's Column (AD 113), a status style of writing seen everywhere in the streets of Rome (Petrucci, 1993). It was 'unicameral' in having only one case, i.e. capital letters; the modern English alphabet is 'bicameral' in having two cases, upper and lower (Bringhurst, 2005: 322). Although the term *case* is unavoidable, it is anachronistic when applied to Roman inscriptions since it refers to the two wooden 'cases' of metal letters used by typesetters a thousand years later, an upper for capital letters, a lower for lower case letters.

The characteristics of capital letters are:

- They normally fit within virtual rectangles, as in < H D G >, etc.
- Their shapes are based on squares and circles as seen in < N O P > etc. Their geometrical properties have been endlessly discussed (Evetts, 1938; Johnston, 1906).
- They are grouped into round letters < O >, symmetrical < A > and non-symmetrical < P > (Haslam, 2011: 136).
- They extend from the baseline to the cap-height.
- They vary in width between wide letters such as < G M O > and narrow letters such as < B E P > (Beier, 2012: 117).
- Their stroke contrast varies between thinnest for horizontal strokes, as in < E > and < L > , and thickest for vertical strokes, as in < T > and < L > and downward left-to-right diagonal strokes, as in < A > and < M >. To Catich (1968: 99), 'the basic identifying trait' of the Roman alphabet is its 2:1 proportion of stroke contrast.
- They have serifs – 'the broadening of triangular forms at the terminals of letters' (Hill, 2010: 186) – at the ends of strokes, for example in Figure 2.7 the feet of the < A > and < L > and the ends of the horizontal strokes of the < E >. The original reason for serifs on Roman inscriptions was that the letters were first painted with a square-cut brush and then cut out by a stonemason, following the marks made when the brush was lifted from the surface (Catich, 1968). Serifs lead to better spacing between letters such as < I > and < L > than letters without serifs (Kinneir, 1980: 34), say <ILLINOIS RAILWAY> (Times New Roman) versus <ILLINOIS RAILWAY> (Calibri).
- Lines of capital letters naturally have more even spacing between them than lines of lower case letters, because of the irregular ascenders and descenders of lower case (Brown, 1921).

The classical Roman alphabet had 22 letters; < H J U W > were later additions, and < K Y Z > occurred only in Greek borrowings. Modern versions of the alphabet for English thus needed to create both compatible capital letters to fill these gaps and also lower case letters to accompany them. The modern English alphabet of 26 letters in two cases has few diacritics compared to, say, the accents, umlauts and other diacritics in French, Swedish or German.

Serif capitals in street signs

Figure 2.8 shows some typical modern street signs with serif capital letters.

Figure 2.8 Street signs in serif capital letters (*Gibson Street, Northumberland House, Alderman Fenwick's House* (truncated), Newcastle)

The standard street name sign *Gibson Street* uses Kindersley, a government-authorised typeface. *Northumberland House* displays the name of an office building in stately incised Roman letters in gold. The eye-level plaque *Alderman Fenwick's House* has white letters raised from a grey metal base.

Street name signs in England are government regulated. Up to 1963, the Ministry of Works recommended a typeface based on the Trajan letters in Evetts (1938) (Gregory, 2020). However, Gray (1960) warned that the classical forms are too thin for street letters. Gurrey (2009) goes further: 'the Roman letter, used other than as a tool for learning, is an aesthetic irrelevance in the contemporary world'. The Kindersley typeface in *Gibson Street* tackled Gray's problem with bolder and fatter letters, and is seen on most streets in England today. It is recommended in the Department of Transport circular (1993), discussed further in Chapter 5. Nowadays the Department for Transport (2015) recommends that the proportion of stroke thickness to letter height should be between 1:7 and 1:4.

Other styles of serif capital letter have been used historically for streets and buildings, as seen below.

Figure 2.9 Naming signs in serif capitals (*Oxford Road,* Colchester; *Sandgate,*
Cordwainers Hall, Newcastle)

Naming signs are particularly affected by the choice of material. The *Oxford Road* street name sign uses white letters on individual black tiles with a fatter letter style than recent signs like *Gibson Street* (Figure 2.8), a style now surviving only in a handful of 19th century neighbourhoods such as Oxford, Hampstead and Colchester. The modern *Sandgate* street name sign is cut in stone, the mid-19th century *Cordwainers Hall* sign in stucco.

The letters on both stone signs in Figure 2.9 are cut into the surface rather than raised out of it, utilising light and shadow in their perception, contrasting with the raised letters of *Alderman Fenwick's House* (Figure 2.8). Incised letters can have more delicate serifs, for technical reasons to do with working stone (Kindersley & Cardozo, 1990). The incised capital < E > in *Sandgate* is cut out into a V-shaped cross-section, while that in *Cordwainer's Hall* is cut into a square cross-section, yielding different shadows. Square-cut letters usually appear stronger (Kinneir, 1980: 107) and more sculptural (Gurrey, 2009: 96). The problem of lighting can be minimised by painting the incised letters in gold, as in *Northumberland House* (Figure 2.8). Roman inscriptions themselves did not rely on throwing shadows, since they were filled in with minium, now known as red lead (Gray, 1960). The use of shadows within letters is thus a later exploitation of the happy accident when the metal fell out.

Figure 2.10 Other signs in serif capitals (*Private*, Blakeney; *Jane & Ann Taylor*, Colchester)

Figure 2.10 shows serif capital letters adapted to a variety of street sign functions. All of these signs rely on the authority of Roman capitals: '... the classical Roman had the regularity and discipline of a Roman army on the march' (Bartram, 1976: 10). The importance of the eye-level *Private* sign is proclaimed by its formal serif capitals. The ornate letters of the brown ceramic wall plaque *Jane & Ann Taylor* give it a late Victorian Arts and Crafts feel.

The wall plaque *Jane & Ann Taylor* shows the further innovation of small caps, i.e. < JANE & ANN TAYLOR >. Small caps are designed separately for each letter size and are usually heavier and wider than full-size capitals.

A variant on serif letters is the concept of block letters. Often printed forms demand to be filled in in block letters, without specifying exactly what a block letter is; the OED (2015) defines it as 'a capital letter written or printed without serifs'. Some see this as increasing legibility for automatic recognition: 'For best recognition results, forms should be completed in block capital letters' (ABBYY, 2009). Yet they are not mentioned in the Royal Mail guidelines (2016). It does seem rather unlikely that, without such instructions, people would fill in forms in serif capitals or lower case.

Sans serif capital letters

Serif capitals were only one of the styles used in Roman inscriptions. The 'rustic' letters of some classic Roman inscriptions were sans serif, as were Greek inscriptions before the 4th century BCE (Kinneir, 1980: 26). According to Bringhurst (2005: 255), sans serif letters were 'emblems of the Republic', serif letters 'symbols of empire'.

There is a minor squabble over whether the spelling should be *sans serif* or *sanserif*. Mosley (2007) claims that *sanserif* is a mistake unwittingly made by the OED (2015) when transcribing a text in their own library. Nevertheless, *sanserif* is the form in Bringhurst (2005), Haslam (2011) and Tschichold (1998 [1928], English translation). A disadvantage of *sanserif* is that it divorces the word *sans* from its historical meaning 'without' – 'Second childishnesse, and meere obliuion, Sans teeth, sans eyes, sans taste, sans euerything' (*As You Like It*, II, vii, 166).

While sans serif capitals have been used for building-name signs in England since the early 18th century (Kinneir, 1980: 36), those in modern street signs often come from the early 20th century modern movement in design led by the Bauhaus. Jan Tschichold famously declared:

> None of the typefaces to whose basic form some kind of ornament has been added … meet our requirements for clarity and purity …. The so-called 'Grotesque' (sanserif) … is the only one in spiritual accordance with our time. … sanserif is absolutely and always better. (Tschichold, 1998 [1928]: 73–74)

Virtually the same opinion is held by the novelist John Updike, who said:

> Serifs exist for a purpose; they help the eye pick up the shape of the letter. Piquant in little amounts sanssserif in page size sheets repels readership; it has a sleazy cloudy look. (Cited in Ogilvy, 1983: 96)

The 20th century saw the creation of many sans serif typefaces such as Johnston Underground and Gill Sans, sometimes regarded as archetypally British.

The characteristics of modern sans serif capital letters can be seen in Figure 2.11, which compares computer versions of serif Times New Roman and sans serif Gill Sans.

A B E G L M O P R T Times New Roman

A B E G L M O P R T Gill Sans

Figure 2.11 Comparing serif and sans serif capital letters

Sans serif capital letters are partly defined by contrast with serif letters:

- Like all-capitals, they normally fit within rectangles, as in the round < O > and the square < M > of Gill Sans.
- Many are based on the geometry of squares <M>, right angles <L> and circles <O>.

- Many sans serif letter styles have constant line-width, evident in the < M > and < O >, a characteristic of handwritten notices since Roman times, and a consequence of the pointed implements with which they are made, whether stylus or biro.
- They lack serifs at the end of strokes, virtually their defining characteristic.
- They define the areas between the letters less well (Smeijers, 2011).

Sans serif letters are often said to be more readable in short displays, serif letters in continuous text. Novels, for example, are rarely set in sans serif letters, one exception being *Pollen* (Noon, 1995). Those who have had the task of reading PhD dissertations forced by university regulations into sans serif will attest to the extra labour involved.

A review concluded that this assumption has no research basis (Poole, 2008). For example, sans serif Arial and Verdana were more legible on screen than serif Century and Times New Roman (Bernard *et al.*, 2001). The comparative legibility of serif and sans serif letters is discussed at length in Beier (2012: 123–130), who argues that it depends more on factors such as letter size and familiarity with the letter style. On the basis of an experiment with sans serif Arial, Fiset *et al.* (2008) claim that letter identification depends on line terminations, suggesting an underlying reason for serifs. Designers indeed use complex formulae to decide the appropriate size for street sign letters according to reading distance (Howet, 1983; Vink, 2015); one rule of thumb states that letter height must be increased by one inch for each extra 10 feet of distance (Signs.com, 2017).

In Figure 2.12, *Leazes Lane* employs Gill Sans, the sans serif typeface approved by the Department of Transport (1993) for street name signs, mostly used for moulded signs in minor streets. *Hospital* is an architectural high-level sign in sans serif letters cut out of a portico. The letters of *The George* hotel sign at roof level are large, gold-painted, sans serif and three-dimensional, part of the native tradition for building signs since the 18th century (Bartram, 1978a).

The function of *Leazes Lane, The George* and *Hospital* is to name streets and buildings, hardly less formal than the serif naming signs of Figure 2.9. The clarity of the sign in different light conditions and its endurance are thus crucial. Sans serif letters have clearer shadows than serif letters due to their comparative simplicity (Kinneir, 1980: 125). Raised letters like those in *The George* may obscure each other from different angles. Again these signs try to impress with their lettering and their expensive-looking materials, whether stone or gold, and in the craftsmanship needed to produce them (Cook, 2015).

Figure 2.13 shows sans serif letters on other signs. *No Entry to Doctor's Surgery* is a large 'amateur' warning sign for drivers outside a building site, painted on hardboard in overlapping strokes. *With Joy* displays a biblical inscription on the arch of an 1864 drinking fountain, intended to decorate and to foster teetotalism in the citizens. Sans serif capital letters can be used on a variety of signs, both informal notices and formal inscriptions, sometimes suggesting practicality and modernity.

Figure 2.12 Street signs in sans serif capital letters (*Leazes Lane,* LPZ; *Hospital, The George,* Colchester)

Figure 2.13 Other sans serif capitals (*No Entry to Doctor's Surgery, With Joy,* Colchester)

Lower case letters

The historical origins of modern lower case letters are complex. One ancestor was the informal handwritten letters with ascenders and descenders that existed alongside the formal Roman capitals used on inscriptions. Another was the minuscule 'insular' unicameral scripts devised by British and Irish monks around 700 AD. A third was the Carolingian letters adopted around 800 AD by Charlemagne's court under the guidance of Alcuin of York (Jackson, 1981: 69). One impetus for their design was the mediaeval demands of the quill pen and parchment compared with those of the brush, chisel and stone used in Roman inscriptions. Books had now taken over from inscriptions as the status form of writing. The mediaeval street was indeed comparatively bare of signs with written texts, reflecting the low level of literacy in the general population (Petrucci, 1993).

Since lower case letters come from different historical and technological sources from capitals, it is often hard to relate them to their upper case equivalents. Lower case letters are sometimes claimed to be more legible than all-capitals. Classic research by Tinker (1963) found lower case was easier to read in print but upper case was easier at a distance; Arditi and Cho (2007) established that capitals are read better in smaller sizes, particularly by those with visual impairment; Sheedy *et al.* (2005) found both x-height and sans serif letters contributed to legibility. Influential research into motorway signs commissioned by the then Ministry of Transport in the 1950s (Kinneir, 1980) showed that a mixture of capitals and lower case is more recognisable from a speeding car, leading to the current UK regulations for motorway signs and the complementary rule that street name signs should be all-capitals (Department for Transport, 2015). Beier (2012: 122–123) sums up modern research in terms of the advantages associated with x-height rather than case, conceding an overall advantage to lower case in some situations. Although capital letters are often called 'big', size is not a defining characteristic, as a 'big' lower case letter is still lower case: < A > is not a bigger version of < a >. Indeed the compatibility of these two distinct letter forms is debatable (Tschichold, 1998 [1928]: 79); Kinneir (1980: 34) sees the concentration on these two letter types as 'a brake on free innovation'.

As seen in Figure 2.14, the characteristics of lower case letters are:

- They vary between wide letters like < m > and narrow letters like < l >.
- While mostly fitting between the baseline and the x-height, some have ascenders that go above the x-height, like < b > and, to a lesser extent, < t >, and descenders that hang below the baseline, like < g > and < p >. Tschichold (1998 [1928]: 80) holds that ascenders and descenders 'make complete words easier to recognise', an argument for basing word recognition on word shapes rather than letters.
- Serif lower case letters vary in stroke contrast, as in <frankie and tony's sandwich bar> etc., while sans serif letters usually have even width <frankie and tony's sandwich bar>.
- To avoid awkward fits, they may overlap in ligatures such as < fl fi st >.

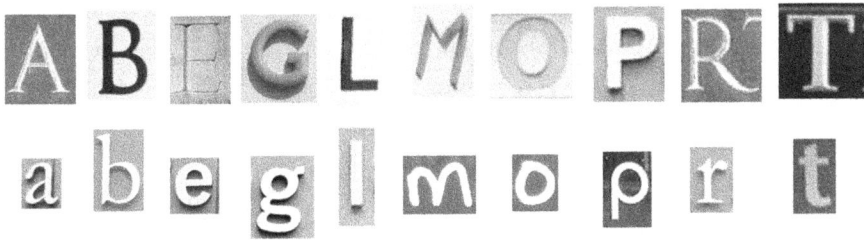

Figure 2.14 Pairs of upper and lower case letters from street signs (Newcastle, apart from capital < O >, Colchester; all taken from signs in this book)

Figure 2.14 shows upper and lower case letters from signs used in this book. While < M m >, < O o > and < P p > are recognisably the same letters, lower case < r b > are open at the top rather than having the closed counters of their upper case equivalents < R B >; lower case < a g > have little in common with upper case < A G >. Kinneir (1980: 30) attributes the differences to the use of a stylus for writing on wax: 'Strokes were dropped (B became b), angles were slurred (M became m), and other strokes were elided (E became e)'.

Figure 2.15 Signs with lower case letters (*Mother's Day, tea sutra,* LPR; *Quayside,* Newcastle)

Figure 2.15 shows a selection of street signs with lower case letters, except for some word- or phrase-initial capitals. The shop sign *Mother's Day* has handwritten lower case letters with word- and phrase-initial caps. The *tea sutra* restaurant sign is in sans serif lower case throughout, as in the vertical version (Figure 2.3). The fingerpost *Quayside* sign has raised metal serif letters, highlighted in different colours.

Italic letters

According to Hill (2010: 185), italics are 'Sloping letters … originally based on handwritten forms'. They were originally used for whole texts but were later combined with Roman lower case within the same printed text (Clayton, 2014). The convention of using italics for emphasis came later. The crucial aspect of italics is suggesting the movement of the pen. Like the shotgun marriage of lower and upper case, it has proved difficult to design compatible italic and non-italic letters within the same letter style, as illustrated by the advice to use vertical brackets with italics (Bringhurst, 2005: 85), i.e. < *(language)* > rather than < *(language)* >.

Figure 2.16 contrasts italic and non-italic lower case letters in typical serif and sans serif computer letter styles.

a b e g l m o p r t Calibri

a b e g l m o p r t Calibri italic

a b e g l m o p r t Times New Roman

a b e g l m o p r t Times New Roman italic

Figure 2.16 Examples of italic and non-italic lower case letters

The characteristics of italic letters are:

- a flow or slope;
- the use of particular letter forms, such as the 'single storey' < *a* > and the elliptical angled counter of < *e* >;
- the use of cursive 'hooks' as if linked to the next letter, as in the < *m* > and < *l* > of Times New Roman, reminiscent of the brush origins of the serif;
- in general, italics are believed to be less readable than other forms and so are used as a contrast within texts rather than for continuous text (Beier, 2012).

Street signs in italics are comparatively rare. In Figure 1.3, *Great Grub* has a painted, shadow italic in a fat letter style with word-initial capitals and a more conventional subheading in italic capitals, <*THE QUALITY SANDWICH*>. Painted shadows get the benefits of incised or raised letters without depending on the vagaries of lighting. The bilingual restaurant sign *Jasmine* emphasises the handwriting origins of italics with a cursive letter style (see Figure 2.17). Interestingly, the Chinese characters also slope, despite italics being frowned on in Chinese printing (Multilingual Typesetting, 2016), so that the two scripts are visually compatible on the same sign.

Figure 2.17 Street signs in italics (*nevisport, Jasmine,* Newcastle)

The occasional use of italics in street signs gives individuality to business names. <*nevisport*> , for example, has lower case italics without initial capitals, the slant suggesting modernity and movement, helped by the arrow-like forms above and below the letters. The italics of *Great Grub* (Figure 1.3) suggest both 'greatness' from the letter forms and informality from the word *grub*. Indeed, according to Magnini *et al.* (2011), customers think restaurant menus in italics are more upmarket.

Overall, the letters of written English come in three separate forms with different origins: capitals, lower case and italics. Gill (1931: 59) calls these 'the three alphabets in common use for the English people'. The distinctive ways in which street signs use these forms are a crucial part of the language of the street. Capitals, for instance, occur far more often than in other varieties of written English, italics less.

Other Symbols

In addition to the conventional modern alphabet used in print, other letters and symbols occur in English street signs, whether numbers, non-alphabetic characters, relics of bygone ages or modern innovations.

Numbers

Roman numbers are represented by letters of the alphabet, i.e. < MDCXLVI >. The so-called Arabic numbers < 0123456789 > were adapted from North African scripts rather than Roman letters, appearing in Europe from the 13th century onward (Clayton, 2014).

Print numbers may be non-lining, 'old style' numerals such as < 0123456789 > (Hill, 2010: 114), characterised by descender and ascender forms. Or they may be lining numerals, < 0123456789 > , which extend between the baseline and cap height, and are now the most common print form. The legibility of the two styles of numbers depends heavily on context (Beier, 2012: 135–136).

Figure 2.18 Numbers (*1914–1918*, War Memorial, Newcastle; *Clock, No 18*, LPR; *149, 274A, Food @ the Mercury*, Colchester)

The dates < 1914–1918 > on the war memorial (Figure 2.18) show non-lining letters incised in stone. Roman numerals in street signs are restricted to dates on memorials, etc., and hours on clockfaces, with a convention that < IV > can also be represented as < IIII > , as seen on *Clock*.

The number signs show the variety of styles for houses available at the owner's whim; currently Amazon.uk have 5822 types on offer. Buildings are required to display their numbers, except on country roads, traceable to Clause *65* of the *Towns Improvement Clauses Act* (1847), embodied in local regulations such as 'Every number, name, or number and name, of any building in any street, shall be marked' (City of London, 2014). Here the materials include brass *18*, tiles *149* and painted brick *274A*. The styles similarly range from classic incised Roman serif in **1914 - 1918** to decorative art nouveau 149 to informal hand-painted *274A*.

The phone number < 01206 368100 > in *Food @ the Mercury* is interesting for the stroke at the top of sans serif < 1 >, which solves the problematic convergence of numeral < 1 > and letter < l > in sans serif letters < l l >. One practical alternative solution adopted in *Pie & Mash* (Figure 2.19) is to disambiguate the capital < I > by adding a dot like a lower case < i >.

Non-alphabetic symbols

A handful of non-alphabetic symbols also occur regularly in English street signs.

Figure 2.19 Non-alphabetic symbols (*Parking, frankie & tony's,* Newcastle; *Pie & Mash, Cock & Pye,* Colchester)

The < £ > character in *Parking* is an arbitrary symbol as baffling to those who have not encountered it before as any Chinese character. It descends from < L > , an abbreviation for Latin *libra* ('pound'). Apart from its continuing international use for the pound sterling, it was also found in Italy as an occasional sign for *lira* in pre-Euro days. These signs involve one-off lexical associations between a symbol and a meaning, not between a letter and a phoneme. Other meaning-based signs are arithmetical characters like < + % > and abbreviations like < Mr. >.

A frequent non-alphabetic symbol in street signs is the ampersand < & >. This started out as a ligature for Latin < et > ('and'): vestiges of the two letters are sometimes visible in its many italic and non-italic forms, for example the italic versions in Garamond < *&* > and Goudy < *&* >. Ampersand was added to the end of the alphabet in readers for Victorian children (Scholfield, 2016). Its name is explained as an abbreviation for *and per se and* (OED, 2015), i.e. 'and in its own right'. In street signs, it connects two words or phrases with the same grammatical structure; *Jane & Anne Taylor* (Figure 2.10) shows a decorative example. It features prominently in shop or restaurant names, joining nouns like <frankie & tony's > , and occasionally appears in name signs like *Cock & Pye Court*. Its appearance in the parking sign *Paid & Displayed* seems odd, not to say ugly. The strange-looking ampersand in *Pie & Mash* demonstrates that ampersands are no longer taught to children in primary school, as my own inability to make one easily attests.

Pointing signs: Arrows

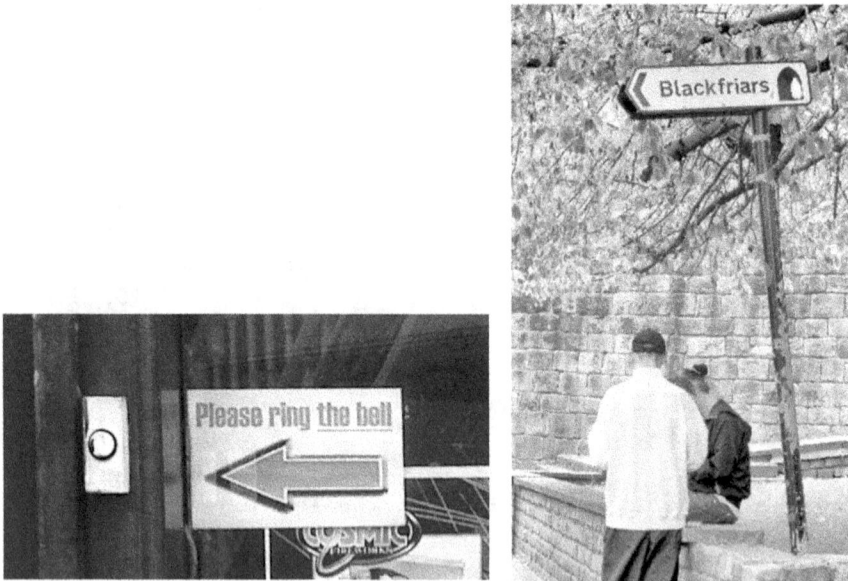

Figure 2.20 Pointing arrows (*Please ring the bell*, LPR; *Blackfriars*, SS)

Figure 2.20 displays direction signs pointing with arrows, such as *Please ring the bell*. In *Blackfriars*, the arrow has become the pointing shape of the sign itself. The use of arrows in signs is described in Chapter 6.

Traditional icons

As many mediaeval street users could not read, tradesmen had to rely on visual icons to lure in passers-by, just as the churches had to use stained glass windows rather than written texts to convey biblical messages. The earliest English pub sign was a bush, derived from the Roman tavern sign of a vine, probably the origin of pub names like *Bull and Bush* (although there are competing explanations), and of quondam proverbs like 'A good wine needs no bush'. The tradition of non-verbal street symbols has been revived in the icons on electronic devices and street direction signs, although more as symbols to which you need to know the key, like ⌛ or 🗑 .

Figure 2.21 Traditional street icons (*Barber's pole, Pawnbroker's balls,* Colchester; *Locksmith's keys,* LPR)

Figure 2.21 documents three of the trade icons that survive on English streets. The spiral red and white striped *Barber's pole* reflects the barber's historical combined role of barber-surgeon, with red representing the blood that was shed, ending in England in 1745 when the Company of Barbers and Surgeons split into the Royal College of Surgeons and the Worshipful Company of Barbers. The pole here is a modern electric version that revolves. Some barbers' signs also use scissors or razors, as seen in Figure 2.26. The three *Pawnbroker's balls* are still found on modern streets, whether solid or painted. They are said on thin evidence to derive from the symbol used by the Medici family for their mediaeval banking enterprises (de Roover, 1946). The *Locksmith's keys* are the logo of the Master Locksmith's Association, an accrediting body for locksmiths.

These icons thus remind us of the three-dimensional nature of street signs and their basis in non-linguistic signs. They prefigure logos like the MacDonald's Golden Arches or the Lloyds Bank black horse, similar to mediaeval signs catering for those who cannot read, whether illiterates or children. However, as Garrioch (1994) points out, this is not a matter of iconic representation so much as an arbitrary memory aid; in the 18th century, a crown may be a sign for a shoemaker, dyer, writing master, linen draper, haberdasher or many other trades (Heal, 1957).

Punctuation marks

English uses a fairly standard set of 'Western' punctuation marks (Nunberg, 1990), which have also found their way into Japanese and Chinese writing systems. The differences between England and continental Europe mainly concern quotation marks. English uses single and double quotation marks at the cap height < " " ' ' > rather than the up and down marks < „ " > used for German and many East European languages, the goose feet < « » > found in French and Russian texts, the reverse goosefeet found in Switzerland < » « > (Cook, 2004a), or the long dashes used in Spanish < – – > (and indeed in James Joyce).

Figure 2.22 Punctuation marks (*Coffee*, LPR; *New's, hypehairdesign*, Colchester)

The signs in Figure 2.22 illustrate the use of punctuation marks in street signs, to be discussed in the next chapter. *Coffee* has an abundance of full stops. *New's* shows the maligned greengrocer's apostrophe. *hypehairdesign* imitates email by using full stops as separators.

A glance at the signs in this chapter soon shows that standard punctuation marks are largely absent. *Cordwainer's Hall* (Figure 2.9) has an unusual final full stop; *Mother's Day* (Figure 2.15) has an exclamation mark. This does not, however, include the use of punctuation marks for creating a unique business identity, seen in Chapter 7.

Perhaps the most crucial but invisible punctuation mark is the space between words. While it may seem obvious that words should be separated, this rarely occurs in the spoken language. Some writing systems do not have word spaces; in Chinese, for example, the characters are evenly spaced, not the words. Word spaces spread across Europe from Irish scribes about the 7th century AD and facilitated silent reading (Saenger, 1997). Street signs use them as word separators in the same way as print. Occasionally the lack of a word space causes confusion as in < ABBEY GATES^t > (Figure 3.4). Sometimes they are absent in texts using messaging conventions such as <hypehairdesign> and in compound business names like *FennWright* (Figure 3.12). For typographers, a word space should be 'the width of a lowercase i' (Hill, 2010: 186).

Alternative Letters

Historical English letters

The street signs seen on English streets today have in some cases survived for long periods, say the 1860s *Cordwainers Hall* (Figure 2.9), although doubtless redone when the city centre was restored in the 1990s, or the 1930s *Dex Garage* (Figure 2.2). So they have letter forms appropriate for their times. Old signs don't die; they just fade away.

Figure 2.23 documents some historical letters of English used in modern street signs. Pub signs assert their antiquity, genuine or fake, by replacing *the* with *ye* as part of 'Olde Tyme' spelling, as in *Ye Olde* (Cook, 2004b). In Caxton's edition of *The Canterbury Tales* (Chaucer, 1473), the first printed form of the word *the* was þ̇, combining the traditional Old English letter thorn < Þ > (originally a rune) with a minute diacritic < e >. The first phoneme in *the* corresponded to the voiced 'th' /ð/ in Old and Middle English, as it does in Modern English; that is to say, there is no reason to believe <the> ever corresponded to /ji:/. þ̇ was one of a conventional set of Middle English 'near' abbreviations (Roberts, 2005: 10), now extinct. By the time of the *King James Bible* in 1611, the straight line of thorn < Þ > had changed to a curve, ẏ, leading to confusion with the letter < y >. By 1716, it had become a full capital Ẏ, crowned with the < e >, ushering in the modern use of <Ye> as a quaint archaism. Nowadays the link between *ye* and thorn is invisible. The *Ye* in *Ye Olde Marquis* is thus trying to appear ancient.

Other genuinely historical letters are absent from modern street signs, such as the long 's' < ſ > found in printed English till the early 19th century (Scholfield, 2016) and the yogh < ȝ >, which had several spoken correspondences in Middle English. The Old

English letter ash < æ > consisted of a ligatured < a e > – a ligature is 'a compound form combining two letters' (Hill, 2010: 185), as in the < AW > in the Edwardian *Law Covrts* or the < NK > in *Space.NK* (Figure 2.25).

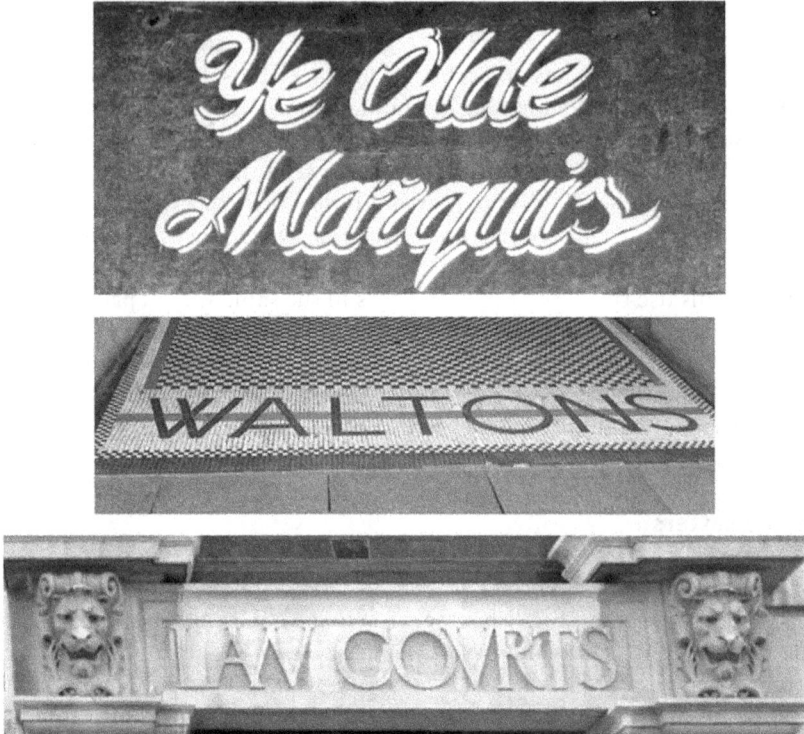

Figure 2.23 Historical letters (*Ye Olde Marquis* and *Law Covrts*, Colchester; *Waltons*, Newcastle)

Double < VV > was combined into < W > about 1300, superseding the Old English letter wynn < p > (also originally a rune), the previous correspondence for /w/ (OED, 2015). A ligatured double-V form is sometimes found in modern logos, such as the mosaic shop floor sign *Waltons* or indeed the capitals of the computer version of Garamond < W *W* >. The alternative letter pairs < I/J > and < U/V > separated into distinct letters in the mid-17th century. Occasionally < V > is used for < U > as an archaism in formal inscriptions, such as the Edwardian sign *Law Covrts* or the 1902 sign on the William Rathbone monument in Liverpool <A FOVNDER OF THE VNIVERSITY>.

Symbols from other writing systems than English

Given the multilingualism of most English cities, it is hardly surprising to find signs using other writing systems than English.

Figure 2.24 Signs using other writing systems (*BreadPoint,* Newcastle; *Push,* SS)

Push, a door sign, and *BreadPoint*, a baker's sign, are partly in Chinese characters, both found in Newcastle's Chinatown. *Push* is a functional everyday notice for the multilingual community it serves, to be discussed in Chapter 8. The letters of the bilingual sign *Push* are brush-drawn, hence the widened lines at the ends of the upright strokes. *BreadPoint* is painted on glass in a one-off red and black design.

Novel spellings

A modern trend extends the uses of written symbols, as seen in Figure 2.25.

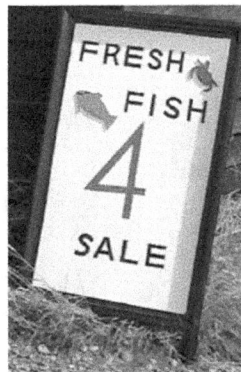

Figure 2.25 Innovations (*Fresh Fish, Blakeney; fabric8,* Colchester; *Space, NK,* Newcastle)

Fresh Fish and *fabric8* show invaders from texting, where numbers replace syllables, < 4 >/ < for> and < 8 >/ < ate>. Other intruders are < # >, the hash mark also
known as octothorpe or the pound sign, and the < . > used as a separator in <SPACE.
NK.apothecary>.

The traditional use < @ > in English bills is *4 bananas @ 25p = £1*, glossed as 'at/
for/per'. Its origins are obscure, possibly an abbreviation for Latin *ad*. It came back to
life in the 1970s in email addresses and social media, imitated in the *Food @ the
Mercury* restaurant sign (Figure 2.18).

As mentioned in Chapter 1, the novel spellings in these signs are not one-off spellings by a single writer, apart from *Fresh Fish*, but draw on the potential for alternative
spellings within the English writing system. Numbers for syllables and words are a
rebus-like tradition, used not just in signwriting but also in text messaging. Full stops
acting as word dividers are found not just on signs but also in internet addresses and,
in a raised form, on War Memorials (Figure 8.6), harking back to some Roman inscriptions. While the < 4 > in *Fresh Fish* may well be the choice of an individual writer for
a one-off sign, the other two signs are the result of a corporate decision by the owner to
have novel spelling in their brand name wherever it appears.

Icons substituting for letters

In Figure 2.26, street signs replace letters with icons of particular objects that resemble them.

Figure 2.26 Icons for letters (*KDIP, LPR; Easi, savers,* Colchester)

The hanging dentist's sign *KDIP* substitutes a screw-in tooth for the letter < I >; the shop sign *savers* a tick for the lower case < v >; *EASI*, a pair of scissors for < A >, plus a novel spelling < i > for < y >. Teeth and scissors link to the businesses involved, once their unexpected shapes have been interpreted. The tick < ✓ > for general approval also occurs in estate agent's signs and the like. These icons show wit by having a double meaning, rather like a pun or a rebus, to be discussed in Chapter 8. They go a step further outside the English writing system, and are again a calculated corporate choice of a distinctive brand name.

Conclusion

To sum up, this chapter has described the basics of the street sign, using mainly writing direction, letter styles and legibility. This corresponds more or less to phonetics in the study of the spoken language. Yet, while every linguist could tell you that an English / p / in *poppy* is an unvoiced fortis plosive, mostly aspirated initially, few linguists could tell you that < p > is a serif lower case letter with varying stroke contrast, a descender and an internal counter. The physical forms of writing have received little attention in linguistics, unlike the vast technical apparatus of phonetics. While the approach used here has been assembled from diverse sources and doubtless needs developing and refining, something like it is essential. Any research into speech or writing that does not build on an adequate descriptive base does so at its peril.

The study of speech has largely been based on the articulatory phonetics of production involving the whole human vocal apparatus and on acoustic phonetics concerned with the perception of sounds. The framework for describing letters here similarly invokes the physical processes of production, involving a variety of materials and tools available to human beings; a shop sign using hand-painted letters is produced very differently from a notice printed by a computer, with different effects on the street users.

A theme that comes through is the extent to which the writing system of street signs depends on their physical properties and precise individual location. What a sign is made of and where it is located within the geometry of the street affect the kind of letter styles available for it, who the potential users may be and the meanings it may convey.

With written language, the history of the means of production is embodied visibly in the letter forms, whether the uniform stroke contrast of pencils and biros or the varying stroke contrast of serif capitals. The historical origins of some spellings and usage are also visible in their modern forms, say the source of silent < e >s in words like *love* and *hate*. The historical origins are often mentioned in this book to make sense of otherwise arbitrary properties of signs.

This chapter has sketched some basic properties of street signs that have gone almost unmentioned in recent studies. The writing direction, the forms of letters, numbers and non-alphabetic characters, their aesthetics and their historical associations all contribute to the meaning of the street sign. Much of the impact of street signs will be missed if these fundamental aspects are ignored.

3   The Language System of the Street

In general, language can be taken to be 'a resource for making meaning' (Halliday & Mattheisen, 2013: 3), here extended to non-verbal street signs. This chapter describes how street signs convey meaning through grammar, letters, vocabulary and punctuation. The English language is seen here both as the abstract entity used in England and as a mental system known by the street user, not necessarily the same as the language recorded in dictionaries and grammar books or invoked in popular discussions (Cook, 2010, forthcoming).

Spoken and Written Language

Aristotle (4th century BCE) believed that 'writing is a symbol of vocal sounds', that is to say, writing represents speech. On no other topic have linguists from different schools, continents and millennia spoken with one voice: speech is primary, writing secondary (Cook, 2004a, 2016a). Consequently, most linguists have only been concerned with the letter-sound correspondence rules between writing and speech, not with the capabilities of written language to express meaning independently of speech.

European linguists within the functionalist tradition have nevertheless treated writing as an alternative form that language can take rather than a parasite on speech. Vachek (1973) maintained that language has both written and spoken norms. Halliday and Mattheisen (2013) claim:

> The sound system and the writing system are the two modes of **expression** by which the lexicogrammar of a language is represented. (Halliday & Mattheisen, 2013: 7)

Despite writing emerging historically after speech, despite children learning to read and write after they have learnt to speak, speech and writing are alternative forms of language that do not necessarily depend on each other in actual use. The crucial synchronic relationship is between writing and language, not between writing and speech (Cook, 2004a).

The letter/sound correspondence links between speech and writing are of course relevant for functions that involve both together, such as reading aloud and the acquisition of literacy. But it seems unlikely that the vast majority of street signs are ever read aloud. As we shall see, they make systematic use of meaningful characteristics of writing, such as line-breaks and capital letters, that do not exist in speech. While most street signs could potentially be read aloud, often this is more like translation than letter-sound correspondence: how would someone set about reading aloud the *Hydrant* sign (Figure 3.1)? And why would they want to?

The Letters of the Street

De Saussure (1976 [1916]: 165–166) made four points about letters that are relevant to the letters of street signs.

- *Letter shapes are arbitrary*: any letter could represent any sound – a spin-off from Saussure's general principle of the arbitrariness of the sign. It wouldn't matter if a letter < d > represented a sound /u:/ provided everyone used it in the same way. Letter-sound correspondences have varied historically, with the vowel letters of modern English far from corresponding to the same speech sounds in Old English. Despite Saussure, it is now claimed that certain letter shapes have non-arbitrary origins, discussed below. Some street signs indeed replace letters with non-arbitrary icons, say a tooth for < I > in *KDIP* (Figure 2.26).
- *Letters work so long as they can be distinguished from each other*: The variations in the letter < e > seen in Figure 2.5 do not matter so long as they suggest an < e > to the user, up to the point of confusion with other letters: a letter can only range so far from its prototype form.
- *Letters work through a system of oppositions*:

  … dans la langue il n'y a que des différences
  ('In language there are only differences'. De Saussure, 1976 [1916]: 166)

  A < b > is not a < d >, an < o > is not an < e >, so <bin> is not <din> and <ore> is not <ere>; at the basic level, computer programs work on the opposition between < 0 > and < 1 >. Oppositions are specific to particular writing systems; the English orthography now opposes 26 letters to each other, with < i > having split from < j > and < u > from < v > in the mid-17th century.
- *The material form of letters is irrelevant*:

  Que j'écrive les lettres en blanc ou en noir, en creux ou en relief, avec une plume ou un ciseau, cela est sans importance pour leur signification.
  ('Whether I write letters in white or in black, recessed or raised, with a pen or a chisel, has no bearing on their meaning'. De Saussure, 1976 [1916]: 166)

  The surface on which a < b > is written or the tool that is used to make it have no effect on whether it is an example of a < b >. So far as the modern printed text is concerned, variations are indeed minimal: the material is paper and the tool is a printer or a printing press; the colour of text is black letters on a white background, occasionally the reverse.

  But street signs make use of many different materials, which *do* contribute to their meaning. An < E > incised on stone with a chisel implies something rather different from an < e > scrawled on paper with a biro. Variations in material contribute over-tones of meaning that are essential to many signs, as discussed in Chapters 4 and 7.

De Saussure's (1916) requirements are only partially true for street signs. Letter shapes and icons may be less than arbitrary; material may be important to their mean-ing. Nevertheless street signs are as dependent as any area of written language on the systematic opposition of letters and their need to be distinguishable.

The Grammar of the Street

Street signs contain not only texts consisting of one or two words and lengthy texts with 'full' sentences but also non-verbal symbols and icons. Grammar applies to all of these in the broad sense of having structured meaning.

Mainstream syntax has taken the sentence as the highest unit of grammatical struc-ture. Traditionally a sentence has been seen as a relationship between a subject and a predicate: *Weston Window Cleaning have moved* (Figure 7.12) has a subject, *Weston Window Cleaning*, and a predicate, *have moved*. Bloomfield (1933: 170–172) rephrased this in terms of 'full' sentences with actor-action constructions like *Dobson designed this charitable institution* (Figure 7.11) or imperatives, *Please ring the bell* (Figure 2.20), and 'minor' sentences that link to previous constructions, say answers to questions, *Yes*, or exclamations, *Oh dear!*.

The sentence is classically defined as a unit 'of written text that is customarily pre-sented as bracketted by a capital letter and a period' (Nunberg, 1990: 22). However, this defines sentences in effect in terms of written language rather than spoken, since there are no direct spoken equivalences for capitals and full stops. It is also rather awkward for linguists who avow the primacy of speech and useless for children who are learning to read, since it presupposes a knowledge of written language they do not yet possess; the National Curriculum (Depatment for Education, 2013) nevertheless requires the word *sentence* to be taught to five-year-olds. The OED (2015) reverses the definition by defining capitals as 'having the distinctive form and size used to begin a sentence, proper name, etc.' Historically, sentence-initial capitals derive from the decorated initial letters found in mediaeval manuscripts (Nesbitt, 1957).

However, the texts in most street signs do not have subjects, predicates, full stops or actor-action sequences. Hence they hardly count as sentences under any of the defini-tions, other than minor sentences. Traditionally they have been treated as reduced or elliptical sentences, 'lacking' articles and verbs. Halliday (1967) talked of 'economy grammar', used when there are constraints on time or space, seen most clearly in the days when telegrams were costed by the word, with traces in the message-length restric-tions in Twitter. Leech (1966) separated 'block grammar' which lacks articles and so on from 'abbreviated grammar', which has a wider range of constructions such as the imperative. But treating street texts as reduction and abbreviation ignores their unique features. The text of street signs needs to be analysed as an independent genre of its own, not just as deviations from print through reduced forms.

Syntax and street signs

A basic requirement for syntax is a hierarchy of units, going from the sentence as the highest unit, down to clause and phrase, then word, and finally morpheme as the lowest unit, each rank consisting of the one below it; a sentence consists of clauses and phrases, a phrase consists of words, a word of morphemes, as displayed in familiar phrase structure trees. Little more apparatus is needed for analysing most street signs.

Figure 3.1 Grammar in street signs (*Hydrant, To Let, red mezze*, LPR; *Planning Notice*, SS, truncated)

Figure 3.1 illustrates the range of grammar in street signs from minimal to maximal. The eye-level *Hydrant* sign uses a letter and two numbers, the positions of which are crucial to their meaning, glossed as 'there is a four-inch mains water pipe 35 feet away'. This is not so much syntax as a code for firefighters. The high-level *To Let* sign has nine lines made up of short phrases or numbers. *Red mezze* shows a typical restaurant fascia board, consisting of two two-word noun phrases, a header and a subheader. *Planning Notice* is in full 'standard' sentences; such notices are usually tied to lamp posts or trees at eye-level and enclosed in plastic that makes them difficult to read.

Nouns and noun phrases make up the bulk of texts on street signs. The bare noun is common in naming signs such as *Sandgate* (Figure 2.9) or *nevisport* (Figure 2.17). The head noun may have elements before it in the phrase (pre-modification):

- adjectives as in *red mezze*;
- *no* as in *No Entry* (Figure 1.8);
- proper nouns with or without *'s*, as in *Gibson Street* (Figure 2.8) and *Rosie's Bar* (Figure 3.3).

Or elements that follow it (post-modification):

- infinitival phrases such as (*the alternative way*) *to pay* (Figure 3.11);
- prepositional phrases such as (*Pay here*) *at machine* (Figure 3.5);
- *only* as in (*Doctors Cars*) *Only* (Figure 3.8).

Both pre- and post-modification can be combined as in *No Entry to Doctor's Surgery* (Figure 2.13). Articles are rare except when *the* is part of the name as in *The Mandarin* (Figure 2.4) and *The George* (Figure 2.12); a few street names in England include a definite article – *The Avenue*, say. Coordination is usually between pairs of nouns as in <BURGER & BEVVY> (Figure 3.2), with *and* often realised as an ampersand < & > (Figure 2.19), unusual in modern printed text.

Adjectives rarely occur as heads of phrases in street signs apart from the ubiquitous *open* and *closed*, as in *Closed for Family Funeral* (Figure 4.7). Verbs are rare; imperatives occur in signs controlling movement like *Look left* (Figure 6.7), sometimes with an object noun like *Push Button* in the *Green Man* sign (Figure 4.12), or *Press Buzzer here to get your taxi* (Figure 7.1). Occasionally a polite *please* creeps in, as in *Please ring the bell* (Figure 2.20) and *Please use alternate means of entry/egress* (Figure 3.17). Infinitival phrases occur like *To Let* (Figure 3.1). Finite verbs chiefly have the present tense such as *SORRY This is* <u>NOT</u> *Part of Mersea Road Surgery* (Figure 3.3) or a future auxiliary, *Unauthorised vehicles will be wheel clamped* (Figure 4.10). Adverbs are mostly for location, *Press Buzzer here to get your taxi* (Figure 7.1), or for manner, *Please drive carefully*.

The few signs that have 'full' lexical sentences with subjects and verbs are official signs at eye-level so that their longer texts can be read by pedestrians. *Planning Notice* (Figure 3.1), for example, has long sentences to cover the obligation on local councils to publicise 'by site display in at least one place on or near the land to which the application relates for not less than 21 days' (*Development Management Procedure*, 2010).

The exact wording of the general *No Smoking* sign (Figure 3.2) is laid down by law. The lack of sentence-final full stops shows that these are nonetheless street signs. The passive voice is very frequent as in *An application for planning permission* (Figure 3.1). Like the dummy subject *it* in *It is against the law to smoke in these premises* in *No Smoking* (Figure 3.2), passives reinforce the anonymity of the writer in speech: it is irrelevant who writes the sign; the passive is the impersonal voice of authority.

The syntax of street signs is limited compared to the language of print, mostly due to their restricted functions. Treating signs as abbreviated versions of print language does not help. Translating *To Let* (Figure 3.1) into *This building is to let* is redundant, as the sign conveys its message effectively in its own way.

Visual grammar and street signs

Kress and van Leeuwen (1996) developed a visual grammar of design based on printed pages and artworks to 'describe the way in which depicted people, places and things combine in visual "statements"'. The crucial aspects of visual grammar are position and prominence, not linear order (Kress & van Leeuwen, 1996: 223).

A key element in visual grammar is the distinction between Given and New, taken from functional linguistics (Halliday & Mattheisen, 2013). Given information is already familiar to the reader, usually appears first and is not prominent. New information that is novel to the reader usually appears second and stands out in various ways. Before-and-after advertisements, for example, often show the before picture of the overweight person in black and white on the left as Given and the after picture of the slender new person, in full colour and with a better haircut, on the right as New. Indeed writing direction has an effect on how people think. Children who speak Hebrew or Arabic will, for example, put pictures of daily meals in a right-to-left sequence, whereas English speaking children will arrange them from left-to-right (Tversky *et al.*, 1991). This dependence on left-to-right direction is not absolute in those who have writing systems with this direction; Botticelli's *Primavera* painting, for instance, has to be interpreted from right-to-left (O'Toole, 1994: 29).

Kress and van Leeuwen (1996) interpret Given as appearing on the left and New on the right; English before/after advertisements do not therefore work for languages with right-to-left direction like Arabic. The influence of the left/right division cannot be separated from the left-to-right writing direction in English signs. In so far as the Given/New distinction relates to the Subject-Predicate construction, this too occurs rarely in street signs, as the signs in Figure 3.1 demonstrate. While *Planning Notice* has 'full' sentences, it is not arranged as a left-to-right sequence apart from reading direction.

Indeed it is not self-evident what Given means in the context of street signs as all the information is effectively New to the street user. Perhaps the Given information is the indexicality of street signs, to be discussed in Chapters 5 and 6. I once joked as a student that the *To Let* sign on a tall London office building had a giant understood subject – many a true word spoken in jest.

Kress and van Leeuwen (1996) make two other relevant distinctions. Centre/Margin separates crucial information at the centre from ancillary information at the margins. Top/Bottom puts Ideal/Real, i.e. 'idealised or generalised essence' at the Top and more specific or practical information at the Bottom (Kress & van Leeuwen, 1996: 194). Both these distinctions cannot effectively be separated from the top-down, left-to-right nature of the English writing system, to be discussed in Chapter 7.

Finally Kress and van Leeuwen (1996: 183) argue for a factor of Salience – attracting the viewers' attention in various ways through foregrounding and backgrounding or variations in size, to be discussed later.

Visual grammar as outlined by Kress and van Leeuwen (1996) and Scollon and Scollon (2003) is a powerful way of interpreting the elements of signs, based on the authors' careful analysis of a variety of visual signs. But how do the actual street users interpret signs? Concepts such as Salience, Centre/Margin and Top/Bottom are empirically verifiable in principle through objective evidence such as how people look at the sign.

The celebrated Ogilvy Formula put forward by the advertising guru David Ogilvy (1983) claims that readers look at advertisements from top-to-bottom as Visual, Caption, Headline, Copy (i.e. prose text of some length) and Signature (i.e. the link to the product). Today the number of words in the Copy element of advertisements has shrunk but the Visual and the Headline are still crucial (PMG, 2015).

Figure 3.2 Street signs and the Ogilvy Formula (*No Smoking*, LPR; *Burger & Bevvy*, Colchester)

Two street signs that conform to the Ogilvy Formula are seen in Figure 3.2. *No Smoking* has a graphic image of a cigarette at the top (Visual), a short prominent text <NO SMOKING.> (Headline), and an amplification text <It is against the law to smoke in these premises> (Copy) at the bottom; this sign also demonstrates the problems of displaying signs through windows, partly the reflections, partly the contact with the glass. The *Burger & Bevvy* sign has a decorative letter < B > and graphic (Visual), <BURGER & BEVVY> (Headline) and a number <£10.95> and opening hours <MON-FRI NOON-5PM> (Copy). But the Ogilvy Formula applies only to the small minority of street signs with Visual and extended Copy texts.

The critical issue is how the street user actually processes and reacts to the sign. Some eye-tracking evidence, for instance, shows that restaurant menus are indeed usually read from top-to-bottom and left-to-right (Yang, 2012), essentially the requirements of the English writing system or indeed the Ogilvy Formula. However, there is almost total disagreement among researchers over the prominence or effectiveness of different zones on restaurant menus (Pearlman, 2018: 255–259).

Research in progress extends the eye-tracker technique to street signs (Cook *et al.*, in preparation). In one experiment, bilingual Chinese/English L2 users and English L1 users were asked to look at simplified estate agent *To Let* signs and brass plate signs modelled on *McCowie* (Figure 4.6). English L1 users tended to look first at the middle of the sign, next at the top and last at the bottom; Chinese/English users looked at the top first, then at the middle and finally at the bottom. In other words, the reading sequence of top-to-bottom is, curiously, more typical of these bilinguals than L1 users. People do not necessarily process the sign in the way experts believe; claims about Visual Grammar thus need the support of empirical evidence. Chapter 7 discusses this further.

Headers

Further important elements of the street sign are the *header* and *subheader*, revised from the analysis in Cook (2015). The term *header* has been preferred to *headline* (Ogilvy, 1983) or *heading*, as it has less association with printed pages. Multi-line signs without headers appear slightly odd, except in formal commemorative inscriptions like *Earl Grey Memorial* (Figure 4.2).

In street signs that have more than one line of text, the header is more salient than the rest. In *To Let* (Figure 3.1) and *No Smoking* (Figure 3.2), the headers are at the top of the sign; in *Hydrant* (Figure 3.1), the prominent header < **H** > fits the numbers < 35 > and < 4 > within its body. In the Ogilvy Formula, the Visual takes precedence, appearing above the header in *No Smoking* and *Burger & Bevvy* (Figure 3.2). Scollon and Scollon (2003) may be correct in claiming that Top typically takes precedence in English signs, although headers can appear in the middle of signs like *Town Wall* (Figure 1.5) or near the bottom as in *No Smoking* (Figure 3.2).

The header in a sense dominates the whole sign. It is the header that attracts our attention and determines whether we will bother to read the rest of the sign. Headers are part of Visual Grammar since it is their visual prominence that is crucial, not their internal grammar. The structures used in headers include noun phrases like *Planning*

Notice (Figure 3.1), particularly for naming signs like *red mezze* (Figure 3.1), and infinitival phrases like *To Let* (Figure 3.1). Indeed, there are different levels of subheaders in a sign, as in print, such as *Rosie's Bar* (Figure 3.3) or *To Let* (Figure 3.1), signalled by different letter sizes, boldness, colour, and so on.

Distinctive Aspects of the Grammar of Street Signs

The syntax of print language and visual grammar only goes so far in explaining street signs. This section looks for their unique features.

Line-breaks as syntactic dividers

A prominent feature of street signs is the use of line-breaks to show grammatical divisions, often in lists.

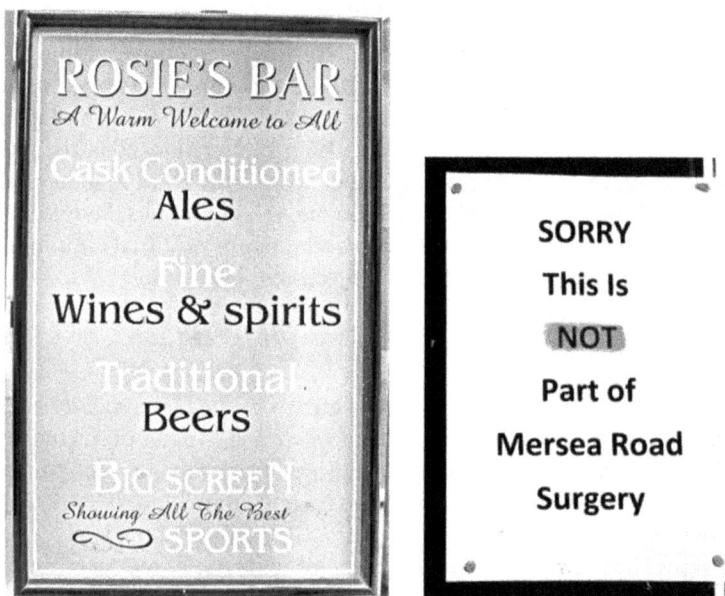

Figure 3.3 Line-breaks in street signs (*Rosie's Bar, SS; Sorry,* Colchester)

Figure 3.3 shows some typical signs with line-breaks, called 'newlines' by Nunberg (1990). *Rosie's Bar* has four pairs of lines, one triplet, alternately in white and black letters in a serif font, with two 'second' lines in a cursive script. Each line starts with a capital letter (although so do all the words except *spirits* and *to*). The line-break marks out complete phrases <ROSIE'S BAR> or separates adjectives from nouns <Traditional / Beers>. In the final triplet of lines, a noun phrase <BIG SCREEN> is separated from a verb phrase <*Showing All The Best*> and the final noun phrase is divided into premodifiers and noun <*All The Best*/SPORTS>.

The *Sorry* sign has line-break divisions marking constituents within a single sentence <SORRY / This is / NOT / Part of / Mersea Road / Surgery>. The final noun phrase is split between the pre-modifying phrase <Mersea Road> and the noun <Surgery>. It is, incidentally, strange how often street signs with *this* inform you what something is *not*; a sign on a Colchester building, for example, warns *This is not the Job Centre*.

Line-breaks are one distinctive way of showing grammatical structure in signs. This parallels the use of line-breaks in printed poetry, which sometimes mark out grammatical or rhythmic divisions, and sometimes occur within units, alias enjambment. In both verse and street signs, new lines usually start with an initial capital letter.

As Waller (1990) points out, line-breaks by themselves may not be sufficient to show meaning as they could be purely arbitrary divisions of text, like those in printed books. So line-breaks may need to be reinforced by bullet points, as in *paybyphone* (Figure 3.11), or by change of colour or letter style, as in *Rosie's Bar*.

Centring as the norm

Lines of text in street signs are centred rather than left-aligned, as seen in *Rosie's Bar* and *Sorry* (Figure 3.3), in *To Let* (Figure 3.1), and indeed in virtually all of the signs in Chapters 1 and 2. Not counting signs without text or those written in other scripts, 78% of the signs in the NCL sample have centred text, 11% left-aligned, 11% mixed alignments. The few signs with left-aligned text mostly involve full sentences, as in *Planning Notice* (Figure 3.1), or street names on direction signs, say *Quayside* (Figure 2.15), that is to say, they are formal and official.

Figure 3.4 Centring in street signs (*PO*, *Function Room*, LPR; *Abbey Gate S^t.*, Colchester)

Function Room shows a centred list of services offered in the Companions Club in all-capitals. The manhole cover *PO* has a design that is centred both horizontally and vertically, again all-capitals. For street name signs like *Abbey Gate St.* that occupy the full width of the sign, centring does not strictly apply (see Figure 3.4). However, the two extra lines <FORMERLY> and <LODDER LANE> are centred neatly below <ABBEY GATESᵗ.>. Incidentally, the lack of a space between <GATE> and <Sᵗ.> led me, for one, into thinking for many years that the street was called *Abbey Gates*, not *Abbey Gate Street*.

Figure 3.5 Centring by columns (*Pay here*, LPR; *Blackfriars Court*, SS)

The sign may sometimes in effect be divided into centred columns (see Figure 3.5). In *Pay here*, the top two lines of text <Pay here / at machine> are centred in a right-hand column, while the iconic < P > is in a left-hand column; the third line <Display ticket> is centred on the whole sign. Similarly, *Blackfriars Court* has the Newcastle coat of arms on the left; <BLACKFRIARS COURT> and <GRAINGER TOWN> centre the rest of the sign on the right, superficially the Ogilvy Formula. Centring within columns is also common in menus outside restaurants like *Gert & Henry's* (Figure 3.15).

Centring extends to the placement of naming signs in their situations (Figure 3.6). *Central Arcade* centres the Edwardian art deco sign around an arch. The name sign *Dog & Pheasant* is centred at high-level within the architecture of the whole pub, in three-dimensional gilt letters. *Headgate* positions both <HEADGATE> and <FORMERLY HOLMER'S LANE ...> centrally at high-level between the windows (which incidentally feature a tromp-de-l'oeil painting of a diminutive maidservant, allegedly starved to death in the cellar of the adjacent pub). There is also a neat contrast between the two letter styles from different centuries used for *Headgate* and *Formerly Holmer's Lane*. In *Nos 30 & 28*, < 30 > and < 28 > are centred on the doors at eye-level height with gold-coloured serif numbers.

Figure 3.6 Centring on objects (*Central Arcade*, Newcastle; *Nos 30 & 28*, LPR; *Dog & Pheasant*, *Headgate*, Colchester)

The fact that centring and line-breaks are important to the grammar of the street seems obvious as soon as it is pointed out. Yet, apart from title pages, headings and the like, centring is not a usual feature of written English, presumably because it would interfere with the eye moving from line to line in connected texts; line-breaks are relevant only to printed verse. The street sign relies on special cues of its own.

Capital Letters in English Street Signs

This section discusses the way in which street signs exploit the contrast between capitals and lower case available in writing.

The conventions for capitals are mostly laid down in prescriptive guides published by self-appointed gatekeepers representing particular institutions. *The Penguin Guide to Punctuation* (Trask, 1997), *The Cassell Guide to Punctuation* (Todd, 1995) and NASA's *Grammar, Punctuation and Capitalization* (McCaskill, 1998) are based on expert opinion and tradition, not on appropriate text corpora, even if such rules are taken as diktats by the general public. Academic writers are subject to similar prescriptivism from dictatorial style guides for journals.

The rule that capitals start sentences is marginally relevant for street signs since they have so few full sentences. *Planning Notice* (Figure 3.1) keeps sentence-initial capitals but dispenses with sentence-final stops. The ubiquitous use of line-initial capitals in combination with line-breaks has been mentioned above. The distinctive features of street signs are word-initial capitals and texts in all-capitals or all lower case.

Word-initial capitals

Initial capital letters are used in the print system for certain classes of words, such as proper names, and for content words in book titles, called 'headline style' in McCaskill (1998).

Word-initial capitals are common in street signs (Figure 3.7). *Motorists* shows the common practice of starting each word with a capital. In *All Time Specials*, a handwritten café blackboard, every word starts with a capital except <in>. The parking notice *Warning* similarly has word-initial caps except for <in operation>. An official sign on Colchester Town Hall, *Customer Service Centre*, capitalises all the words apart from the function words *in, of, for, the, or, be* and the verb *deposited*. Capitalising content words but not function words harks back to 17th century English in which content words were capitalised in some styles, similar to modern German, seen in the capitalised nouns of the *Constitution of the United States* (1787). It survives in book titles such as *Lord of the Rings* or *Across the River and into the Trees*. Subjectively, these street signs seem quaint and amateurish rather than everyday.

All-capitals

In the print system, phrases in all capital letters are used for title pages of books, headlines in printed editions of tabloid newspapers, and some restricted uses such as acronyms. Texts in all-capitals are attacked as 'shouting' in web netiquette and indeed in contemporary advice to university students, although this goes back to at least the mid-19th century:

"YOU DIDN'T GO IN, Rawdon!" screamed his wife. (W.M. Thackeray, 1847, *Vanity Fair*)

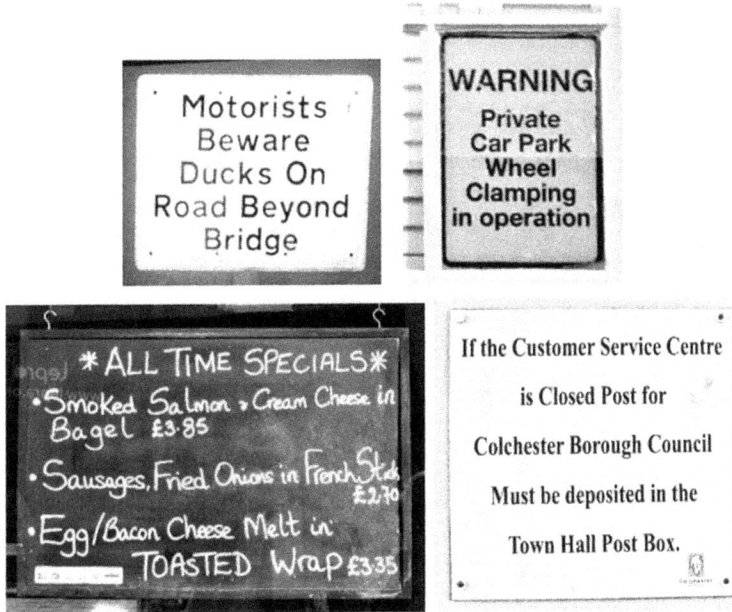

Figure 3.7 Notices with word-initial capitals (*Motorists*, Coggeshall, Essex; *Warning*, Newcastle; *All Time Specials*, *Customer Service Centre*, Colchester)

All-capitals are, however, almost the default mode for street signs: perhaps shouting is necessary for signs to get attention. Street and building name signs are typically in all-capitals, as seen in *Abbey GateS*[t] (Figure 3.4), *Central Arcade* (Figure 3.6) and through-out Chapter 5. Even entire texts may be written in all-capitals, like those in *Alderman Fenwick's House* (Figure 2.8).

Figure 3.8 shows the use of gilt capital letters for pub names in *The Percy Arms* in the serif all-capitals of the native English signwriting tradition, with the additional twist of non-word-initial letters being small caps. Parking signs like *Private* and *Parking for Doctors* tend to be in all-capitals, reinforcing their authoritative tone. The shop window sign *You are man?* has all-capitals <YOU ARE MAN?> for a man, and initial capital plus lower case <You are woman?> for a woman; the heroically bearded man is natu-rally in the left-hand window.

Memorials such as the *Welcome* plaque on the pavement of Eldon Square or *Castle Park* at eye-level at the park entrance (Figure 3.9) are usually incised or raised letters on stone or metal, the materials suggesting permanence, as discussed in Chapter 4. *Welcome* skilfully highlights the golden letters in black so that they stand out from the same-coloured bronze background. *Castle Park* illustrates how to emphasise incised noun-initial capital letters by colouring them red as well as making them larger.

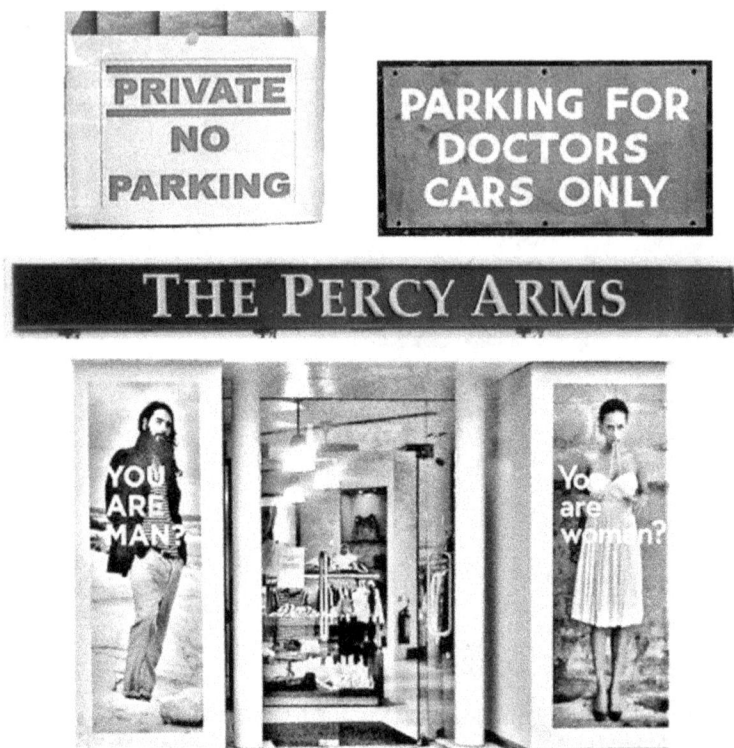

Figure 3.8 Signs in all-capitals (*Private*, LPR; *Percy Arms*, LPZ; *Parking for Doctors*, Colchester; *You Are Man?*, Newcastle)

At the opposite end come unique signs made by 'non-expert' writers with a pen or a brush, which also favour all-capitals (Walker, 2001). *Wet Paint* and *Sweet Mother's Day* (Figure 3.10) epitomise these straightforward temporary notices. *Wet Paint* has a large brush-pointed sign. *Sweet Mother's Day* makes partial use of slightly larger word-initial capitals like the first < S >, made with a felt-tip. It seems to be assumed that capitals are more legible and easier to make, particularly on a large scale with brushes and paint, as in *No Entry to Doctor's Surgery* (Figure 2.13).

All lower case letters

A text in all lower case letters can be a deliberate rebellion against the print system and so become a mark of the avant garde poet, as with Archie, the cockroach:

i was once a vers libre bard
but i died and my soul went into the body of a cockroach (Marquis, 1927)

Figure 3.9 Commemorative signs (*Welcome*, Newcastle; *Castle Park*, Colchester)

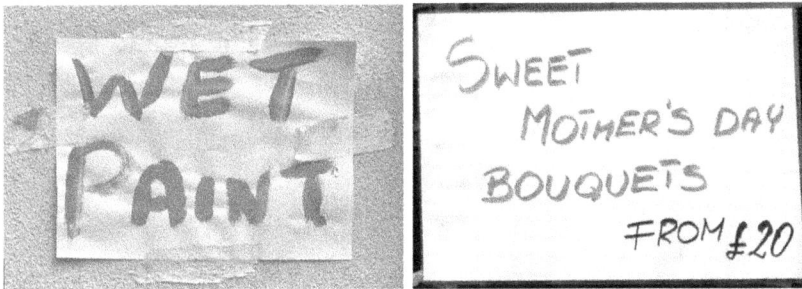

Figure 3.10 All-capitals in 'non-expert' hand-drawn signs (*Wet Paint, Sweet Mother's Day*, LPR)

although here caused by his inability to use the shift key on a typewriter. This seems another spinoff from the Bauhaus, which adopted all lower case in its official publications in 1923, and the Swiss school of typography it inspired: Tschichold (1998 [1928]) talked of 'the great advantage to the national economy' that would arise from the sole use of lower case.

Figure 3.11 shows three street signs in all lower case letters. Elegant signs like *the terrace* seem more about corporate identity than artistic rebellion. The fascia-level *mercurytheatre* illustrates an unusual use of lower case letters for a building name, and also omits the word space as if it were an email address. Capitals are absent from the official eye-level parking sign *paybyphone*, with full stops also lacking, giving a more informal tone than usual in parking regulations, together with the sans serif letters. But, to my eye, this notice is less legible than one with a more liberal use of capital letters.

Mixed capitals and lower case within the same word

The print system uses capitals within a word in Irish- and Scottish-derived surnames, which may or may not have a capital after *Mac-*, *MacWhinney* versus *Macgregor*.

Figure 3.11 Signs with no capital letters (*the terrace*, Newcastle; *paybyphone*, LPR; *mercurytheatre*, Colchester)

Figure 3.12 illustrates the use of word-internal capitals in modern cross-media signs for company names. Usually capitals signal morpheme splits within compound words, often blended names, as in *StarkHartleyAtkinson*. The familiar logos *NatWest* and *FennWright* for high street businesses are used across many media, and so are more part of the naming conventions for businesses than of the language of street signs. To take some non-street examples of capital use, an experimental system to minimise mistakes in dispensing medications found that printing the second part of the name in capitals led to fewer errors (Filika *et al*., 2004); a modern novel is titled *HHhH* (Binet, 2012).

Figure 3.12 Mixing capitals and lower case within the same word (*StarkHartleyAtkinson*, LPR; *NatWest*, *FennWright*, Colchester)

The ways of using capitals and lower case in street signs clearly differ from those in the accepted print system. Sentence-initial capitals are rarely seen and then only in 'official' long-text notices. All-capitals are the norm for inscriptions, warning and non-expert notices, naming signs and text artwork, rather than 'shouting'. All lower case letters make a statement about individuality and modernity. Line-initial capitals punctuate by separating phrases. Word-initial capitals are used not only for proper names but also sometimes for all words, sometimes for content words alone.

The Punctuation of Street Signs

Punctuation started as a way to help poor readers read manuscripts aloud (Parkes, 1992) by indicating pauses, intonation, etc. (Cook, 2004a) – a system for symbol-sound correspondence. Since we have argued that street signs are rarely read aloud, this use of punctuation is of marginal relevance here.

But, as the habit of silent reading spread in the Middle Ages, punctuation developed into a way of helping the reader to understand the text by marking out its grammatical structure. Grammatical punctuation marks show the boundaries of syntactic units and the relationships between them, and abbreviation where words are shortened by omitting letters. Sentences begin with a capital and end with one of the punctuation marks < . ! ? >; clauses and phrases are separated by < – , ; : >; words are delimited by word spaces. Marks like < ' ' " " – > separate units for purposes such as quotation (Cook, 2004a). Punctuation links grammatical units through the hyphen < - > in compound words <tea-cup> and the apostrophe <ROSIE'S BAR> (Figure 3.3). The emphasis here is on grammatical punctuation.

Punctuation marks occasionally have a meaning in themselves. The from-to dash < – > in < pp. 25–27 > has a meaning equivalent to 'from X to Y'. The colon in <Man proposes: God disposes> implies a link between the two clauses, paraphrasable as 'but'. Other uses of punctuation marks include < ' . > for single or multiple letter omission, as in <doesn't> or <St.> (Figure 3.14). More details are given in Cook (2013b).

Like the shibboleth spelling mentioned in the last chapter, some punctuation 'mistakes' have been ascribed to illiteracy or lack of class. Confusing the uses of <its> and <it's> as in <Its head/it's head> <It's new/its new>, using an 'Oxford' comma before the *and* that concludes a list <the birds, the bees, and the sycamore trees>, or referring to <Newcastle-upon-Tyne> go beyond simple mistakes to show a depravity of soul. Yet, like the shibboleth spelling rules, no authority has the right to lay down such regulations: linguists describe what occurs, as physicists describe electrons. Nevertheless, writers of street signs have to take into account the risks of going against popular opinion by deliberately or accidentally using non-standard punctuation.

Table 3.1 compares the frequency of punctuation marks per thousand words in the NCL sample with the print sample described in Cook (2013b), which consisted of 459 thousand words from diverse text types. Given the large number of variables involved, such comparisons must be suggestive rather than definitive.

Table 3.1 Punctuation mark frequencies per 1000 words

	NCL	Print
Full stops	12	65.3
Commas	11.4	61.6
Overall	37	235.2

Source: Cook (2013b, 2020b).

The street signs in the NCL sample had an average of 37 punctuation marks per thousand words, considerably less than the 235.2 for print. Stops used as separators in money expressions like < £10.95 > are common in menus and are also found in numbers < 3.142 > and web addresses – the decimal stop (Cook, 2015). Setting these aside, full stops averaged 12 per 1000 words in street signs, 65.3 in print. Commas occurred 11.4 times per 1000 words, compared to 61.6 in print; 46% of the commas in street signs were for listing items, compared to the 20% found by Bayraktar *et al.* (1998) in newspaper texts.

The NCL sample averages one punctuation mark for every 11.5 words, the print sample one for every 4.3 words. Overall, after excluding decimal and abbreviation stops and from-to dashes, 53.7% of signs in the NCL sample had no punctuation and only 4.1% had sentence-final full stops. The NCL sample thus uses punctuation sparingly. While the NCL sample is fairly small, it includes all signs, not just, say, shop names.

Although the punctuation in the general sample cannot be reliably quantified because the signs were selected, the figures confirm the sparseness of punctuation. Sentences in street signs are mostly not signalled by full stops, nor phrases and clauses by commas. The <ST THOMAS STREET.> sign (Figure 3.14) is unusual in ending a street name with a full stop. Social media texts also frequently do without full stops, which can communicate insincerity (Gunraj *et al.*, 2016).

The typical full stop in street signs shows abbreviation in nouns such as *street* < St.> as in <Abbey GateS^t.> (Figure 3.4) and *saint* <St.>, seen together in <St. Thomas St.> (Figure 3.14), or <Ltd.> as in *McCowie & Co Ltd.* (Figure 4.6). The abbreviation full stop does not always occur where the letters are expected but after the whole word, as in <St.>, often beneath the < t > as in <St. James St.> (Figure 3.14). Other familiar examples are <Ave.> and <Mr.> (Figure 4.6). Road marking signs for drivers on the roadway sometimes have almost impenetrable abbreviations like *So'ton* (Southampton) or *Bps Stortford* (Bishops Stortford). Novel punctuation in naming signs is discussed in Chapter 7.

A minor use of the full stop is to divide up numbers, for example < £3.99 > in *Scampi* (Figure 3.16) and < £10.95 > (Figure 3.2), known as the decimal point; some countries prefer the decimal comma. Interestingly, several handwritten street signs show the raised dot formerly used in England for decimal numbers < £3.85 > (Figure 3.7), < £8.95 > (Figure 3.15) before the currency was decimalised in 1971, presumably giving away the writer's age.

Use of the Apostrophe

When the apostrophe < ' > came into English in the 15th century, its first use was to show that a letter had been left out, as in <don't>, <I'm> or <it's> (Scholfield, 2016). Indeed, the missing letters in < 'em > in *Give 'em hell*, reflect an even earlier Old English <hem> of 1200 years ago rather than the <them> of the invading Viking word *them*.

Many final < e(s) > endings on modern nouns are reduced forms of the Old English cases, which died out over the centuries. When the Middle English genitive inflection <es> became irrelevant to speech, the < e > could be replaced by < ' >, i.e. become silent, so <fatheres>, for example, could be written as <father's>. The replacement of < e > by < ' > was extended to other genitive noun inflections regardless of whether they had < e >, plus an added convention that the apostrophe should follow the genitive < s > when the noun was plural, <fathers'>. The apostrophe shifted from indicating the absence of a sound in speech to showing the genitive case, i.e. from correspondence punctuation to grammatical punctuation. But this usage was not extended to personal pronouns like < hers > (Scholfield, 2016), let alone to plural nouns not in the genitive case.

The English writing system had therefore come up with a novel way of disambiguating words with the same pronunciation. It is useful to be able to distinguish *fathers*, *father's* and *fathers'*, or *it's* and *its* in writing, even if it is unlikely that people actually confuse them in speech. Nevertheless this seems to have perplexed English writers ever since.

Apostrophes in shop names and building names

The genitive apostrophe < ' > thus shows ownership in street and building names.

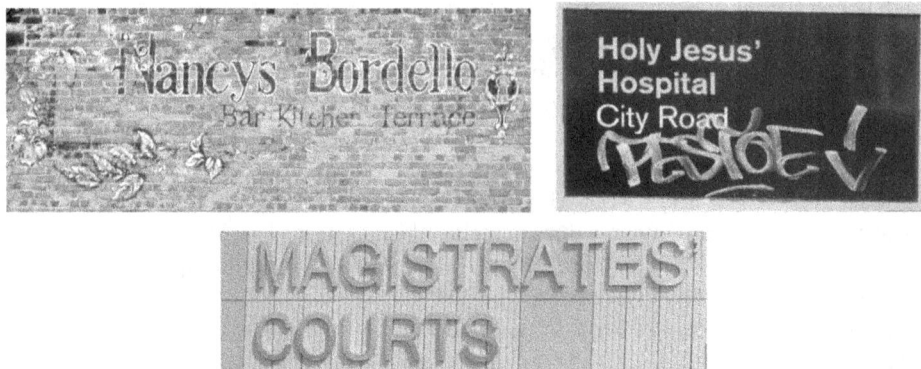

Figure 3.13 Building names with apostrophes (*Nancy's Bordello, Holy Jesus' Hospital*, Newcastle; *Magistrates' Courts*, Colchester)

The high-level sign *Nancy's Bordello* painted on brick has the singular genitive <Nancy's>; despite its fadedness, the restaurant still exists. The apostrophe of *Holy Jesus' Hospital* in a way shows <Jesus's> lack of two letters. The sign has a more modern sans serif letter style than might be expected on a historical religious building. It stands out by being left-aligned rather than centred. It also incidentally illustrates the use of graffiti writers' tags, to be discussed later. *Magistrates' Courts* is a plural genitive <MAGISTRATES'> in silver applied all-capitals in the high zone.

Apostrophes in street names

The question of whether an apostrophe is needed in street name signs has never been resolved, as Figure 3.14 shows.

The *St Thomas* signs come from the LPZ area adjoining Leazes Park Road, the *St James* signs from the area adjacent to St James' Park stadium. They highlight the inconsistency of apostrophes in street signs, sometimes even for the same street. *St James' Park* names the football stadium, home of Newcastle United, 100 yards or so from Leazes Park Road; the apostrophe here relates to two missing letters <es> <Jameses>, a form for words ending in < s > seldom found in street signs apart from, say, <St Gileses-Terrace> in Oxford.

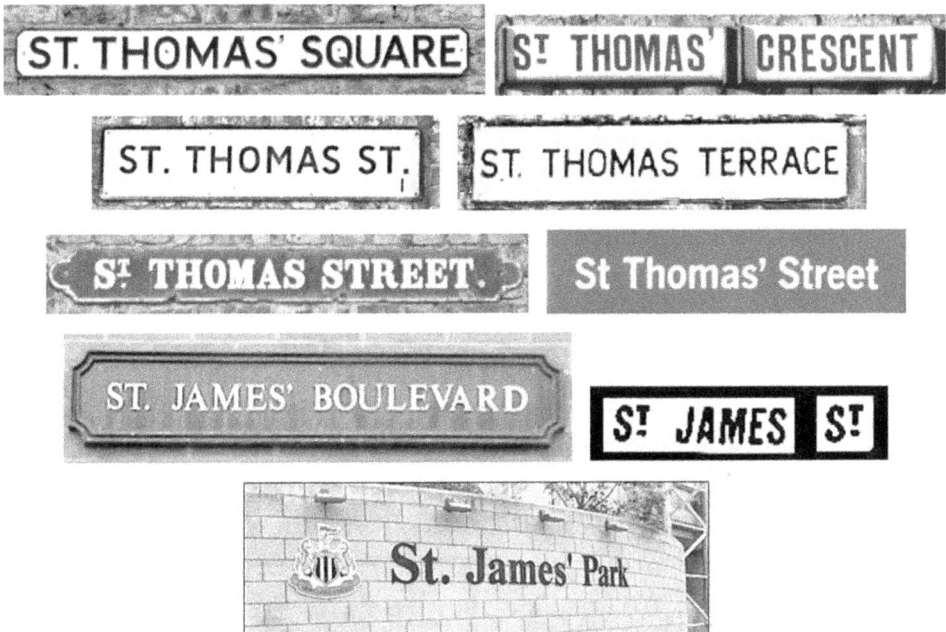

Figure 3.14 Apostrophes in street names (*St Thomas Square/Crescent/Street/Terrace, St James Street* (edited), LPZ; *St James Boulevard/Park*, Newcastle)

Whether the stadium is <St. James Park> or <St. James' Park> is a great concern for Toonies, the fans of Newcastle United, and debated about with much passion and a host of folk etymological arguments in local newspapers and the like. A university colleague and I were interviewed separately by local television about which was correct – and came to opposite conclusions. Nothing much hinges on the choice except some sense of identity.

Building and shop names with and without apostrophes

Traditional grammarians for many years had their own version of the apostrophe debate in terms of whether one wrote *Harrods* or *Harrod's*, *Woolworths* or *Woolworth's*. Zandvoort (1957: 105) related this 'local genitive' to an unexpressed noun, say *Harrod's (shop)*, even when this form never actually appears.

– *Greggs* is a classic all-capitals name sign without an apostrophe, despite still being run by the Gregg family in Newcastle.
– *Waterstone's* bookshop changed in the 2010s to *Waterstones*, having lost its original owner, Tim Waterstone; the apostrophe is being faded out almost literally in their logo to make it 'more versatile' (BBC, 2012), and the letters are now lower case black rather than gilt capitals.

- *Master Mariner's*, a house sign, shows the local genitive with implied noun.
- *Gert and Henry's* restaurant in York appears as <Gert and Henry's> on Facebook but as <Gert and Henry> on Tripadvisor.
- *Our Lady* sign has a curiously logical form <Our Lady and St Annes' Primary School> where the genitive < s > belongs to the compound noun phrase <Our Lady and St Anne> and so has been given a plural form; their website (http://www.olsa. org.uk/), however, gives it throughout as <Our Lady and St Anne's Primary School>, as do other schools with this name.

Figure 3.15 Name signs in < s > with and without < ' > (*Greggs*, LPR; *Waterstone's*, Colchester; *Master Mariner's*, Blakeney; *Our Lady*, Newcastle; *Gert & Henry's*, York)

Missing apostrophes on signs are also common, like <DOCTORS CARS> in *Parking for Doctors* (Figure 3.8). Clearly the use of the genitive apostrophe is still as variable as it has ever been.

The greengrocer's apostrophe

The greengrocer's apostrophe is called after their widespread habit of labelling their wares <Banana's> and <Carrot's>. The everyday 'mistake' is generalising the apostrophe to all nouns with plural *s* rather than just those genitive singulars, with some leeway for dates <1600's>, abbreviations <CD's> and the like, at least for some gatekeepers – book editors seem peculiarly hostile to these exceptions.

The failure to observe the < 's > conventions has become a shibboleth of literacy and public discussion of language. What started as a useful minor convenience became a millstone on writer's shoulders, treated with scorn in books such as the massive bestseller *Eats, Shoots and Leaves* (Truss, 2004). It inspired a 'grammar vigilante' in Bristol to paint apostrophes on street signs where he thinks they are needed (BBC, 2017). Ironically, from photos, he seems to paint primes < ' > rather than apostrophes < ' >, a mistake of a different type (Bringhurst, 2005: 316).

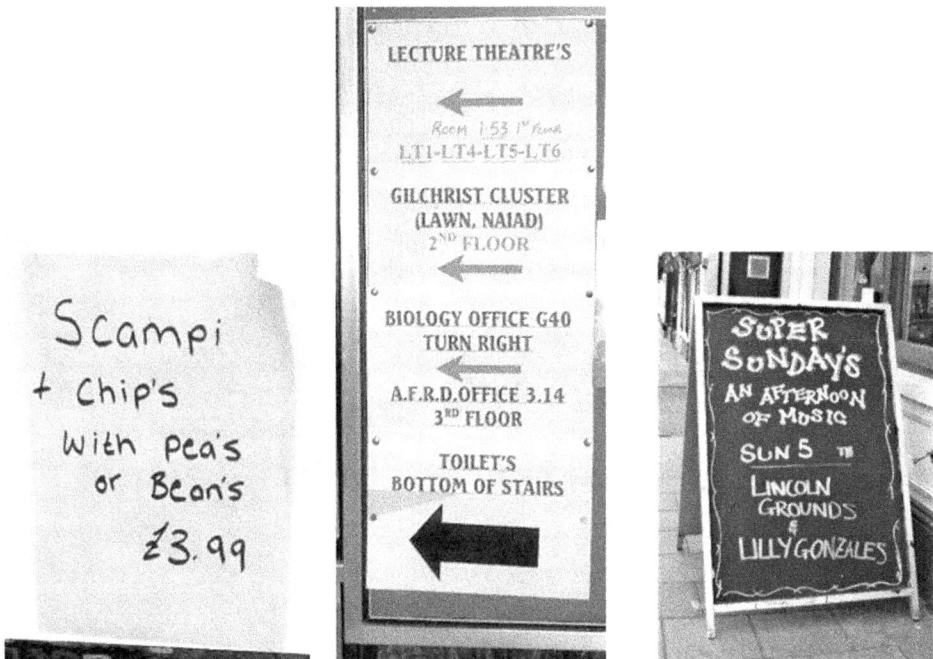

Figure 3.16 Greengrocer's apostrophes (*Scampi*, LPR; *Lecture Theatre's*, Newcastle; *Super Sunday's*, Colchester)

Scampi shows three greengrocer's apostrophes on a restaurant sign <Chip's with Pea's or Bean's>, *Super Sunday's* a single prominent example <Sunday's>. Although *Lecture Theatre's* is in an entrance not a street, <LECTURE THEATRE'S> and <TOILET'S> illustrate how widespread this practice is, even in higher education.

The greengrocer's apostrophe is an established and enduring element in the language of unique street signs, however much self-nominated pundits may complain. Further examples can be found on such websites as *The Greengrocer's Apostrophe* (Cook, 2020a) and *The Apostrophe Protection Society* (2020). Its critics elevate knowledge of apostrophe use to a shibboleth for literacy. A similar shibboleth is against *'till* (Figure 4.7). *Till* and *until* have been distinct words since Old English rather than *till* being an abbreviation (Cook, 2004b).

The Vocabulary of Street Signs

As a distinctive genre of written language, street signs employ words that are rarely heard in speech. Street signs in Colchester say *Don't park on the greensward* and *Cyclists must dismount*, vocabulary usually associated with Robin Hood. The Newcastle Metro still warns *Before boarding let people alight first;* I cannot remember ever hearing anyone say *alight* and I do not know whether its past tense is *alit* or *alighted*; OED (2015) gives both.

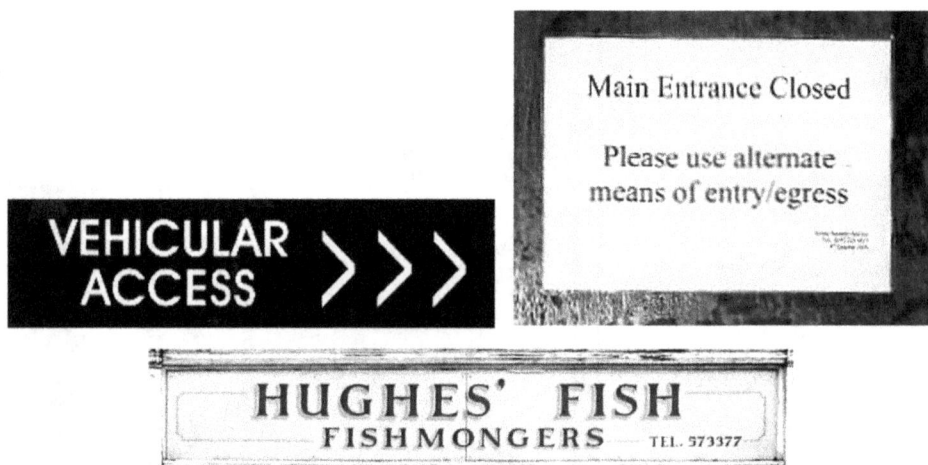

Figure 3.17 Old-fashioned written words (*Vehicular Access, Hughes' Fish*, Colchester; *Main Entrance Closed*, Newcastle)

One curious pocket of street sign vocabulary is the preservation of archaic trades and shops, usually in unique signs. *Hughes' Fish* has *fishmongers*, rarely heard in speech. Signs also feature *cheesemongers, apothecary, haberdashers* and *fleshers*, although the latter was only glimpsed in Scotland. Such names are either genuine historic survivals or self-conscious attempts at antiqueness as in *SPACE.NK.apothecary* (Figure 2.25), chosen for the images of corporate businesses.

Other street vocabulary items seem to be selected for their connotations of formality and officialdom, say, *vehicular* or *egress* found in *Main Entrance Closed*, although both do occur in the British National Corpus. The vocabulary of traffic signs and of street and building names is also restricted by regulation, as seen in Chapter 5; the word *Road* is, for instance, banned from the City of London proper.

Graffiti and Text Art

Graffiti and text art are often considered the most distinctive and interesting of street signs. The term *graffiti* is defined by English Heritage (1999) as 'words, scribbling or drawings used in the deliberate, unauthorised defacement of a surface', adopting an owner's perspective that graffiti detract from the objects on which they are placed and that the motive for making them is defacement, not enhancement or challenge. In Ross (2016: 476), graffiti are 'words, figures, and images that have been written, drawn, and/ or etched into or on surfaces where the owner has NOT given permission', concurring that graffiti are additions to existing surfaces and lack permission but assigning no motive to them.

Defacement and lack of permission represent the traditional way of looking at graffiti in, say, the classical signs of Pompeii and Rome (Baird & Taylor, 2016) or those in mediaeval churches (Champion, 2015). Linguists have mostly seen graffiti as transgressive, 'the process of writing/drawing illicitly' (Pennycook, 2009: 306): Soukup (2020) talks of 'illegally placed stickers' on signs in Vienna without explaining which laws they break.

When graffiti writers are prosecuted in English courts, it is, however, for the offense of criminal damage, not for lack of permission. Many graffiti could be said to be licensed through deemed permission under the *Outdoor Advertisements* (DCLG, 2007) regulations. In England, it is the physical damage the signs cause that needs to be punished:

> 1) A person who without lawful excuse destroys or damages any property belonging to another intending to destroy or damage any such property being reckless as to whether any such property would be destroyed or damaged shall be guilty of an offence. (*Criminal Damage Act*, 1971)

It is then criminal to write *Coca-Cola* on a lorry with a spray can but legal to cover the whole lorry with an advertisement for Coca-Cola. Banksy claims it is not so much graffiti writers that vandalise our streets as 'the companies that scrawl giant logos across buildings and buses trying to make us feel inadequate unless we buy their products' (Banksy, 2005: 8).

The signs in Figure 3.18 illustrate the pervasive use of all-capitals in graffiti and text art. Of the 300 English examples of text art in Cook (2021, unpublished), 64% have all-capitals, 2.4% all lower case and 10.1% the usual prose style of sentence and proper name initial capitals.

Graffiti like *Mark Lvz Liz 4eva* are an English tradition that has endured for generations, whether protestations of love, scatological remarks or mock identities such as Chad looking over a wall, often accompanied by the text *Kilroy woz here*. These shade into political slogans like the renowned London campaign *Free George Davis* that successfully freed an unjustly convicted bank robber, only for him to be caught red-handed while robbing another bank shortly after his release; signs were still visible on railway bridges 40 years later. Social media have now largely taken over this protest role; tweeting a message is easier than climbing a railway embankment in the dark.

Figure 3.18 Graffiti and text art (*Mark Lvz Lizs 4eva*, Newcastle; *Self portrait*, Mark Wallinger, Gateshead; *Is this the place of your dreams?*, Mark Titchner, Colchester)

Traditional graffiti like *Mark Lvz Liza 4eva* can be readily defined in terms of defacement and lack of permission. Owners of historic buildings see them as a threat in that many can only be removed with difficulty, if at all (English Heritage, 1999).

Ironically some graffiti are themselves historical monuments, like those inscribed on Hadrian's Wall by Roman soldiers or Lord Byron's tag preserved in a dungeon at the Château du Chillon.

Graffiti now usually refers to signs like the name tag on *Holy Jesus* (Figure 3.13) that spread from 1960s New York streets around the world as fast as McDonald's, covered in books such as Ross (2016) and Waclawek (2011). Tags, for example, proclaim gang membership and self-identity within a subculture and show off skill and originality (Waclawek, 2011); they involve an element of risk from prosecution and from the physical danger of placing signs in spaces only accessible through climbing or a ladder, like high zone *Invader* (4.13). However, in the New York epicentre of modern graffiti, most works are now done legally with the permission of the site owner and an illegal graffiti writer only lasts six months (Kramer, 2016).

The hanging banner < I > is a work by Mark Wallinger called *Self Portrait*, repeated in many versions in different locations; the one seen here is on the Baltic Gallery, Gateshead, in Times New Roman on a gigantic scale 20 metres high. *Is this the place of your dreams?* forms part of a project by Mark Titchner that appeared in several unused Colchester shop windows in 2020 in forceful sans serif capitals.

Invader provides a link to the parallel cultural movement of text art in public spaces, glimpsed in *I* and *Is this the place of your dreams?*, as likely to be seen in a gallery as in a street. Rather than lacking permission, text art is commissioned by owners as artwork and commands enormous prices, say the $26,485,000 paid for *Apocalypse Now* by Christopher Wool (Christie's, 2020). Banksy and Invader straddle both traditions – prestigious art originally done without permission in public places – but the motivations are rather different. The graffiti coverage in *The Routledge Handbook of Graffiti and Street Art* (Ross, 2016), for example, has little overlap with the text art in *Art and Text* (Beech *et al.*, 2009).

While graffiti and text art need to be mentioned here, they fit uncomfortably because their functions and meanings go beyond social life and movement (Cook, 2021, unpublished), and they belong to international cultural movements rather than being specifically English. The language of the street framework can at best comment on the prevalence in these signs of all-capitals, the crudeness of the execution of much text art compared to the work of signwriters, the use of distinctive materials in graffiti such as spray paint, and the characteristic language content involved, whether slogans, aphorisms or name tags.

Conclusion

In the light of this chapter, the language of the street is a special genre of written language that is rarely read aloud and is sometimes effectively impossible to read aloud. Letter-sound correspondences are more of historical interest than relevant for the modern street sign. Meaning depends on how letters contrast with each other and on their variable forms, plus the connotations to be dealt with in Chapter 7.

Above letters come grammatical and lexical systems, partly a small subset of the standard language, with obvious biases towards nouns and noun phrases, a minimal use of verbs and punctuation, some archaic vocabulary and common use of novel spelling forms. But, in addition, street signs include: a level at which arrangement in space creates meanings, such as the Ogilvy Formula; a notion of salience in which headers, etc., are made prominent in various ways; the use of distinctive punctuation such as line-breaks and apostrophes; a complex system of capitals and lower case letters conveying diverse meanings; and a reliance on centring of text within the sign and of the sign within the environment. This goes further than Halliday's economy grammar in establishing a genre of written language all of its own, differing from the written language of printed books in more ways than the absence of certain features.

A final coda is needed to remind the reader of the standard axiom mentioned in Chapter 2 that linguistics is descriptive, not prescriptive. The point of street signs research is not to decree what should or should not appear on signs. It is not a matter of whether line-breaks, greengrocer's apostrophes etc. are correct in terms of some prescriptive account of English but of how they are used. Although often inappropriate in other genres of English, such as printed books and newspapers, they succeed in conveying the meanings appropriate to street signs.

4 The Material of the Street Sign

Written language uses visible and tangible material and has an enduring physical reality, whereas speech consists of transitory soundwaves. Street signs may be made of stone, glass, metal, paper or pixels; their letters may be cut by chisels, written with felt tips, painted with brushes, moulded in metal, printed with printing presses or displayed on screens. As Levy (2001) points out:

> For most of the five thousand years of writing history, all our techniques and technologies have been aimed at making visible marks stick to surfaces. (Levy, 2001: 34)

The dictum from de Saussure (1976 [1916]: 166) that the material forms of letters are arbitrary, discussed in Chapter 3, thus misses an important aspect of street signs. For the street user's interpretation of street signs *is* affected by the materials they are made of and by the physical processes used to create them (Kress & van Leeuwen, 1996: 232). This chapter explores the meanings that the material of the street sign conveys to the street user, building on Cook (2015).

Figure 4.1 demonstrates the wealth of materials to be found on the signs of any street.

- *The Trent*. A pub blackboard propped against a wall, handwritten in chalk in capital letters, a movable sign taken in at night, neatly displaying the Geordie meaning for *canny* of 'great, nice', etc. See Pearce (2017) for more discussion.
- *Millennium Trail*. A small metal sign of Newcastle Castle Keep embedded in the pavement movement zone, marking out a route for sightseers to follow, now long defunct.
- *Wet Paint*. A flimsy bilingual English/Chinese notice on paper, pinned to a door at eye-level for a few hours – an informal warning.
- *Chef Canton*. Cursive italic letters painted in gold on a glass fascia that reflects the other side of the street – an elegant restaurant sign.
- *Turn Right*. An elongated traffic signwritten on the cobbled road surface, applied in skid-proof paint – the standard for roadway markings.
- *Erected AD 1844*. Sans serif capital letters cut into a stone plaque at low-level – a classical style for commemorative foundation stones.
- *City Hall*. A building name sign with large individual gold-painted serif capital letters, applied to stone in the high zone – a proclamation of respectability and stability.

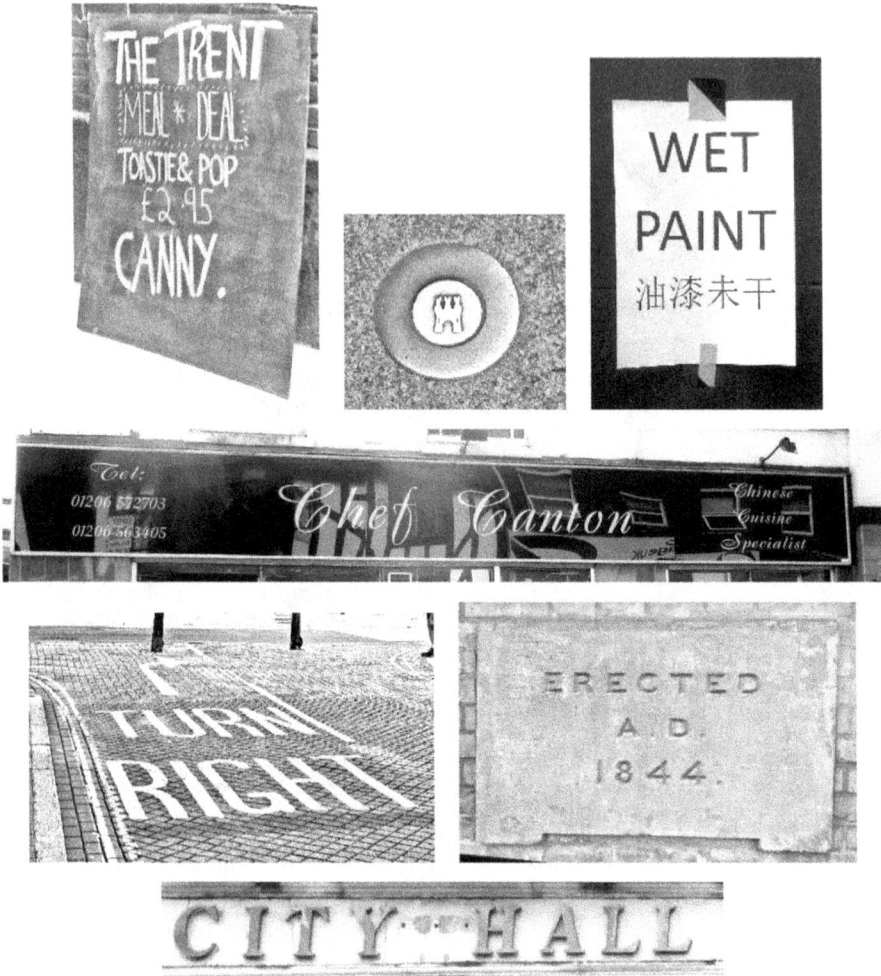

Figure 4.1 A sample of materials in street signs (*The Trent, Millennium Trail*, LPR; *Wet Paint, Erected AD 1844*, SS; *Chef Canton, Turn Right*, Colchester; *City Hall*, Newcastle)

Could the *Wet Paint* paper notice be engraved on stone like *Erected AD 1844*? Could *Millennium Trail* be painted on glass like *Chef Canton*? Could *City Hall* be painted on a road like *Turn Right*? Materials are chosen to suit a given genre or purpose, as detailed comprehensively in Haslam (2011) and Kinneir (1980).

Appearance counts for more than substance; it does not matter whether a street sign is actually made of stone or painted in real gold so long as the street user sees them as stone or gold. A surface may well appear to be stone or metal, but may be made from materials like stucco, plastic or concrete.

The material aspects of signs were described by Scollon and Scollon (2003: 135–136) in terms of:

- **permanence/durability**: the material may show 'the signs are to last the life of the building itself', like *Erected AD 1844*;
- **temporality/newness**: signs 'attached to or superposed on more permanent signs', like *Wet Paint*;
- **quality**: signs that involve 'a longer time of preparation and a greater expense in production', like *City Hall*.

These categories provide an initial frame for the discussion.

Street signs and location

The meanings of many street signs are bound to specific locations. Scollon and Scollon (2003: 146) speak of 'situated semiotics ... any aspect of the meaning that is predicated on the placement of the sign in the material world'. Building name signs like *City Hall* or inscriptions like *Erected AD 1844* are meaningful only when they are attached to particular buildings; they lose their point if they are moved somewhere else. *Wet Paint* is local in referring to the immediate vicinity and its effective meaning has a brief timespan.

The brass plates *Newcastle Companions* (Figure 1.11) and *McCowie & Co* (Figure 4.6) announce the registered offices of those businesses; the street name signs *Maldon Road* (Figure 4.6) and *Abbey Gate S^t.* (Figure 3.4) occur meaningfully only at the ends of those streets or along their lengths: their meanings are tied in to their location. Controlling signs additionally depend on the user's orientation, that is to say on which way they are facing, to be discussed in Chapter 6.

Integrated street signs are called 'architectural' if they form an integral part of the object they name (Baines & Dixon, 2002), typically cut into stone in an arch or portico, as in *Hospital* (Figure 2.12) or *Dex Garage* (Figure 4.3). The large signs of casinos and hotels identify the businesses of the Las Vegas Strip, where 'the sign is more important than the architecture' (Venturi *et al.*, 1977: 13). Times Square in Manhattan and Piccadilly Circus in London are recognised by their signs, not by their buildings. Venturi *et al.* (1977) regret that modern architects have seen signs as tacked on to buildings rather than integral to them.

The physical relationship between the sign and what it is attached to is thus important. Kinneir (1980: 72) describes:

- 'letters integrated into the building during the course of construction', such as the foundation stone *Erected AD 1844* or the brick *CIU* (Figure 4.13);
- 'letters applied after completion to the surface of buildings', such as *City Hall* (Figure 4.1) or *Laing Art Gallery* (Figure 5.4);
- 'letters which are related but separate', such as movable signs like *The Trent* blackboard (Figure 4.1) or paper signs like *Wet Paint* (Figure 3.10).

Location also relates to legibility: does a sign need to be read from a few feet away like the *Millennium Trail* sign (Figure 4.1) or from many yards like *City Hall* (Figure 4.1)? Signs are usually placed in the vertical plane facing the users, sometimes on horizontal surfaces beneath their feet or on banners above their heads, and many are some way from them, distance dictating the letter size (Vink, 2015).

Yet sheer legibility is not necessarily the goal (Kinneir, 1980). Well-known signs may be instantly recognisable even if they are scarcely legible: the McDonald's Golden Arches or the Starbucks siren do not need words. The difficulty in reading *Conservative Club* (Figure 4.5) hardly prevents the members of the Conservative Party from finding it.

Street signs must be visible at all times and in all conditions. Fingerposts and direction signs, for instance, must be readable regardless of lighting or weather. During daylight hours, the visibility of the sign relies on the availability of natural light. Raised and hollowed letters depend on the angle of the light bringing out shadows. In some instances the signs themselves provide the light source, discussed below. Light coming from behind the sign has different colour properties from light bouncing off it: the backlit sign is effectively filtering the light rather than reflecting it selectively. The typeface FF Transit designed for public signage systems has different versions for front- and back-lighting (https://www.fontshop.com/families/ff-transit).

Writing technology

Writing has always reflected the materials and techniques of its time, as described by calligraphers like Donald Jackson (1981) and Ewan Clayton (2014). Chinese writing, for instance, started by carving symbols on bones and metal, developed into painting with pointed brushes, leading to the present-day Chinese characters seen in *Wet Paint* (Figure 4.1) and *Mangos* (Figure 4.9). Writing with a brush lends itself to flowing curves and strokes of varying width, imitated in modern signs by italics.

Each technological change in how writing was produced affected the written sign. The forms of the serif capital letters on Roman monuments reflect both the chisel that cut them out and the square brush that made temporary marks for it to follow (Catich, 1968), echoing down the millennia to the serifs in *City Hall* (Figure 4.1). Paper was first made from reeds, later from old clothes and from vellum, still used for recording Acts of Parliament and for the calligraphic masterpiece the *Saint John's Bible*, created by Donald Jackson (2002–2011). Paper only became cheap and disposable in the 1840s when methods were invented for making it out of wood pulp (Clayton, 2014). Paper affected the shapes of letters because of the way ink interacts with it; some print letters, for example, are designed with 'ink traps' to prevent ink silting up internal corners (Beier, 2012: 94). Computer screens light the surface from behind and so a printout never looks like the version on the backlit computer screen: 'The screen mimics the sky, not the earth' (Bringhurst, 2005: 193). Hence screens too demand specially designed typefaces like Verdana and Lucida.

So, just as modern English spelling shows the changes in a language over centuries, the shapes of English letters on street signs incorporate elements of their previous historical forms. The choice of serif rather than sans serif letters for a sign, for example, arose out of the mason's skill with stone letters but has developed into a contrast between tradition and modernity. The technical demands of electronic display led to distinctive letters that may in turn feed back into print forms, where their subtle adaptations may be unneeded. Street signs evolve continually while preserving within them hints of their past.

Three-dimensional Signs Written on Stone and Metal Surfaces

Renaissance printers once 'revelled in the physical depth and texture' their printing technology could produce on the paper of their time (Bringhurst, 2005: 138), nowadays largely confined to book covers. Letters with three dimensions are now found chiefly in street signs and a few indoor public signs in, say, churches.

Recessed letters on stone

Cutting marks into solid surfaces formed an early writing technology.

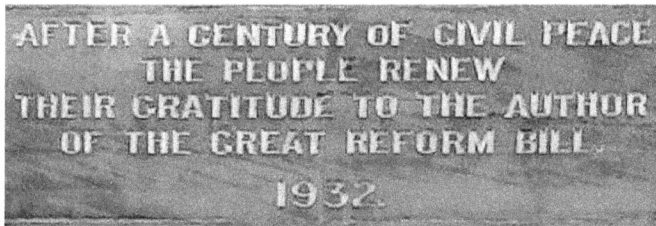

Figure 4.2 Stone surfaces with recessed letters (*Earl Grey Memorial, Osborne Terrace*, Newcastle; *Town Hall*, Colchester)

Recessed letters can be cut into the stone surface with chisels, gouges or machines, as in *Earl Grey Memorial* and *Osborne Terrace* (Figure 4.2). Following the Roman tradition, some recessed letters are coloured in gold as in *Earl Grey Memorial*, in black as in *Osborne Terrace*, or in pink as in *Hospital* (Figure 2.12). According to Kinneir (1980), letters have to be cut deeper into the stone in London than in Rome to compensate for the weaker sunlight. Painted letters often have painted-in shadows to increase their visibility, as in *20* (Figure 5.5). Most stone signs are in the high vertical zone like *Osborne Terrace*, or the fascia zone like *Earl Grey Memorial*. Hence the letters are mainly large capitals with a dramatic impact. Earl Grey was once more famous for his political reforms than his taste in tea, particularly the 1833 Slavery Abolition Bill passed while he was Prime Minister.

Figure 4.3 Solid surfaces with raised letters (*Dex Garage*, Newcastle; *Leazes Crescent*, LPZ)

Raised letters on stone surfaces

Relief letters are raised from stone, stucco or metal by cutting or moulding (Figure 4.3). As the letters do not contrast with the background material, shadows are crucial. Raised letters are more difficult to make and less durable because the edges are more susceptible to damage.

– *Dex Garage*: an architectural sign three storeys high, an integral part of a 1930s building, in squared sans serif capitals with some diagonal line endings, moulded in concrete to appear modernist;
– *Leazes Crescent*: part of the original roof-level façade of this 1829–1830 terrace, in stucco; fat letters with heavy square serifs.

Figure 4.4 Applied letters in metal (*Aspers*, SS; *Leazes Arcade*, *50*, LPR; *Next*, Newcastle)

Applied letters and numbers

Three-dimensional letters are cut out or moulded and then 'applied' by sticking or screwing them onto the background surface. They are often made of metal or look like metal, whether gold in *Leazes Arcade* or silver in *Aspers Casino*, *Next* and *50*, contrasting with the background in material and colour (Figure 4.4). Most have traditional serif capitals, apart from the modernity of the sans serif lower case in *Next*. Applied letters and numbers can be bought in sets, such as *50* or *149* (Figure 2.18). They too have surprising powers of endurance; originally a synagogue, Leazes Arcade became a shopping arcade, then student accommodation, and is now being redeveloped.

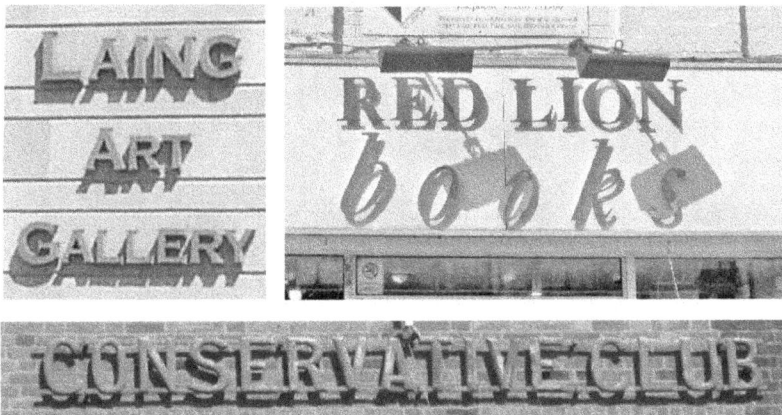

Figure 4.5 Letters and shadows on applied names (*Laing Art Gallery*, Newcastle; *Conservative Club*, *Red Lion Books*, Colchester)

The three-dimensionality of lettering is crucial to the legibility of raised or cut letters, since they rely on shadows (Gray, 1960), seen dramatically in *Laing Art Gallery*. In general, the simpler lines of sans serif letters cast better shadows than the serif letters of, say, *Red Lion Books*. Problems arise when there is a gap between the letters and the wall, as in *Conservative Club*, or when shadows from other objects interfere, as in *Red Lion Books* (Figure 4.5).

Letters moulded in metal

Figure 4.6 Integrated metal letters (*Dutch Quarter, Maldon Road*, Colchester; *McCowie, Mr. M.F. Lee, Water*, LPR)

Metal street signs are mostly moulded or cast from aluminium. They are often information signs at eye-level like *Dutch Quarter*, street name signs like *Maldon Road*, or service signs on the movement plane like the manhole cover *Water*. The scale is usually smaller than for stone signs (shown in Figure 4.6); *Millennium Trail* (Figure 4.1) is barely two inches across. Some of the main types are:

- *Brass plates*, with recessed letters, as in *McCowie* or *Mr. M.F. Lee*, are usually made of brass- or silver-coloured metal; see also Figure 1.11. These are required by law to be displayed 'at or near' the doors of the registered offices of businesses (*The Companies (Trading Disclosures) Regulations*, 2008).
- *Service signs* such as manhole covers like *Water* are addressed to specialist readers servicing underground cables and pipes, mostly located in the horizontal movement zone, although some may be in the low vertical zone, like the *Hydrant* sign (Figure 3.1). Manhole covers are usually moulded in cast iron, because of its strength and durability (Stinson, 2016). The shape and material of many is determined by practical considerations: it is impossible for a circular manhole cover that has been lifted up to fall into the hole, unlike rectangular covers.
- *Street name signs* like *Maldon Road* have raised letters in the Kindersley typeface in moulded aluminium on low posts.

Stone and metal signs typically assert respectability and importance through all-capital letters. Building names such as *City Hall* (Figure 4.1) and inscriptions like *Earl Grey Memorial* (Figure 4.2) mostly have serif letters derived from the Roman monumental scripts.

The audience for most metal and stone signs is passers-by on foot. The text is not authored, in that it consists only of the names of the buildings, streets or services with no choice of wording, other than its initial naming. Because of the skill involved in working with stone and metal, the writers are professional signwriters and stonemasons such as Andrew Ziminski (2020).

Light and shadow are particularly important for three-dimensional letters. Raised letters where letters and background are the same material, as in *Non sibi sed* (Figure 8.6), would be unreadable without a shadow. Light and shadow are equally necessary for recessed letters, although painted fill-ins can help. The letters of *Osborne Terrace* (Figure 4.2) depend upon the shadows from its deep square-cutting, while the shallow rounded cutting of *Earl Grey Memorial* (Figure 4.2) needs colour to compensate for the lack of shadow. The applied metal letters in *Aspers Casino* (Figure 4.4) are brought out by shadows, while reflections in brass plates like *McCowie* (Figure 4.6) distort them. Indeed Abousnnouga and Machin (2013: 51) claim that 'glossy, shiny surfaces ... suggest luxury and also the clean minimalism of modernity', as in *next* and *Aspers* (Figure 4.4).

Stone and metal signs convey:

- *Extreme permanence/durability.* Stone identifies public buildings such as hospitals, halls and law courts with capital letters and is used for inscriptions on public monuments. Metal letters show the permanence of house numbers *50* (Figure 4.4) and of businesses *next* (Figure 4.4). Street name signs such as *Maldon Road* or manhole covers such as *Water* (Figure 4.6) need to last for decades – **functional permanence**

(Cook, 2013a). Name signs like *Aspers Casino* (Figure 4.4) claim permanence for something whose timespan is comparatively short – **asserted permanence**. Some commemorative inscriptions have lasted for millennia: *Town Hall* (Figure 4.2) is a mere hundred years old. Signs that aspire to permanence need to be inscribed in stone like *Town Hall* (Figure 4.2) or moulded from metal like *Leazes Park Road* (Figure 5.2). Ironically, *Town Hall* was recut in 2019 due to the deterioration of the surface. Commemorative signs proclaim their enduring messages by being engraved on stone. While banks used to claim permanence through carved stone letters, they now prefer a designed logo as it is more visible on the High Street (Gray, 1960).

– *Temporality/newness.* Age goes with stone and metal; formality and respectability are the keynotes. Stone signs try to be traditional in appearance even when they use sans serif letters, as in *Erected AD 1844* (Figure 4.1), as do signs like *Aspers Casino* (Figure 4.4) with silver metal letters. The life of a sign like *We will be closing* (Figure 4.7), handwritten on paper in felt-tip, is limited to today. The connotations suggest something new and fleeting. Nothing is more annoying than the common sign *New Road Layout Ahead*, when it stays in place for more than a year.

– *Quality.* Stone and metal are regarded as high-quality materials, more expensive to buy and to work with than, say, paper or plastic. Gold lettering in monumental inscriptions like *Earl Grey's Memorial* (Figure 4.2) and *Leazes Arcade* (Figure 4.4) is a clear indication of quality, as is the brass of brass plates like *Newcastle Companions* (Figure 4.9). Name signs like *City Hall* (Figure 4.1) vouch for the respectability and status of their owners. Each stone sign is a unique one-off design by a stone cutter, and so there are subtle variations between signs, most notably in the street name signs of Bath (Bartram, 1978b). However, mechanical or computer-controlled systems are now used to cut letters into some gravestones, for instance in British war cemeteries (Haslam, 2011).

Signs Written on Paper

Handwritten or printed paper signs inform potential customers on foot about temporary circumstances and products for sale, authored and written by the staff of the shops and restaurants (as seen in Figure 4.7). They are typically A4 size and are fixed in the vertical eye-level zone to doors, windows or even trees with sellotape, drawing pins, blu tack and so on.

Handwritten signs

Handwritten paper signs in the eye-level zone usually have constant stroke contrast made by pens of different types and sizes or by brushes, as in *Push* (Figure 2.24). They make extensive use of colour, combining orange, blue and green letters in *New Stock*, and of capital letters, except for *Special Clearance*, which has word-initial capital letters. Punctuation is absent, apart from multiple exclamation marks, as in *Sorry*;

line-breaks, layout and size of letter serve in their place, except for *Closed*, where each phrase finishes with a full stop. *Special Clearance* stands out with its triple exclamation marks, ellipsis and inverted commas (and the classic apostrophe 'mistake' *'till*). The texts consist of noun and adjective phrases, with the occasional imperative, except for the full sentences of the unorthodox *Sorry*.

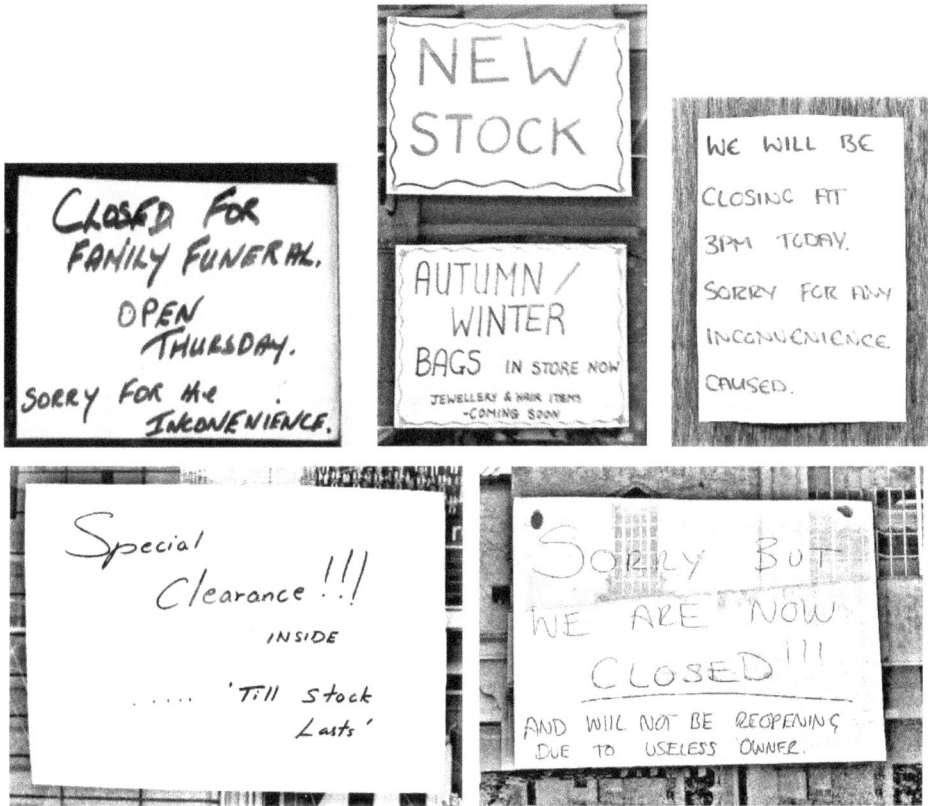

Figure 4.7 Handwritten paper signs (*Closed, Sorry, Special Clearance, We will be closing*, Colchester; *New Stock*, Newcastle. *Sorry* edited because of glass reflections)

These signs appear amateurish and informal, particularly the *Sorry* signwritten by a disgruntled employee; some chain stores do, however, distribute printed 'handwritten' signs. Hence they are the natural home of the greengrocer's apostrophe, as seen in *Scampi* (Figure 3.16), and of typos, as in <inconenience> in *Closed*. Amateurishness is not necessarily a defect as it can imply informality, homeliness, immediacy and sincerity. While these signs are definitely unique, they do not carry the aura of quality that this often brings.

Printed signs

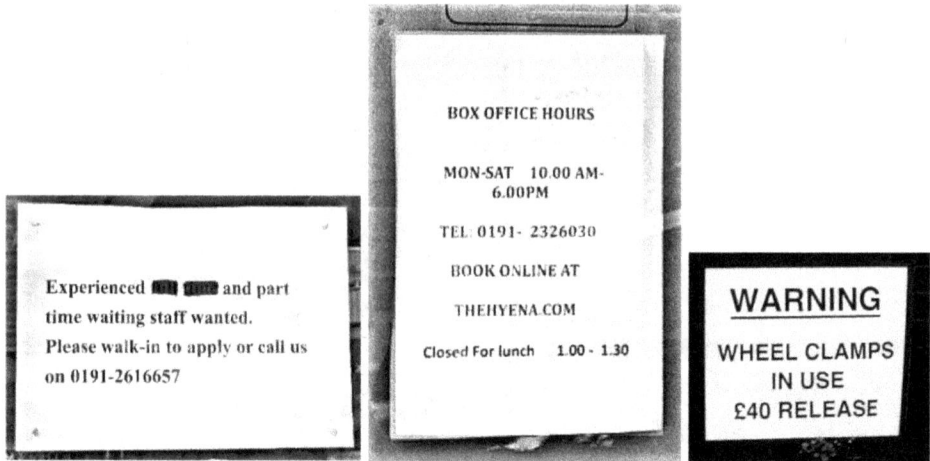

Figure 4.8 Printed paper signs (*Job ad*, SS; *Box Office Hours, Warning*, LPR)

Paper signs printed on PC printers are mostly one-off signs rather than professionally printed in multiple copies. They often use all-capitals, serif typefaces and minimal street-type punctuation. Grammatically, they are dominated by noun and adjective phrases, separated by line-breaks and spaces rather than punctuation marks, as in *Box Office Hours*. Occasionally they have longer phrases in lower case <Experienced and part / time waiting staff wanted.>. They are more impersonal than the handwritten signs, giving factual information such as opening times (*Box Office Hours*) and job specs (*Job ad*).

A paper surface suggests:

- *Permanence/durability.* A paper sign is temporary rather than permanent. One exception is the bilingual door sign *Push* (Figure 2.24).
- *Temporality/newness.* Informing notices such as *Wet Paint* (Figure 4.1) tell pedestrians about temporary hazards, short-term bargains, lost cats, jobs currently available, etc.
- *Quality.* Most handwritten signs have little pretension. The writing is evidently the writer's normal handwriting executed on a larger scale, as in *Sorry we are closed* (Figure 4.7). Other writers take more care, such as the carefully drawn serif capital letters and characters in *Push* (Figure 2.24). All-capitals signifies seriousness, particularly the underlined capitals of *Warning* (Figure 4.8), similar to the 'necessity' signs in South African townships (Stroud & Mpendukana, 2009).

These paper signs seldom separate the roles of owner, author and writer. The *Closed* paper sign (Figure 4.7), for instance, is owned by the shopkeeper who devised the wording and wrote it, unlike the unique *Sorry* sign (Figure 4.7) where the owner has no control over the rebellious author.

Painted Signs

Most signs painted on wood or other permanent surfaces are name signs and information boards for restaurants and the like, at fascia or eye-level height in the vertical plane.

Shop and restaurant fascias

Figure 4.9 Shop and restaurant fascias (*Newcastle Companions*, LPR; *Mangos*, SS; *artcafé*, Colchester)

These classic fascia-level signs proclaim the name of the business and are intended to be read from some distance. Painted or printed fascias try to project unique and arresting identities (Figure 4.9). They are effectively permanent, conveying a lasting identity without the pomposity of the stone signs in Figure 4.2. Fascias are discussed further in Chapter 7.

Fascia signs employ a vast range of lettering types – the faux Chinese white-outlined letters of *Mangos*, discussed in Chapter 8, the respectable shadow serif letters of *Newcastle Companions*, and the high x-height of the sans serif letters of *artcafé*. Mostly they have word-initial capitals, although some are all lower case, as in *artcafé*, or all-capitals, as in *Magic Box* (Figure 1.7). The bright blue and orange of *Mangos* are striking, as are the rainbow colours of *Magic Box*. Each sign proclaims an idiosyncratic identity: uniqueness plus quality.

Information boards

Figure 4.10 Information signs (*Warning, Great Grub, For sale*, LPR)

Informing signs may also be printed or painted, like the elegant no parking sign *Warning*, the *Great Grub* menu sign and the complex *for sale* sign (Figure 4.10). The letters are mostly sans serif and all-capitals, as in *Warning*. The menu of *Great Grub* partly uses word-initial capitals and has the Geordie word *stottie* for a kind of bread roll. The *for sale* sign combines all lower case sans serif <for sale> with an all-capital wide-spaced serif <SANDERSON YOUNG>. Layout rather than punctuation is used to show grammatical structure. The *Warning* sign has a passive *will be wheel clamped*, a conventional way of menacing through impersonal authority, and a curious use of *occur* in *A release fee of £75 will occur*, presumably meaning 'will be incurred', perhaps to stress the inevitability of being caught.

Fascia and information signs come in between stone and paper signs in terms of meaning.

- *Permanence/durability.* Both naming and informing signs are relatively permanent and durable, as *Wm Rodgers* (Figure 1.7) shows, painted in expensive gold and surviving long after the business has folded. These signs are not here and gone tomorrow.
- *Temporality/newness.* Printed signs can be readily replaced, suggesting newness, unlike stone; estate agents' *for sale* signs are licensed as temporary attachments to walls, etc. The naming signs like *Mangos* and *Magic Box* (Figure 1.7) are also lively and idiosyncratic.
- *Quality.* Painted signs can indicate quality, like the individualised colourful designs in *Magic Box*, rather than the formality of letters in stone or the amateurish designs on paper. This shades into the logos used by companies to establish an identity across all the media, seen in *for sale* in <SANDERSON YOUNG>.

Signs Written on Other Materials

Almost any material can be used in street signs. Other common materials include:

Letters on glass

The visibility of signs written on glass varies according to whether the interior lights are on or off and how reflections from outside appear on the glass, as in *Chef Canton* (Figure 4.1). Several of my photos of glass and brass signs are not usable as they reflect me taking the photo. Showing these signs without reflections would not give a fair idea of how they appear to the eyes of street users. A variety of techniques for creating signs on glass have been used, whether etching, back-painting or back-gilding.

Figure 4.11 Signs on glass (*Cutlery, Stoll Picture Theatre*, Newcastle; *hyena, 46*, LPR)

- *Cutlery* is a stained glass window on the first floor of a former Newcastle department store, now an unusual material for signs, with stacked, vertically aligned capitals.
- *Stoll Picture Theatre*, now the Tyne Theatre, was made of leaded stained glass in 1919 using Art Nouveau serif capital letters.

– *hyena* is the sign for a comedy club, painted on the inner side of a glass window and viewed from outside, like *Percy House* (Figure 1.4); a neon version of *hyena* is seen in Figure 4.12. The cut-about letters of *hyena* resemble the distortions in a CAPTCHA online security test; recognition is important rather than legibility.
– *46* is a house number on the fanlight above the front door, in painted gold italics. These signs are often hard to see because of both the reflections on the glass and the shade within the doorway, as in *46*. They are readily available as stick-on signs for the inside of fanlight windows.

Lit-up letters

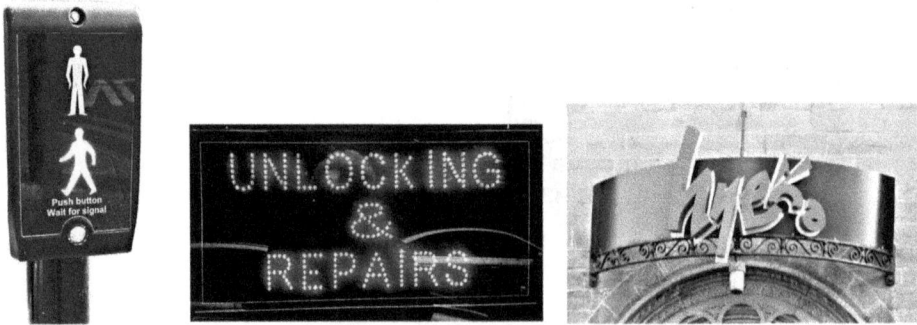

Figure 4.12 Signs consisting of lights (*Green man, hyena*, LPR; *Unlocking*, SS)

– *Green man.* Signs to control pedestrians at traffic lights depend on the appropriate green and red lights switching on and off. Meaning then depends upon the international symbolism of the striding green man and the stationary red man, lighting up in sequence. In addition bleeps, etc., accompany the changes, the only sign in the NCL corpus with synchronised sounds.
– *Unlocking* has letters made up of mini-lights behind glass. The letters are themselves the light source, here in sans serif with a dotted effect.
– *hyena.* Cursive letters are easier to use in neon signs as they accommodate the necessary glass and electric connections better. This fascia sign for the comedy club is unlit in the daytime and so is more insistent at night. Recently glass neon signs have been largely superseded by LED-based signs (Vink, 2015).

Bricks and tiles

Brick and tile signs usually integrate the sign with its host during construction (Figure 4.13).

– *CIU* is a large, almost invisible sign on the wall of the Newcastle Labour Club in the high vertical zone, made of yellow half-bricks integrated into the grey brick wall. The simple square letters use the modular technique in which each letter is composed of a number of repeated shapes, here half-size bricks. *CIU* shows the club is a member of the Club and Institute Union.

–   *Kings Arms.* <FH 1760> adorns the roof of a country pub, picked out in contrasting roof pantiles, showing the date when these three cottages were converted into a pub, not the much earlier date when they were built. Again the letters are modular, in this case made up of pantiles. The technique is not dissimilar to the digital dots or pixels used in screen displays.

–   *Ireton Road* is a further example of Colchester letter tiles, to be compared with the modern sign in *Ireton Road* (Figure 5.2). This Victorian style is only found in a few areas of England, as discussed in Chapter 2.

–   *Space Invader* is an example of street art, graffiti in the broadest sense, in Stowell Street (SS), made by an anonymous artist known as Invader, who has 'invaded' 77 cities by installing artworks based on images from the early video game *Space Invaders* (http://space-invaders.com/home/). Newcastle's invasion in 2006 amounted to 25 signs in the high vertical zone of central city streets, many still visible. This technique for creating graffiti involves a prefabricated sign that can be quickly installed, here in the form of small tiles.

Figure 4.13 Bricks and tiles (*Kings Arms*, Blakeney; *CIU*, LPR; *Ireton Road*, Colchester; *Space Invader*, SS)

Blackboards

Although blackboards may have disappeared from classrooms, they are everywhere in the amenity zone of English streets (Figure 4.14). Many are painted to withstand rain rather than written in chalk. They are common because they are both movable and reusable for new messages.

Figure 4.14 Blackboards (*Fresh Pheasants, Daily Specials, In a hurry, Look*, Colchester)

- *Daily Specials* is a painted blackboard in an ornate calligraphic style with word-initial caps in separated letters in the names of food dishes and a more cursive lower case italic in the subheadings, implying quality.
- *In a Hurry* has idiosyncratic capital letters in disconcertingly mixed sizes and styles with a rather weak <11am – 5pm>. It gives an impression of liveliness by implying that the writer is making up the letter shapes as he or she goes along.
- *Fresh Pheasants* has chalked letters on a blackboard outside a butcher's, using standard centred all-capitals.
- *Look* is a traditional way of attracting attention through the filled-in 'eyes' of < oo >, with centred all-capitals apart from the line-initial capital of <More dresses upstairs>.

These are examples of the double-sided A-boards that have proliferated on shopping streets, to the annoyance of those in wheelchairs and with poor eyesight; *In a hurry* is in fact standing on the tactile warning surface of a beer cellar trapdoor.

As street signs, blackboards represent a kind of folk art, untouched by print technology or signwriting but dependent on handwriting and the writer's whim. They are unique signs, done for one place at one time. They tend to have spelling mistakes, such as <avaliable> (*In a hurry*), and <guiena> (*Fresh Pheasants*). The street use of blackboards covers a wider range of establishments than their interior use for restaurant menus, which is mostly restricted to, on the one hand, genuinely artisanal greasy spoons and, on the other, gentrified, fine-dining bistros and pubs.

In terms of meaning, these less common materials demonstrate:

- *Permanence/durability*, varying between the semi-permanence of glass (Figure 4.11) and the deliberate impermanence of chalk (Figure 4.14).
- *Temporality/newness*, ranging from the traditional look of numbers painted on glass like *46* (Figure 4.11) to the sprightliness of *hyena* (Figure 4.12).
- *Quality*. Only the painted signs on glass (Figure 4.11) claim respectability through workmanship and design; the rest assert individuality rather than quality.

Conclusion

This chapter has developed the relationship between street signs and material, of peripheral interest to most genres of writing but particularly important to street signs research. It started from the three material factors described by Scollon and Scollon (2003: 135–136) and found that permanence needed to be split two ways: functional permanence in signs that genuinely need to last, and asserted permanence in signs that wish to claim the respectability of lasting signs (Cook, 2013a). Temporality/newness included temporary paper informing signs, whether handwritten or printed, not only disposable but also tacked up in informal ways, showing they are valid for a limited time period.

Quality, the third property, seems more useful as a superordinate category built out of permanence and temporality than as an independent dimension of its own, made up of the quality of the surface material and of the writing material, the skill of workmanship, the letter style, and so on. These build a notion of respectability and authority out of an accumulation of features, say the carved serif capitals of *Town Hall* (Figure 4.2) versus the felt-tip sans serif of *We will be closing*. Quality signs use enduring materials and are made with skill and expense. Uniqueness can be a sign of quality when used with quality materials, unlike the down-market virtues of unique handwritten signs.

Street signs depend on material far more extensively than other forms of language. Speech is here and gone; street signs are with us till our attention shifts; they last from a few seconds up to millennia. They thus permit rereading whenever we like, up to the time when they are no longer available. Speech is constrained by the properties of air and of the human speech processing apparatus; street signs vary the material according to their purpose and their location within street space, from pen on paper for close-up reading to chisel on stone for permanent display at a distance. This affects the kind of message they can convey and their form in terms of length, letter style, layout, etc. The use of capitals or lower case, serif or sans serif, short noun phrases or 'full' sentences depends on the sign's material and on its physical location.

The unique property of street signs is that they are seen as wholes before their parts are considered. Their meaning is compounded from their overall form as well as their constituent parts. Some, like McDonald's signs, function as wholes for recognition. Others, like traffic signs, require an integration of their shape, colour and specific text before they are understood, to be discussed in Chapter 6. As suggested earlier, many street signs can be processed through recognition rather than read as text, enabling access for those who cannot read text.

5 Naming the Street

According to Unwin (2009: 32), 'architecture ... begins with a mind's motivation to make that mark, with its desire to identify that place'. Streets and buildings are identified through their name signs. Identifying something not only says what it *is* but also implies what it is *not*; in a sense it establishes a border around it. This chapter explores the issues that arise from naming signs, ranging from linguistic to political. The focus is on signs that are physically attached to the particular objects they name.

Figure 5.1 Percy name signs (*Percy Building*, *Percy St.*, *Percy Terrace*, LPZ; *Percy House*, LPR; see also *Percy Arms*, Figure 3.8)

The speech act of 'emplacement' places 'a sign in its physical location to activate its meaning' (Scollon & Scollon, 2003: 210); *Percy Building* comes alive as a sign when it is placed on the right building. But the opposite also holds true: an anonymous building acquires its name when the sign is attached to it; a building becomes Percy House when it is named *Percy House*.

The naming signs of the street are bound to the architectural places where people live: naming turns space into place (Tuan, 1991). Naming signs employ 'nomination': 'the bestowal of an expression on an individual to serve as a distinguishing mark' (Coates, 2009: 434). Naming, on the one hand, creates the name for the street object; on the other, it labels it for the street user.

The meaning of naming signs is exophoric, that is to say, 'the identity presumed by the reference item is recoverable from the environment of the text' (Halliday & Mattheisen, 2013: 624). The sign *Percy St.* labels the street it is attached to, just as *Percy Building* labels the building. If the *Percy Terrace* sign were put up in Stowell Street (SS), the words would be the same but they would be decorative rather than meaningful. The meaning of naming signs is inseparable from their location.

Naming signs may provide a legal sign of ownership or demarcation. While the names of restaurants and businesses confer individuality, street and building name signs claim an enduring identity. The name of the building, say *Percy House*, is not necessarily that of the business that occupies it, even if sometimes they are one and the same. Business names serve different functions from building names in that they project onto the street the identity of the business, usually the choice of the owner, not that of the building itself.

So naming gives a street or a building a unique label; naming signs are site specific. The actual name is largely arbitrary; *Percy Terrace* could just as well be called *Carnaby Street* or *Kings Road*. In naming signs, the nominating link between the name and the physical object is crucial: *this* street *here* in Newcastle is called *Percy Terrace*. Street and building name signs primarily refer to unique objects, with some indications of the type conveyed by the head noun: a terrace does not typically consist of bungalows nor a mews of large detached mansions; a hall is usually bigger than a cottage.

The modifying words that make up the name convey different levels of meaning. The family name *Percy* belongs in Newcastle to the Dukes of Northumberland, a title revived in the 18th century rather than directly descended from the Percys of Shakespeare's history plays and the Thomas Percy who took part in the Gunpowder Plot. The original purpose in naming them may have been to commemorate a family, still a major landowner in the area, and to assert land ownership. But there is little need for the street user to be aware of these meanings – who cares who Percy is or was? The plethora of *Percy*s in name signs in this part of Newcastle contributes to local identity.

The names of celebrity streets often have associations quite distinct from the words. The Champs Elysées, the Via Veneto and the Kurfürstendamm do not, however, conjure up the Elysian fields, a WWI battle or the prince electors of Brandenburg that their names commemorate any more than Percy Street makes Geordies think of the Duke of Northumberland. Looking at the literal meanings of the words in street or building names is rather like discussing the etymology of words: where they originated is irrelevant to their primary naming function. Do the words in *Buckingham Palace*, *Saville Row* or *New Scotland Yard* have anything to do with their modern meanings or connotations? Who are Buckingham and Saville? Where is *Old* Scotland Yard?

It is then important to distinguish the different layers of meaning involved in naming signs, as discussed in Schmitt (2018) and Nystrom (2016). Chapter 7 outlines further meanings based on the forms of street signs, here called connotations.

The Naming of Things

Street name signs

The *Public Health Act 1925*, *Section 19* (1925) requires local authorities to ensure that 'the name of every street shall be shown in a conspicuous position'. Street name signs in England are usually attached to buildings in the high vertical zone, as in *Percy St.* (Figure 5.1), or are embedded in walls, like *Percy Terrace* (Figure 5.1), or sit on short poles in the frontage zone, as in *Ireton Road* (Figure 5.2). They do not hang centrally over the street or project from lamp posts at street corners, as they do in, say, New York.

Figure 5.2 Street name signs (*Ireton Road*, *Constantine Road*, Colchester; *Leazes Park Road*, LPR; *High Street* x2, Blakeney)

Street name signs identify and delimit streets, with at least one sign at each end; these are general signs written in the same form, the same type of location, etc., even if each sign has a unique meaning *in situ*. Figure 5.2 displays some typical examples in all-capitals. The faded *Ireton Road* sign is on short posts in the frontage area and uses the serif Kindersley letter style, discussed in Chapter 2, as does the lower *High Street* sign. *Leazes Park Road* has Gill Sans in the high-level zone. These three metal signs thus conform to the typefaces laid down in street regulations (Department for Transport, 2015). The much older *Constantine Road* sign has fat letters on individual tiles embedded in a wall at a low-level; the upper *High Street* sign has an old format of raised white serif letters on a black background, now barely legible.

The choice of head nouns for street names is governed by local and national regulations. New street names need to go through a process of approval from the local council. Building developers tend to choose names that sell better: a house on a *lane* costs twice as much as that on a *street* (Mask, 2020: 232; Wallop, 2016).

The spelling of street names may involve unusual sound-letter correspondences, such as *Cholmondeley Avenue* /ˈtʃʌmlɪ/, *Leicester Square* /lestə/ or *High Holborn* /həʊbən/, all in London. Holders of proper names seem to have a right to choose how to spell them, as seen in Chapter 2. Street names rarely have punctuation other than an apostrophe or an abbreviatory full stop, such as < RD. > in *Ireton Rd.* and < S! > in *Percy Street* (Figure 5.1).

Their structure consists of noun phrases with a pre-modifier and a head noun, as in *Ireton Rd.* The article *the* sometimes forms part of the name. The most frequent names with *the* in London are *The Drive*, *The Avenue* and *The Green* (Room, 1992). The head noun comes from a limited range of words, most of which are listed in Box 5.1, sometimes specified by local regulations.

Box 5.1 Head nouns used in Newcastle street names

Arches, Approach, Avenue, Bank, Bungalows, Boulevard, Chare, Close, Corner, Cottages, Court, Courtyard, Crescent, Croft, Cross, Dene, Drive, Ends, Farm, Field, Flatt, Foot, Gardens, Garth, Gate, Grove, Hamlet, Haugh, Haven, Heads, Hill, Homes, Houses, Lane, Lodge, Lea, Lonnen, Lough, Manor, Market, Meadow, Mere, Mews, Moor, Mount, Nook, Parade, Park, Place, Rise, Road, Row, Square, Stairs, Station, Steads, Street, Sykes, Terrace, View, Villas, Walk, Way, Wharf, Wynd, Yard

The layout of most English town centres is usually based on the vagaries of mediaeval roadways and the whims of 19th and 20th century developers rather than on grids or radiating avenues imposed by a central planning authority. Colchester town centre is unusual in partly preserving its 1st century Roman grid, while central Newcastle keeps its mid-19th century development of streets converging on Grey's Monument, both of them untypical of the largely unplanned historical centres of English towns.

It is rare for streets to be named with ordinal numbers in England, unlike, say, *52nd Street* and *Fifth Avenue* in New York. The few exceptions occur mostly in new towns like Milton Keynes or in post-war housing estates rather than grand thoroughfares.

Box 5.2 Most frequent street names in Greater London

(1) Church Road
(2) Park Road
(3) Station Road
(4) High Street
(5) Manor Road

Source: Room (1992).

The City of London (2014) has a typical set of regulations for street names. (Note: the City of London refers to the historic business area, a fraction of the whole city of London – an illustration of the usefulness of capital letters for disambiguation.) These forbid the use of 'Names of persons (living or dead)', 'Names that endorse commercial marketing' and 'Names … capable of being misconstrued into inappropriate meanings'; the word *road* is now specifically prohibited. Box 5.2 gives the most popular street names in Greater London (Room, 1992). (Greater London usually refers to the whole city consisting of 33 boroughs, one of which is the City.)

Historically, many London streets are named after the aristocratic families who owned the area, and often still do, like Lord Grosvenor, alias the Duke of Westminster, in *Grosvenor Square*, *Russell Street* and *Cadogan Square*, or the developer and his family, like Edward Harley with *Harley Street*, *Cavendish Square* and *Wimpole Street* (Jenkins, 1975), rather than the historic figures and liberators honoured in many countries. Perhaps the oddest such scheme in London once spelt out the full name of the Duke of Buckingham: <u>George</u> *Street*, <u>Villiers</u> *Street*, <u>Duke</u> *Street*, <u>Of</u> *Alley* (now *York Street*), <u>Buckingham</u> *Street*. Central Newcastle street names show similar preferences for aristocratic owners, *Percy Street* and *Northumberland Street*, and for developers and architects, *Grainger Street* and *Dobson Street*. English street names thus often commemorate local families and events rather than major aspects of English history.

Local dialects vary particularly in the head nouns for alleyways. Newcastle has *Chare* (Figure 5.7), *Garth*, *Wynd*, *Entry* and *Haugh*; Colchester adds *Folley*; other parts of England use *Lane*. The word *gate* often historically meant 'way' rather than 'opening in the city wall', and survives in some compound street names, *Scheregate* and *Headgate* (Figure 3.6) in Colchester, and *Gallowgate* in Newcastle, and everywhere in York, say *Fossgate*, *Nessgate* and *Micklegate*.

According to the OED (2015), a *road* is 'A path or way between different places, or leading to some place', a sense first recorded in 1580. Most towns and suburbs around London have a *London Road*. *Leazes Park Road* (Figure 5.2) is a 19th century renaming showing the way to Leazes Park. Sometimes streets are named after a direction, like the *Great North Road*, which connects London with Edinburgh, a short named stretch in Newcastle separating two parts of Newcastle University. The spoken stress is usually on the word *road*, i.e. *London Road*. Street names with *Road* are often preceded by a definite article *the* – *the London Road* – while those with *Street* are not.

A *street*, on the other hand, is a built-up urban road 'usually running between two lines of houses or other buildings' (OED, 2015) that does *not* lead to the place it refers to (Room, 1992), such as *Liverpool Street* in Newcastle. The spoken stress is usually on the pre-modifying noun *Liverpool Street*.

Figure 5.3 Street name signs in languages other than English: *Stowell* Street (edited), SS (English/Chinese); *Via Urbis Romanae*, Colchester (Latin)

While bilingual signs in Welsh/English and Gaelic/English are found in Wales and Scotland, English is used for virtually all street name signs in England. Bilingual street name signs cluster in a few areas where non-indigenous minority languages are spoken, say Bengali in Bethnal Green in London. Bilingual English/Chinese signs such as *Stowell Street* in Newcastle are a common feature of Chinatowns worldwide, to be discussed in Chapter 8. The *Stowell Street* sign also has a distinctive green background, usually not permitted on street name signs as it provides less contrast with black letters than a white background.

A new road in Colchester was christened *Via Urbis Romanae* (Figure 5.3) ('Road of the Roman town', Latin) to draw attention to the Roman origins of the town, without an English translation. This is the only monolingual street name sign in a classical language that I have been able to find in England.

Names of buildings

Building names are also restricted by various types of regulation in a similar fashion. Building name signs in England are usually placed on a vertical wall at high-level, a few underfoot, such as the mosaic entrance tiles in *Waltons* (Figure 2.23). Their characteristics (as seen in Figure 5.4) overlap with the names of restaurants and shops, to be considered in Chapter 7.

–   *Bamburgh House* is a high-level 'applied' letter sign for an office block using a serif letter style.
–   *Laing Art Gallery* is painted high on a brick wall in fat serif letters with an even stroke contrast (see also Figure 4.5).
–   *Grand Theatre* is a 19th century roof-level sign in raised stone serif letters, an architectural sign built into the structure itself.
–   *St Peter's Church* is a painted board in serif word-initial caps, doubling as an information notice; the name forms a prominent header, for once not all-capitals.

Figure 5.4 Building names (*Bamburgh House, Laing Art Gallery*, Newcastle; *Grand Theatre, St Peter's Church*, Colchester)

Many building name signs are enclosed in rectangular panels, either with borders marked out, as in *Laing Art Gallery* (Figure 5.4), or framed by a rectangular window frame, as in *Percy House* (Figure 5.1). The text is usually single lines in landscape mode, like *Percy Building* (Figure 5.1), occasionally square, like *Laing Art Gallery* (Figure 5.4) in centred lines. Vertical naming signs are rare, apart from some shop and restaurant signs (Figures 2.2 and 2.3).

In the City of London, building names should not be difficult to pronounce or spell, and should not have more than three syllables. They 'should not be named after living persons, with the exception of the Royal Family' (City of London, 2014). Displaying a building name is no guarantee that the name is still current: *Grand Theatre* (Figure 5.4) is now a nightclub.

While the local authority licenses all aspects of street name signs, this applies only to new names and numbers. Older signs often breach the regulations in one way or another. Unapproved street names in the City of London include *Austin Friars*, *Bevis Marks*, *Cloth Fair* and *Old Bailey*, and indeed the banned word *road* in *Goswell Road*, brought into the City by a boundary change.

Numbers of buildings

Numbers are in a sense the purest form of nomination, free from other connotations, save perhaps for the avoidance of unlucky numbers such as 13. For official purposes such as receiving mail or contacting emergency services, it is the number that is critical, not the name. The numbering of buildings was systematically imposed on many European cities during the 18th century (Rose-Redwood, 2008). From the start, some owners objected that building numbers diminished their individuality or social status (Simmel, 1997); you do not number palaces and castles, apart perhaps from The White House, 1600 Pennsylvania Avenue.

Figure 5.5 House numbers in Newcastle (*20, 34–32*, LPR) (see also Figures 2.17, 2.18 and 4.11)

The **meaning** of numbers is indexical and exophoric: the sign *20* belongs to one building in one street, and to that building alone. In England, the numbering of buildings is by street. Odd numbers are allocated consecutively to one side, even numbers to the other, as in *34–32* (Figure 5.5), exceptions being the consecutive numbering on the same side in cul-de-sacs and a few older streets. Most famously the Prime Minister officially lives in *10 Downing Street*, next door to the Chancellor of the Exchequer in *11 Downing Street*; the numeral < 0 > displayed in the number < 10 > on the Prime Minister's door is in fact a rounder letter < O >, originally a mistake, now a tradition. In addition 'Main roads should be numbered so that when travelling away from the centre of town the odd numbers are on the left hand side and even numbers on the right' (Department of Transport, 1993).

UK street numbering thus differs from block numbering, both the Japanese system based on the order in which houses were built and the Philadelphia system (Rose-Redwood, 2008) in which 100 numbers are allocated to each block, which provides more flexibility by allowing for unallocated numbers. The linear system in England often does not work strictly in sequence: a vanished property may leave a hole in the system, sometimes literally as the result of a WWII bomb; a divided property can have numbers followed by A, B, etc., as in *274A* (Figure 2.18). This is not, however, consistent; I live in a semi-detached house called *149* (Figure 2.18), the other half being *149A*, to the confusion of posties and visitors.

The City of London (2014) forbids the spelling out of numbers as letters: 'authorised addresses must be numeric and not textual … an address should be 1 Smith Street as opposed to One Smith Street'. Their own website nonetheless lists the controversial building *No 1 Poultry* as *One Poultry* (City of London, 2015).

Crosby and Seale (2018) relate styles in number signs to changes in the urban environment and report three 'families' of number signs:

- *do-it-yourself signs*, made from the materials to hand, like the painted brick *274A* (Figure 2.18);
- *transactional signs*, designed for purely practical identification on business premises;
- *transitional signs*, trying for a gentrifying effect on residential properties, like those in Figure 5.6 or the art nouveau *149* (Figure 2.18).

These three categories could be applied usefully to other signs. DIY signs, for example, might include *No Entry to Doctor's Surgery* (Figure 2.13) and parking notices (Figure 6.10), transactional signs *Lecture Theatre's* (Figure 3.16) and pseudo-archaic signs like *Ye Olde Marquis* (Figure 2.23).

House names

While house numbers are integral to the addressing system in England, house names are optional. Hence many are unique signs subject to the whim of the owner: my parents lived in a house called *Heron's Ghyll*, an archaic spelling of *gill* meaning 'brook'; my grandfather in one called *Meiringen*, a town in Switzerland; and my aunt in *The Cottage*.

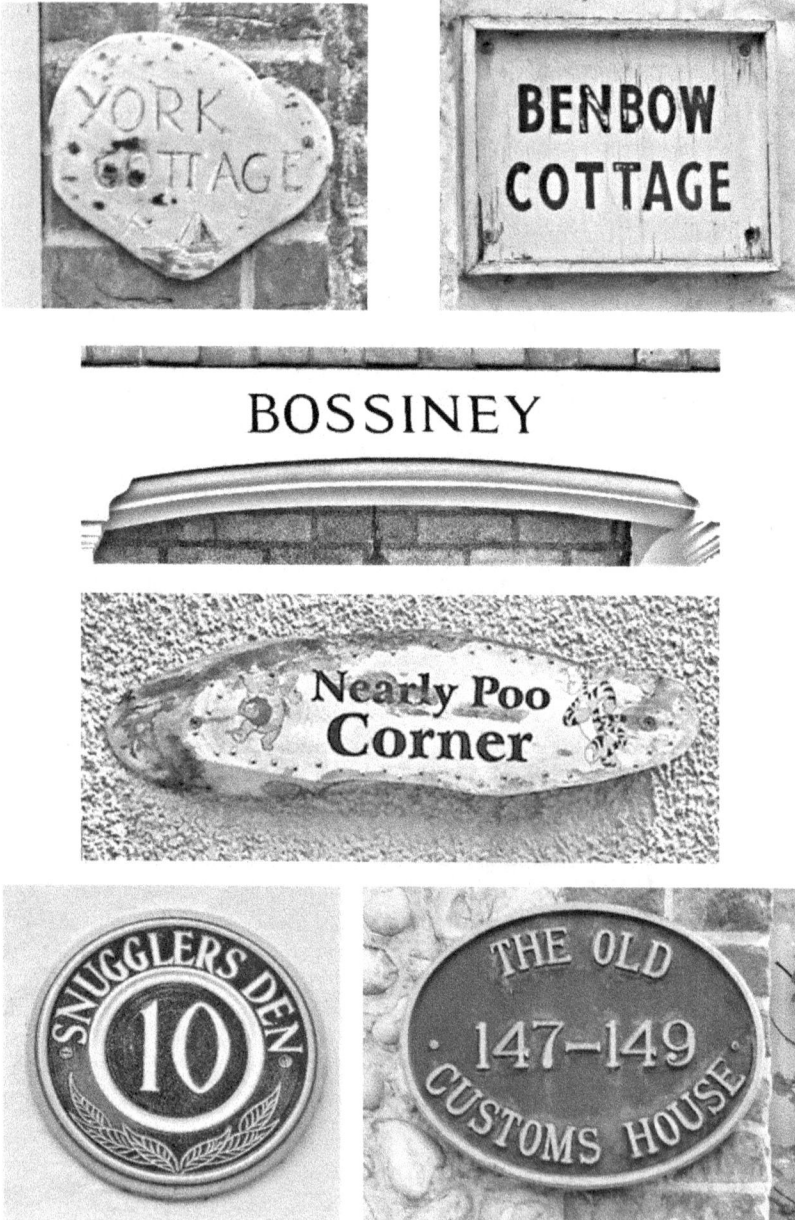

Figure 5.6 House names (*York Cottage, Snugglers Den, Benbow Cottage, The Old Customs House,* Blakeney; *Bossiney, Nearly Poo Corner,* Colchester)

The sample of house names in Figure 5.6 shows the freedom of house owners to choose names for their properties and to design house signs in a multitude of ways.

- *York Cottage* has serif capitals cut into a pottery slab, not altogether legible but suggesting informality and creativity.
- *Benbow Cottage* has plain sans serif letters in graceful simplicity but with slightly awkward letter spacing.
- *Bossiney* has formal elegant serif capital letters.
- *Nearly Poo Corner* uses word-initial caps painted on a piece of wood, with a pun on *poo/Pooh*.
- *Snugglers Den* and *The Old Customs House* have raised serif letters with a high contrast in stroke conveying dignity and elegance.

Cook (2004b) lists some of the methods for coining house names, such as: reversing the sequence of letters, *Emoh Ruo*; making a pun, *Snuggler's Den*; mentioning the building's alleged history, *The Old Customs House*; and borrowing a place name, *Bossiney*, a Cornish village, or sometimes fictional, such as *Rivendell*. House names are described in more detail in Miles (2001) and Koopman (2016).

Letters in Name Signs

All-capitals in street name signs

Street name signs are almost invariably written in all-capitals, as seen in those cited in this chapter, unlike the use of lower case letters in countries such as Norway, Germany and France. The exceptions are the small capitals < T > and < D > in abbreviations for *Saint* or *Street* in *Percy St.* (Figure 5.1) and for *Road* in *Ireton Rd.* (Figure 5.2). The official rationale for having all-capitals in street name signs is 'to avoid confusion with traffic signs, which generally employ lower-case lettering' (Department of Transport, 1993), as discussed in Chapter 3.

Capitals and lower case in building names

Most building name signs are written entirely in capitals, such as *Percy Terrace* (Figure 5.1). Word-initial capitals occur in *Bamburgh House* (Figure 5.4) and *Percy Building* (Figure 5.1). A few signs with all lower case letters are also found, like *Percy House* (Figure 5.1).

While street name signs are in the hands of the local authority, building name signs are the responsibility of the owner and the writer. The capital letters of building name signs lend them more individuality, contrasting, say, the old-fashioned dignity of all-capitals *Grand Theatre* (Figure 5.4) with the modernity of lower case *Percy House* (Figure 5.1).

Serif and sans serif letters

Serif capitals and varying line-width are used in *Bamburgh House* (Figure 5.4) and *High Street* (Figure 5.2). Sans serif letters with even line-width are seen in *Leazes Park Road* (Figure 5.2) and *Stowell Street* (Figure 5.3). The two characteristics are not necessarily found together; serif *Laing Art Gallery* (Figure 5.4), for instance, has almost even stroke-width.

Functions of Naming Signs

The primary functions of name signs include:

(i) Identification: You need to name something to be able to refer to it

The sign *Percy St.* (Figure 5.1) identifies the street and delimits it at both ends; *Grand Theatre* (Figure 5.4) forms part of the building it identifies. GeoPlace (the official body for addresses in the UK) (2021) proclaims, 'Everything happens somewhere'. The precise identification of places is the basis for maps, title deeds, etc. In England, this comes down to entries in the Land Registry (HM Land Registry, 2020), which records ownership rights for all property that has changed hands since 1862, an example of '*a legal cadastre*, intended to define the ownership rights attached to each plot' (Farvacque-Vitkovic *et al.*, 2005: 33). While registration has been fully compulsory for land since 1990, many large English estates have never been sold, and so remain unregistered.

The display of numbers has been required in England since 1762: 'Every number, name, or number and name, of any building in any street, shall be marked' (City of London, 2014). If property starts from land ownership, the identification and naming of one's property is indispensable.

(ii) Location: You need to know where something is to be able to get to it

People have to recognise when they have reached their destination. The Royal Mail and other delivery services need a postal address, now in part superseded by postcodes or Zip codes. These are not displayed on buildings, although occasionally added to street name signs, as in the *NR25* on the lower *High Street* sign (Figure 5.2). The location system does not work well for 'vanity' addresses which claim to be somewhere they are not: *520 Park Avenue* in Manhattan is located 150 feet west of Park Avenue in East 69th Street (Mask, 2020).

(iii) Durability: Name signs need to last

The material of name signs must be as indestructible as possible.

– Stone or moulded stucco are historic choices for imposing building name signs such as *Worswick Chambers* (Figure 5.7) or *Grand Theatre* (Figure 5.4), with raised or incised letters. These materials are less common in modern street name signs, an exception being the stone sign *Sandgate* (Figure 2.9).

- Metal is used in most approved street name signs, as in *Plummer Chare*, typically pressed letters in aluminium, although older signs were made of cast iron like the upper *High Street* sign (Figure 5.2). Other signs have a metallic finish, whether silver, *Percy Building* (Figure 5.1), or gilt, *Percy Arms* (Figure 3.8), particularly the brass of numbers like *32* (Figure 5.5).
- Ceramic tiles with individual white-on-black letters placed on brick walls were a Victorian style, as in *Constantine Road* (Figure 5.2).
- Painted black-on-white signs are exemplified by *Percy St.* (Figure 5.1). Street name signs are rarely painted on a surface, presumably for reasons of durability, and are not allowed under current regulations.
- Building names are often painted or stuck on the inside of glass windows, as in *Percy House* (Figure 5.1); numbers are stuck on the glass or painted in gilt, as in *20* (Figure 5.5). Originally this was achieved through gilding and other glass techniques, showing quality both by the expense of the gold leaf and by the skill needed to apply it to the glass.
- Individual raised letters made of different materials are also applied to buildings, like *Bamburgh House* (Figure 5.4), as discussed in Chapter 4.

Figure 5.7 Names and materials (*Plummer Chare, Worswick Chambers*, Newcastle)

(iv) Visibility: You need to be able to read the sign

Visibility depends on there being enough light to see the signs by. Most naming signs rely on what is available in the dark from street lights, etc., rather than being lit individually: street name signs are required to 'be fixed so that they will be illuminated by light from street lamps' (Department of Transport, 1993). Light also plays an important role in signs on glass lit from behind, say *20* (Figure 5.5), and in three-dimensional signs where shadows help or hinder visibility, say *Grand Theatre* (Figure 5.4), as discussed in Chapter 4.

Addressing systems

A modern influence on overall addressing systems has been Kevin Lynch's idea of the 'legible city' – 'the ease with which its parts can be recognised and can be organised into a coherent system' (Lynch, 1960: 2–3), reminiscent of Barthes (1997: 168), 'The city speaks to its inhabitants, we speak our city, the city where we are, simply by living in it, by wandering through it'. The city should make sense to its residents as they walk or drive through it, using multiple cues to experience how it fits together. In England, this led to projects like *Bristol Legible City* (2019), intended 'to improve people's understanding and experience of the city through the implementation of identity, information and transportation projects', and inspired some of the wayfinding signs seen in the next chapter. Legibility also suggests to some the '"physical typography" of the city-text', with 'page numbers', an 'index' and a 'page layout' (Rose-Redwood, 2008: 289). O'Toole (1994) developed a similar approach in terms of Halliday's textual meta-function.

Mental images of cities are nevertheless subject to cultural variation. The Japanese addressing system is spatial rather than linear in that an address consists of a number within a block within a district, and so on. In other words, Japanese buildings are not located by streets, nor by number in linear order. Although doubtless both English and Japanese systems now rely on postal codes, What3Words and GPS for practical purposes, these are different ways of looking at the world, and street users must map out routes and destinations very differently in their minds. I should admit to terror while trying to find a house in a Tokyo suburb after dark from a map written only in kanji.

From a political perspective, the naming and numbering of streets and buildings is crucial for planning and administration (Tantner, 2015). It is thus part of development, as in the street addressing projects in Sub-Saharan Africa reported in the World Bank manual, *Street Addressing and the Management of Cities* (Farvacque-Vitkovic *et al.*, 2005), which lays particular stress on taxation and the control of epidemics.

> Street addressing is therefore the foundation on which civic identity can develop and a prerequisite for the development of civic institutions. (Farvacque-Vitkovic *et al.*, 2005: 21)

Systematic addressing systems originated in the mid-17th century as a way of recruiting soldiers and gathering taxation in many European cities like Paris and Venice, not without protests both from the nobility, who saw it as reducing them to the level of the commoners, and from the commoners, who saw it as the growth of state control (Tantner, 2015).

In England, local authorities now stress the pressing need for emergency services to be able to identify locations (City of London, 2014). Street and building numbering represents the state consolidating its power over the land and its citizens. Having an address has become more and more a necessary part of one's identity, as a citizen for asserting the right to vote, as a patient for collecting prescriptions, as a customer for receiving mail orders, as a parent for getting one's child into a particular school, and so on. The street addressing system is not just a convenience but a method of control. Without a street address, you are a vagabond, suspect in every country whether homeless, Roma or nomad. The street addressing system suggested by the World Bank is arguably a Western way of looking at the world that originated in European cities and so a form of cultural imperialism imposing one world view on others.

Conclusion

Naming signs are a complex area of the language of the street, impinging on different aspects and functions of language.

(1) *They have unique relationships to meaning.* On the one hand, they are indexical in that their meaning relates to their precise location – the building or the street they are attached to: moving signs destroys their meaning. On the other hand, they are performative: installing the sign gives an object its name. In this function, the naming sign is not there to be read but to stake a claim. Interaction with a passing street user is virtually beside the point; it is the visible presence of the sign that counts. In addition, they have layers of meaning for the words that make them up and the connotations of their diverse forms.

(2) *Street addressing systems are only valid if sanctioned by the relevant authority,* ultimately through Acts of Parliament and the Land Registry. Street name signs are integrated with the law of the land in precise ways, not only in the choice of words, but also in the letter forms and display and in their exact location. A two-way choice between top-down and bottom-up signs (Ben-Rafael *et al.*, 2006) does not do justice to the complex functions of naming signs, which are licensed from above, nationally or locally, but owned, authored and written by different people.

(3) *Name signs have connotative and decorative characteristics.* Their identity and quality derive from the materials they are made of, the choice of letter forms, and so on, as discussed in Chapters 4 and 7. The decorative qualities may come from their integration into the whole building, for example *Dex Garage* (Figure 2.2) where the visual art deco character of the building is partly created by the sign. Hence the actual form and material of the letter is crucial. In speech, allophones of one phoneme rarely represent meaningful alternatives; a speaker does not have the option of saying *Bill* /bɪɫ/ with the clear /l/ of *lip*, except to mimic a particular accent. But the choice between different forms of the same letter contributes to the meaning of the street sign: a < P > means something different from a < p > or a < *p* > or even a < p >.

(4) *Naming signs have three dimensions.* Unlike printed books or notices, the letters can be raised from the surface as in *Welcome* (Figure 3.9), cut into it as in *Worswick*

Chambers (Figure 5.7), or stand free of it as in *Bamburgh House* (Figure 5.4). Even metal street name signs like *Stowell Street* (Figure 5.3) or the standard *Ireton Rd.* (Figure 5.2) have slightly raised letters. Their three-dimensionality relates to the kinds of shadow they show and to the solidity they display. They thus have to work from different viewing angles. The most extreme three-dimensional form is when the sign is a free-standing sculpture of numbers or letters.

6 Controlling Signs

Some signs try to control what we do on the street – help us move about as pedestrians or road users, deal with hazards, ring doorbells, and so on. Typical examples are seen in Figure 6.1. Controlling signs regulate the behaviour of the street user, whether physical movement, *Authorised vehicles*, obedience to regulations, *No Smoking*, or avoidance of hazards, *Watch yer heed!*. Some are general signs governed by national regulations, like *No Smoking*. Others are unique signs that reflect the whims of individuals, like *Watch yer heed!* (a spelling attempt at representing a Geordie accent) on a door lintel.

Figure 6.1 Controlling signs (*Authorised vehicles*, Colchester; *No Smoking*, LPR; *Watch yer heed!*, Newcastle)

The meaning of a controlling sign is firmly rooted in a precise point in space and time. Some, like *No Smoking*, are permanent, or at least long-lasting, and emanate from authorities that have to be obeyed. Others, like *Watch yer heed!*, are temporary one-offs valid for hours or days, the work of individuals.

Most controlling signs are in effect licensed by what English law calls 'deemed consent' (DCLG, 2007; see Chapter 3), without need for specific permission, like all street signs. Traffic signs are additionally governed by *CIRCULAR ROADS 3/93* (Department of Transport, 1993), with later emendations (Department for Transport, 2015). Legally mandated, national controlling signs also include specific pedestrian signs such as *Fire Assembly Point* signs and *No Smoking* signs, which have to be displayed at the public entrances to enclosed premises and must show 'a burning cigarette graphic in a red circle with a red bar across it' (*Smoke-free (Premises and Enforcement) Regulations*, 2006). It should perhaps be pointed out that the interpretation of regulations and statutes in this book is not that of a qualified lawyer.

Controlling signs are all effectively anonymous, the identity of the owner being implied rather than stated. In *No Smoking*, the owner and licensor take over the author and writer roles by dictating the very icons, dimensions and colours of the sign. Unique controlling signs like *Watch yer heed!* are authored and written by the people who work or live at the structures they are attached to.

Controlling signs make particular use of icons, in Peirce's sense of images of actual objects (Peirce, 1906), and of conventional symbols like mortarboards, motorcycles and shopping bags, some derived from national or international conventions, some ad hoc. Icons and symbols can be accessed by those who cannot read text. The Department for Transport (2004) believe:

> For simplicity of content and layout, ideographic representation of the message is most effective ... Abstract symbolism is less satisfactory since its meaning must be learnt and remembered. (Department for Transport, 2004: 12)

That is to say, icons are preferable to symbols that need to be remembered and to be interpreted.

Signs Controlling Action

Signs that control action mostly tell people which way to move. Traffic signs are discussed later.

Pointing signs: Arrows and hands

The direction signs in Figure 6.2 point with hands and arrows.

— *Samphire* (a tasty salt-water marsh plant) shows a chalk-drawn blackboard in green and pink with capitals that have ball-shaped serifs. The sign also shows that a drawback with blackboards is getting them clean; a closer look reveals that the board was previously used to advertise *The Bike Shed*.

- *53 North Hill* is a faded notice in peeling paint in vertically stressed serif capitals, showing a pointing hand index, known to printers as a manicule (Sherman, 2005).
- *Beethoven* is a scrawled post-it showing the way to a Beethoven concert.
- *Press to Open* is computer-printed in red, the dominant street colour in Newcastle Chinatown: the bilingual texts are centred in a right-hand column.

Figure 6.2 Pointing arrows and hands (*Samphire*, Blakeney; *53 North Hill*, Colchester; *Beethoven*, Newcastle; *Press to open*, SS)

These signs demonstrate three basic characteristics of direction signs.

- *The use of standardised images and icons* such as arrows and hands. The pointing hand in *53 North Hill* is first recorded in marginalia on the pages of 14th century books, used to draw attention to a note; it appeared in print in the late 15th century (McPharlin, 1942). Pointing hands were reduced to typographic ornaments until revived as cursors on computer screens. Their use as a direction sign is rare in modern times, although it can be traced back to drawings of feet and other parts of the body for showing direction in Ephesus in the 1st century BC (Finkel, 2015). As direction signs have a limited lifespan, other signs with pointing hands may have gone unrecorded.

The use of an arrow for direction is now global. A line with a pointed end is universally meaningful, even if arrows themselves are nowadays largely confined to sport. The first use may have been in 18th century technical drawings, where arrows showed the direction of flow in waterwheels, etc., with arrow heads and feathers (Gombrich, 1999: 228). Over the years, the image lost its fletching, i.e. < ↦ > became < → >, as in the spear-like arrows in felt-tip in *Beethoven* and in chalk in *Samphire*, the word-processor arrows in *Press to open* and the arrows in *Authorised vehicles* (Figure 6.1). The endpoint in the arrow's evolution is when it loses the line itself, becoming < > >, seen in traffic signs like *City Centre* (Figure 6.8) or the pointed ends of fingerposts like *Colchester* (Figure 6.3).

– *The control of people's actions.* Pointing signs guide people's movement in public places. They are addressed to road users or pedestrians, whether directing them in a particular direction or instructing them to press a push-pad. The arrows in *Authorised vehicles* (Figure 6.1) direct vehicles to go in particular directions, effectively with no choice and implicit penalties for disobedience. *Beethoven* (Figure 6.2) tells pedestrians how to get to the concert hall. *Samphire* (Figure 6.2) influences people to buy something rather than facilitating what they are going to do anyway; that is to say, it crosses over into selling.
– *Indexicality.* Direction signs are indexical in terms of place, orientation and, in some cases, time (Scollon & Scollon, 2003). The indexical meaning of direction signs depends on:
  • precise location – *53 North Hill* has to be visible at the entrance to the alleyway;
  • facing in a particular direction – *Press to open* points towards a push-pad;
  • sometimes, being valid for a limited period of time. *Beethoven* is useful only for the evening of the concert.

The indexicality of direction is dynamically based on movement rather than on the static identification of name signs: direction signs mark the routes between places, not the places themselves. Fuller (2002) points out that 'An arrow is a sign that has no referent; it assembles movement, it doesn't identify things', and so it is no longer an index that relates to things in Peirce's (1906) sense. The design of arrows for wayfinding is covered in Uebele (2007).

Some direction signs point towards specific features of the street, such as *Press to open* and *Beethoven*, the exophoric function where language makes the city legible. Others point to a route towards a place rather than the place itself, so that they may appear to point in unexpected directions.

Pointing signs for pedestrians and cyclists

Fingerposts take the arrow/hand icon a stage further by making the sign itself point in the appropriate direction in three-dimensional space (Figure 6.3). From the 17th century onwards, signposts made of wood or cast iron had multiple arms pointing road users to different destinations. Nowadays these traditional signs have largely disappeared, apart from a few at country crossroads. The modern equivalents are used primarily for local directions for non-car users and are found in 92% of English towns (Streetwise, 2013). The minimal form is seen in *Colchester*, white on a blue background as required by the traffic regulations described below, usually on poles in the amenity zone. Occasionally the sign may be on the 'wrong' side of the pole in that the 'finger' points in the reverse direction to the whole sign, as in *Christ Church*, the local church, probably to avoid obstructing the roadway. Typical fingerposts use icons or symbols to represent destinations, such as the railway logo in *Colchester* and the mortarboards in *RVI fingerpost*, or they show means of transport such as the bicycle in *Colchester* and the coach pointing to Haymarket bus station in *RVI fingerpost*. The minimalist notice-board in *Berrick Saul Building* leaves just the arrows to show general direction rather than more precisely pointing multiple arms. The *RVI fingerpost* is the most common type of metal sign, with white lower case sans serif letters against a black background, present in 78% of English towns (Streetwise, 2013).

Monolith signs in which the fingers have reverted to tiny arrows occur in 28% of town centres (Streetwise, 2013). The name suggests a resemblance to the monoliths in *2001 A Space Odyssey*. Monoliths are part of the legibility movement (Bristol Legible City, 2019), discussed in Chapter 5, and have smaller siblings, *midiliths* and *miniliths*. The circular pillars for advertising and notices common in Paris and elsewhere on the continent (Gorter, 2019), called Morris columns, have never been popular in England outside a few university campuses, although they do have a worldwide presence (JCDecaux, 2019).

Fingerposts are indexical because they point: in other words their meaning relates to their precise orientation at a particular location in space. They may also incorporate icons of walking men or bicycles that change direction to agree with the direction of pointing; the running man on emergency exit signs is a parallel case where the figure runs towards the exit, whether left or right (Scollon & Scollon, 2003: 30).

Describing these signs as controlling people's actions implicitly takes the owners' top-down view. Looked at from the street users' perspective, they are part of the legible city, enabling them to see its organisation and to choose where they are going within its overall information structure. With direction signs, users have a certain freedom of choice outside the planners' control.

Other controlling signs for pedestrians

Some controlling signs are intended primarily for those on foot. Hence they tend to be small, at eye-level and to have short snappy texts (Figure 6.4).

–   *Colchester Town Trail* is a round metal sign embedded in the pavement movement zone every few yards, designed to be legible after being trodden on many times. Like *Millennium Trail* (Figure 4.1), it marks a Town Trail for visitors on foot, combining commemoration with tourism. Many such trails appeared in England around the celebratory year 2000 but have not been maintained since.

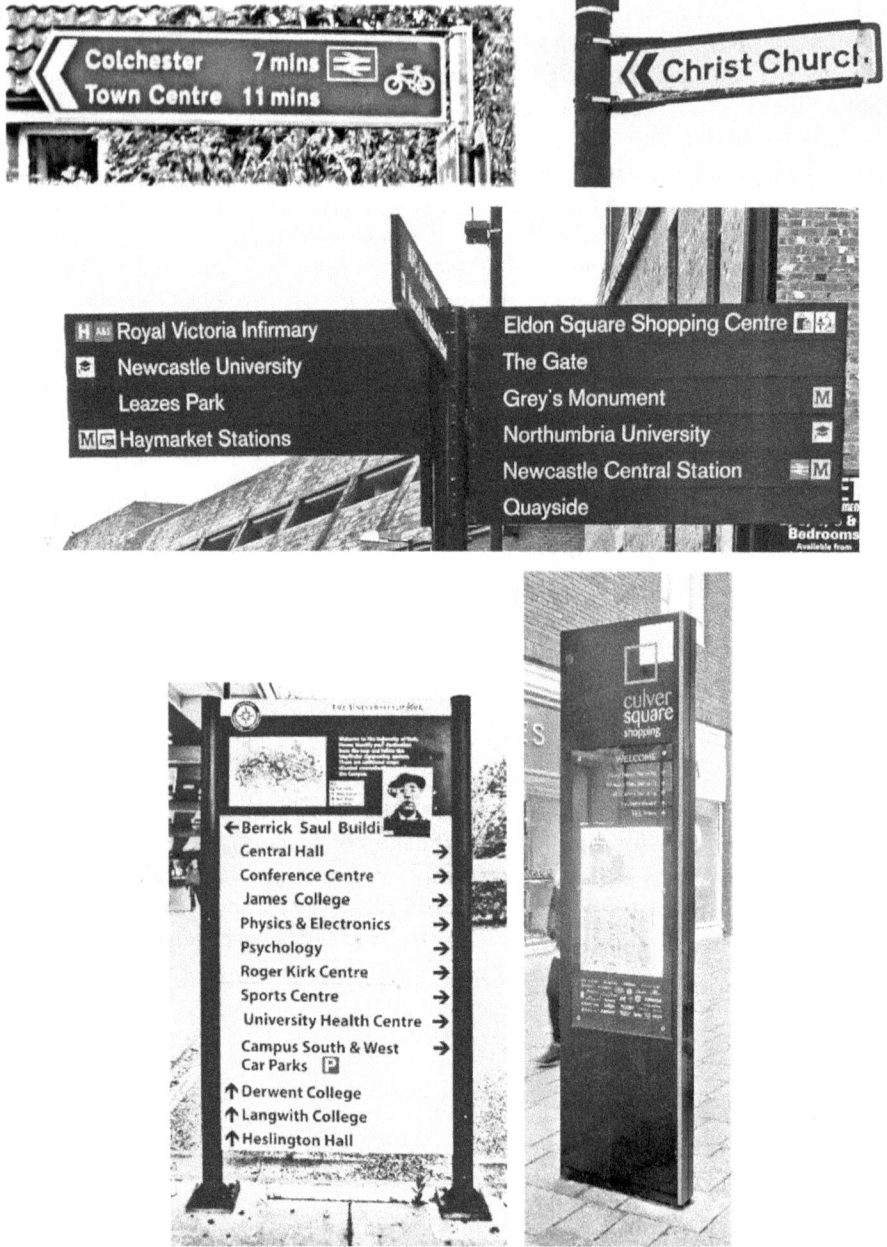

Figure 6.3 Pedestrian direction signs (*Colchester, Christ Church, Culver Square Monolith,* Colchester; *Royal Victoria Infirmary (RVI) Fingerpost,* LPR; *Berrick Saul Building,* York University)

Figure 6.4 Controlling signs for pedestrians (*Colchester Town Trail*, Colchester; *Thieves*, SS; *Danger*, *No dogs* (edited), Newcastle; *Pull*, LPR)

- *Danger* doubtless has an addressed audience of roofers but an unaddressed audience of passers-by. *Slippy* is a Geordie variant of *slippery*, as my Newcastle students told me with glee when I claimed it was a spelling mistake; the OED (2015) indeed has examples from several sources including Dickens. *Danger* incorporates maximum visibility black letters on yellow backgrounds, reinforced by the triangular warning sign.
- *Thieves will be prosecuted* on a shop door discourages a different type of misbehaviour, rather like *No Smoking* (Figure 6.1). Its dramatic effect comes from its closely spaced capitals with fat strokes and vertical stress, even if the point of the indistinct person in the prohibitory triangle is obscure. It borrows the triangular warning shape from traffic signs.
- *No dogs* similarly uses the traffic convention of the left diagonal negative line on a circular sign. Once such symbols are devised, they can be transferred to other uses, whether the red circles and negative diagonals in *No Smoking* (Figure 6.1) and *No dogs*, or the warning triangles in *Danger* and *Thieves*. The red diagonals on *No Smoking* (Figure 6.1) and *No Right Turn* (Figure 6.5) forbid the activities depicted, while that on *No Dogs* forbids the presence of dogs. The negative meaning of the diagonal is highly context dependent (Dobson & Dobson, 2018).
- *Pull* has sans serif all-capitals. A door that needs permanent written instructions is, however, a failure of design, as it should be obvious what to do if door handles and push-pads are used appropriately (Norman, 2002).

Traffic Signs

Traffic signs control road users, whether pedestrians, drivers, cyclists or anyone else. They are general signs sanctioned by government regulations:

> A traffic sign for conveying a description of a warning, information, requirement, restriction or prohibition specified under regulation 3 must be of the size, colour and type provided for in these Regulations. (*Traffic Signs Regulations*, 2016: 22)

The general public have access to these regulations through the booklet *Highway Code* (1999) 'issued with the authority of Parliament'. Each element of the traffic sign is licensed, owned and authored by the local government or highway authority acting on behalf of the national government, as regulated an area of language as it is possible to imagine. This section concentrates on traffic signs found in urban streets rather than those on motorways, etc.

Traffic signs attach rigid legal meanings to arbitrary aspects of language. Colours and shapes take on particular functions: circles with red borders or blue backgrounds, triangles with red borders, white rectangles with black borders – all ultimately implement the *Vienna Convention on Road Signs and Signals* (1968). The meaning of yellow lines along the edge of the roadway as 'You MUST NOT wait or park' does not derive just from the grammar and lexicon of English but from 'Law RTRA sects 5&8' (*Highway Code*, 1999: 54). And indeed only a particular yellow colour is permitted, namely BS381C No.355 (lemon), although 'No.309 (canary) is also acceptable' (Department for Transport, 2003: 144). Traffic signs in England reflect the UK interpretations of these internationally agreed signs, and differ from those in countries that have not signed the Vienna Convention, such as the United States.

The system of road traffic signs in the UK emerged from the *Worboys Report* (1963), named after its chairman Sir William Worboys. This is still in use in England, whether for the classification of signs, the coding of colours and shapes, or its library of icons. The letter styles were standardised to the sans serif Transport (Kinneir, 1980), in deliberate contrast with the typefaces prescribed for street names, namely Gill Sans and Kindersley (Department of Transport, 1993).

The Worboys research established that all-capitals <NEWCASTLE> are less legible from a vehicle moving at speed than lower case letters combined with initial capitals <Newcastle> (Kinneir, 1980). The mixed-case of traffic signs thus complements the all-capitals of street name signs (Department of Transport, 1993), as described in Chapter 5.

The three main official classes of road sign are regulatory, warning and informatory (Department for Transport, 2003).

Most traffic signs function as symbols rather than as icons in that the user needs to know the coded meanings assigned to them, say the green man for 'You may cross' or right-diagonal for negation versus left-diagonal for removing negation, occurring together in *Zone Ends*, a kind of double-negative construction in which two negatives make a positive, 'You may (not) (not) park here'.

Figure 6.5 Regulatory signs (*Turn left, 30 mph limit, No entry, No right turn, Give way*, Colchester; *Stop*, Essex)

Figure 6.6 Warning and informatory signs (*Left junction, Zone ends*, Colchester)

The overall meanings arbitrarily attached to features of traffic signs in England are (Department for Transport, 2003: 9):

Regulatory: circles (Figure 6.5):
    Mandatory: white border, blue background – 'Must be done': *Turn left* arrow
    Prohibitory: red border, white background – 'Mustn't be done': *30* and *No entry* circle; diagonal bar for specific prohibition: *No right turn*
    Others: octangular shape with red background: *Stop*, and downward-pointing triangle: *Give way*
Warning: upward-pointing triangle with red border: *Left junction* (Figure 6.6)
Informatory: rectangular (Figure 6.6)
    Blue background, white border (except motorways): *Authorised vehicles* (Figure 6.1)
    Green background, white border (motorways)
    White background and black border: *Zone ends*
    Brown background, local and tourist signs: *Maldon* (Figure 6.8)

While the meaning of colour in traffic signs is arbitrary, some uses are internationally agreed, for example the green in emergency exit signs. Other shared features relate to how humans see road signs. A coloured background, for instance, contrasts better with white text than with black text (Uebele, 2007), although this depends also on factors such as hue and density; compare, say, *Stop* (white on red) (Figure 6.5) with *Give way* (black on white) (Figure 6.5). The red border of prohibitory signs and the red of the stop light on traffic lights are intentionally intrusive; the brown background of tourist signs like the *Colchester Zoo* sign in *Maldon* (Figure 6.8) is deliberately subdued.

The conventions for shape are also arbitrary. Traffic signs use red circles for prohibitions, upward-pointing red triangles for warning and white rectangles for information. The rationale for the eight sides of the *Stop* sign decreed by the Vienna Convention (1968) is obscure, leading to various folk explanations such as: an octagon is recognisable to vehicles coming from the other direction; the more sides a sign has the greater its force – a circle is one power, a triangle is three, and so on.

Figure 6.7 Pedestrian signs (*Look left*, LPR; *Pedestrians*, Newcastle)

Look left illustrates how the meaning of street signs can depend on the perspective from which they are read. The meaning of *Look left* written on the pedestrian crossing only works for the direction the pedestrian is facing; the complementary sign *Look right* on the far side of the crossing is perfectly legible, although upside down, but invalid from this side of the road (Figure 6.7). It is hard to think of other uses of written language where meaning depends literally on point of view. The *Look left* sign also shows tactile meaning on the pavement for those with poor sight, where 'Dots in a grid mean a dropped curb for crossing the road' (RNIB, 2019). Tactile paving is a complex area of its own in street signage, regulated by Department of the Environment, Transport and the Regions (2007).

The all-capitals *Pedestrians* sign has extra line space after *pedestrians* to punctuate it as direct address followed by an imperative – *Pedestrians! Do not walk on the road* – rather than as a proverbial saying – *Pedestrians do not walk on the road*. It also uses a strong yellow background, often found in warning signs.

Figure 6.8 Traffic direction signs (*City Centre*, Newcastle; *Maldon, Lexden*, Colchester)

The main direction signs are divided by the Department for Transport (2007) into:

- **Motorways**: blue with white border;
- **Primary routes**: green with white border;
- **Non-primary routes**: white with black border: *Maldon, Lexden, City Centre.*

Signs such as *City Centre* (Figure 6.8) indicate direction of travel and are arrow-shaped with a minimal arrow-head. They resemble informing signs in presenting a menu of destinations line by line.

Again colours have explicitly specified meanings. The coloured backgrounds to road numbers on non-primary route signs indicate the status of the roads, matching the full size signs, so that, in *City Centre*, the blue background to *A167 (M)* shows that it is a motorway, the green background to *A19* that it is a primary route, the white background to *A188* that it is a non-primary route. Whether the average road user is aware of these distinctions is debatable.

Some traffic signs are applied to the surface of the roadway, as seen in Figure 6.9.

Figure 6.9 Roadway signs (*No Through Road*, Colchester; *Yellow lines*, SS; *Bicycle*, LPR)

The horizontal roadway signs with text like *No Through Road* or images like *Bicycle* aim at a 'stretched' version of the Transport Medium typeface (Department for Transport, 2003: 139), whose tall, sans serif letters aid visibility for drivers who see them from an angle at a distance, also found in *No Entry* (Figure 1.8) and *Turn Right*

(Figure 4.1). They consist of words or minimal phrases reminding people of parking restrictions, cyclists' rights and the like. The material of the sign has to contrast with the asphalt road surface, must be durable and skid-resistant, and should not hinder drainage. It may consist of 'thermoplastic, cold plastic, preformed material or paint' (Department for Transport, 2003: 142), although paint is only suitable where it gets little wear. Texts on roads relate to the driver's or cyclist's point of view: *No Through Road* implies 'from this direction'.

Parking signs

Signs to control parking proliferate in urban streets, shading between 'private' signs to protect parking spaces and official general signs dictated by regulations.

On-street parking

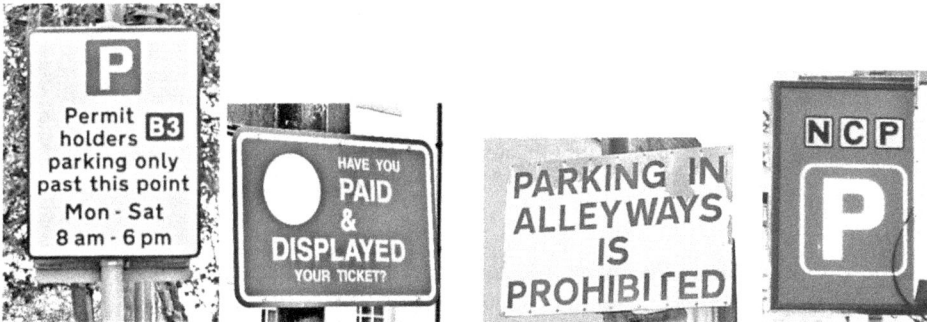

Figure 6.10 On- and off-street parking signs (*Permit holders*, Colchester; *Paid & Displayed, Parking in Alleyways*, LPR; *NCP*, SS)

The first defence against parking is roadway markings like double yellow lines (Figure 6.9). Next come local council signs controlling parking zones like *Permit holders* mounted on a pole sign in the amenity zone, oddly centred in Gill Sans, mostly featuring a white sans serif < P > on a blue ground. In addition, there are diverse signs for off-road car parks, as in *Paid & Displayed* and *NCP* (Figure 6.10). The car park sign *Parking in alleyways* is slightly baffling as *alleyways* refers to the car lanes rather than to narrow streets, not attested in the OED (2015).

Private parking signs

Private parking signs like those in Figure 6.11 are authored by the owners of the property and written by the owners themselves or by signwriters, licensed by deemed consent, although *£50 fee* does look too wide to be legal; they are then unique signs. Virtually all the Leazes Park Road (LPR) buildings with off-road parking seen in Figure 1.1 right discourage parking through signs like *Private Parking*.

Figure 6.11 Private parking signs (*Private Parking*, LPR; *Please don't park, Polite notice,* Colchester; *£50 fee*, Newcastle)

These signs look as imposing and deterring as possible, with *£50 fee* becoming almost menacing. The very amateurishness of unique handwritten signs like *£50 fee* and *Please Don't Park* suggests that something unpleasant might happen to your car if it were parked there. *Polite Notice* follows a tradition built upon the convenient confusability of *polite* and *police*. All these signs have sans serif letters, centred lines and all-capitals – emphatic warning without permanence.

Green man and *Traffic lights* raise questions about the meanings of colour and on/off lights. Traffic lights are often used in introductory linguistics courses as an example of a system in which each of the three colours has meaning only in relation to the other two. The red of *stop* contrasts with the green of *go*; in the UK the amber light combined with red effectively means 'get ready to go'; by itself amber means 'stop' if you can do so safely (although the Highway Code (1999: 70) calls both ambers 'Stop'): red means 'not-green'; stop means 'not-go'. The order always runs from red at the top of the sign to green at the bottom, partly to assist the colour-blind. Traffic lights in Quebec are an exception in having a horizontal display, sometimes with different shapes for the three lights: red square, yellow diamond and green circle.

The UK three-colour scheme goes back to the *Ministry of Transport Roads Dept. Mem.* No. 297 (1929), globalised through the Vienna Convention (1968: 15), which laid down:

(i) A green light shall mean that traffic may proceed …
(ii) A red light shall mean that traffic may not proceed …

(iii) An amber light ... when appearing alone it shall mean that no vehicle may pass the stop line ... When shown at the same time as the red light, it shall mean that the signal is about to change.

Figure 6.12 Timed light signals (*Green man, Traffic lights*, LPR)

Given the variation in colour terminology across the world's languages, the Vienna Convention is not always easy to implement. In Japan, the bilingual traffic regulations call the colour in traffic lights *blue* 青 in Japanese and *green* in English (Backhaus, 2013). To my English eye, it certainly looks blue. The UK regulations specify the infrequent colour word *amber*, a word with only 235 examples in the British National Corpus of a hundred million words, rather than *yellow* with 3766. The relationship of colour and meaning is arbitrary, being decided for traffic signs by government and decreed by law: language dictated by the state.

Since traffic signs need to function 24 hours a day, light is crucial. The illumination of traffic signs is to be specified in the forthcoming Department for Transport (in preparation). For *Green man* and *Traffic lights*, the red and green colours are only valid when lit, a type of meaning peculiar to controlling signs.

Conclusion

Controlling signs are a unique form of written language because:

- *The meanings of controlling signs depend upon precise location and orientation.* The signs have to be in the correct place and facing the user in the correct direction;

when encountered in other locations or with other orientations, they can be ignored. While naming signs depend on attachment to the streets and buildings they name in zones of street space that any street user can access, controlling signs need to be embedded in appropriate zones in locations that are visible to the group of street users they are aimed at, say those on wheels versus those on foot.

– *Controlling signs lead to dynamic action or avoidance by the street users.* Most other street signs require cognitive activity by the street user in identifying places, commemorating events, considering what to buy, etc. Controlling signs, however, ask the user to do something by moving in a certain way, such as turning left, or by avoiding an action, such as smoking. The anonymous voice of authority is telling the street user how to behave and asserting implicitly that they have the right or the knowledge to do so: go this way, press this button, do not smoke.

– *Controlling signs are largely available to street users who cannot read*, whether children, illiterates or users of different writing systems. By their nature, controlling signs need to affect any relevant user whether for direction, control of driving or moral behaviour. Hence their meaning utilises people's ability to comprehend objects depicted in icons, indexes or symbols, akin to pictograms and rebuses. The same factor applies to logos and names of international businesses and products like KFC, instantly recognisable without accompanying text.

– *Every aspect of general traffic signs is subject to minute control by government or international regulation.* No other kind of language is so regulated by an outside authority, dictating not just the wording but also the very shape, colour and size of the letters. The regulations run to hundreds of pages, issued in separate 'chapters' over several decades (*Department for Transport Traffic Signs Manual*, 2003, in preparation). Traffic signs thus represent control of people through nationwide general signs, deliberately chosen by the appropriate body, often based on research and testing.

– *Traffic signs rely on consciously assigned meanings of colour and shape.* Colours and shapes do not have the natural associations and connotations for particular cultures but explicitly defined meanings. In turn, these may become part of the language of street signs, whether 'negative' diagonal lines or upward-pointing 'warning' triangles. Street signs both borrow from other genres and contribute to them.

– *The texts of controlling street signs are minimal.* Mostly the sentences consist of imperatives, like *Press to open*, location names like *Christchurch*, and present tense injunctions, like *It is against the law to smoke on these premises*. While nouns giving the names of buildings and places are frequent, these are always instrumental in that they show how to get to them rather than naming them.

7 Connotations of Letter Forms in Street Signs

The overtones of meaning that street signs convey are often as important as their explicit messages. The yellow background and the letter style of the sign *Danger of Death* (Figure 7.9) warn how serious the threat may be; the fat red lower case letters of *red mezze* (Figure 3.1) suggest the liveliness of the restaurant; the incised stone letters of *Remember* (Figure 1.5) highlight the solemn commitment of the memorial. This chapter concentrates on the connotations of street signs rather than their indexical or referential meanings. It complements in a sense the legibility research mentioned in Chapter 2 and the materials discussion of Chapter 4. The term 'typeface' is used for much of the chapter rather than 'letter style', partly because it is common in typographical research, partly as a reminder that this research is not directly about street signs.

Some typographers believe that nothing should come between the reader and the message. In her celebrated essay 'The Crystal Goblet', Beatrice Warde (1932) asks the reader to choose whether they would prefer to drink wine from a goblet of solid gold or one of clear crystal:

> … you will choose the crystal, because everything about it is calculated to reveal rather than hide the beautiful thing which it was meant to contain. … Type well used is invisible as type, just as the perfect talking voice is the unnoticed vehicle for the transmission of words, ideas. (Warde, 1932: 1)

The author's message is paramount; connotations of letter form are by the way. Can anyone remember the typeface in which they first read *Harry Potter*? (Actually, it was most likely Garamond; Agarwal, 2012). Traffic and servicing signs have a similar aim: the less attention we pay to the messenger, the more we pay to the message. Hence official general signs of national and local government are concerned with visibility and legibility expressed through plain uniform letter styles; connotations are largely reduced to their sober, uniform and official appearance. Indeed the World Health Organisation's (2016) recommendations concerning cigarette packets state:

> plain packaging that only allows brand and product names in a standard colour and font style will make health warnings more noticeable and further disrupt the attractiveness of the packaging.

Street signs other than official signs, however, need the visual impact of the golden goblet, not the transparency of the crystal. If they do not arouse our interest instantly, we do not notice them. Cross-media and unique signs require very different effects from the anonymous transparency of traffic signs or, indeed, books. A maxim in Bringhurst (2005: 95) is, 'Choose faces that can furnish whatever special effects you can require', leading to the anonymity of traffic signs on the one hand, and the individuality of street blackboards on the other.

Most published discussion of the connotations of letter forms is based on the personal judgment, skill and experience of the analyst and on the traditional consensus of opinion, not on empirical evidence of readers' behaviour (Thangaraj, 2004: 5). Semiotics research too has discussed the letter shapes used across typefaces mostly in terms of beliefs such as:

> Roundness can come to signify 'smooth', 'soft', 'natural', 'organic', 'maternal' and so on, and angularity 'abrasive', 'harsh', 'technical', 'masculine', and so on. (Van Leeuwen, 2006: 149)

These judgments are inevitably influenced by the analysts' culture or the first writing system they learnt.

In addition, experts do not see the same connotations as non-experts (Bartram, 1982), and 'amateurs' have less extreme judgments than 'pros' (Tannenbaum *et al.*, 1964), sometimes called the 'design disconnect' – 'the measurable difference between the design preferences of design professionals and everyone else' (Iovene *et al.*, 2019). Hence expert interpretations of street signs need to be supported by empirical research with the street users themselves, such as that proposed in Dyson (2014).

But can such claims be justified empirically rather than subjectively? In principle, opinions about the connotations of letter forms can be elicited from many actual users rather than one analyst, no longer the judgment of one person or a clique of experts but of actual street users, similar to the accent perception surveys used in dialect research (Giles, 1970). At the very least, such research can provide a brake on the pronouncements of experts.

Much of the research on letter forms concerns the effects of display on consumers, whether in restaurant menus, logos or fascias, that is to say, with how cross-media signs like the McDonald's Golden Arches project a commercial identity to the world. As direct research into street users' perceptions of street signs has been sparse, typographic research here stands in as a pro tem solution, eventually to be replaced by research based directly on street signs.

Connotations also involve history. Given that signs may endure over long periods of time, what do the classical letters in *Town Hall* (Figure 4.2) based on Roman letters from the AD 2nd century say for the early 20th century when the sign was erected or for the 21st century we are now in? Speech is typically produced for an audience that is physically present at a particular moment, even if recordings nowadays potentially give it a longer life; street signs project backwards in time, like the 19th century names carved in stone all over Newcastle, such as *Leazes Crescent* (Figure 4.3). The equivalent in speech would be a modern street dotted with elegant people speaking 18th and 19th century English; the past is still alive in the English street. These relics resemble the novel written by Pierre Menard, the Borges character, which is word for word the same as *Don Quixote*, but is a new creation because the world around it has changed.

Typographic Research

Typographical research that tries to evaluate the feelings that typefaces convey to readers looks promising as one avenue for firming up the evidence used in street signs research. Its methods are largely surveys and experiments with hundreds of participants. The typical approach is to ask a large panel of people to judge texts in various typefaces via a number of scales. Doyle *et al.* (2010), for example, tested 102 typefaces against three scales, Evaluation, Potency and Activity, derived from the Semantic Differential Test (Osgood *et al.*, 1957), widely used for assessing connotations in psychology and business. Kastl and Child (1968) originally found that curved, sans serif letters felt sprightly, sparking and dreamy, whereas angular, bold serif letters felt sad, dignified and dramatic.

More recently, the experiments of Velasco *et al.* (2018) investigated how round or angular letters influence perception of taste. Participants rated the taste of jelly beans inside bags labelled <**eat me**> (VAG rounded) versus <**eat me**> (London 2012) or with questions <**tastes like?**> versus <*tastes like?*>. The rounder letters and thicker type went with increased perceptions of sweetness.

An alternative approach measures letters in terms of brightness, interpreted as values on a greyscale (Nedeljković *et al.*, 2017). Franklin Gothic as in <**Bamburgh House**> (here Franklin Gothic Demi) came out as the darkest typeface and scored high on loud, masculine, cold and cheap, while Gill Sans <Bamburgh House> was among the lightest, scoring highly on elegance and femininity. The sheer forms of letters influence people in ways they are unaware of, in street signs as much as in other genres.

To explore how this typographic approach might be applied usefully to street signs, Figure 7.1 shows a sample of four familiar typefaces, seen in:

— *Press Buzzer* (Figure 7.1) is in Times New Roman printed on A4 paper, in all-capitals, with <***HERE*** > in bold underlined italics, protected by a plastic file folder: the materials shout temporary. Times New Roman has become a default serif typeface on personal computers and is often stipulated for journals and dissertations. It is a serif typeface with variable line width and medium x-height, its name overtly linking it to classical Roman letters.

The sign highlights how thin and frail the capitals of Times New Roman appear in street signs compared with the more forceful look of the bold italic letters. Gray (1960: 26) points out that, while the Romans used Trajan-style letters on inscriptions, they preferred heavier letters for their triumphal arches and building name signs. The typographic research showed Times New Roman to be academic (Hyndman, 2016), direct (Brumberger, 2003), low on activity (Doyle *et al.*, 2010) and traditional (Shaikh *et al.*, 2006). Overall, these judgments suggest that *Press Buzzer* is not so much conservative as old-fashioned.

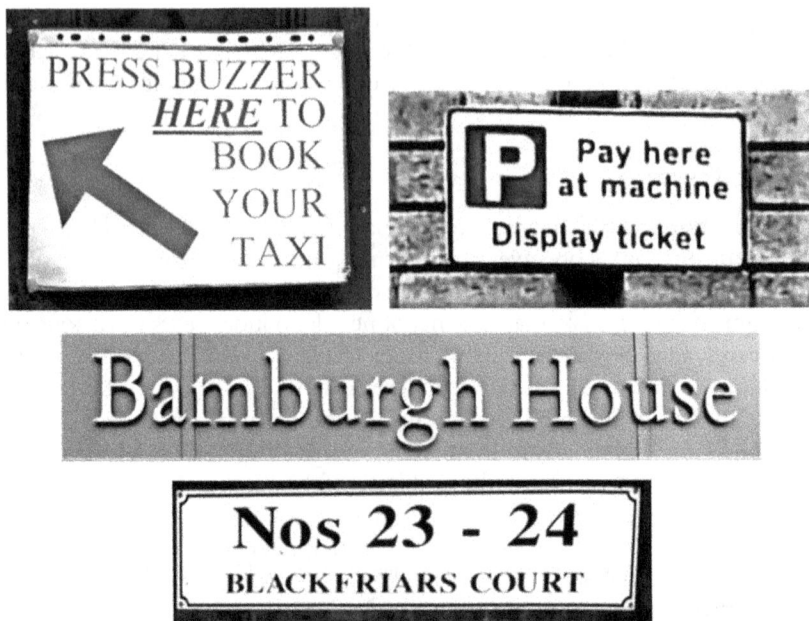

Figure 7.1 Street signs showing four typefaces: Times New Roman (*Press Buzzer*, SS); Gill Sans (*Pay here*, LPR); Garamond (*Bamburgh House*, Newcastle); Bodoni (*Nos 23–24*, SS)

— *Bamburgh House* (Figure 7.1) shows Garamond on a building name sign on a large scale). This 16th century typeface was revived in the 20th century in many different forms (Carter, 1995). It is a serif typeface with a short x-height and variable line-width. It was used in writing this book as I find it easy to read, both on screen and in printout.

Garamond comes across better than Times New Roman on these street signs, perhaps because of the shadows from the raised metallic letters, but this may well reflect our familiarity with it rather than its intrinsic virtues, as Beier (2012) points out. In the typographic research, Garamond is intellectual (Hyndman, 2016), direct (Brumberger, 2003) and low on activity (Doyle *et al.*, 2010). Garamond is thus judged as being just as old-fashioned as Times New Roman. Incidentally Garamond uses less ink than other typefaces on computer printers (Agarwal, 2012).

— *Pay here* illustrates the common use of Gill Sans on controlling signs). Gill Sans is a sans serif typeface with a medium x-height; although appearing in the same era as the sans serif types of the new typography advocated by the Bauhaus, it was less geometrically based (Bringhurst, 2005: 258). Gill Sans is one of the typefaces offi-cially allowed for street name signs such as *Leazes Lane* (Figure 2.12) and suggests seriousness and authority. In the typographic research, Gill Sans comes across as everyman (Hyndman, 2016) and low on potency (Doyle *et al*., 2010), but elegant and feminine (Nedeljković *et al*., 2017).

– *Nos 23–24*. The building name sign is painted with a decorative border and a prominent header in larger letters, using Bodoni, a historical revival of an 18th century design that became a hallmark of 20th century fashion magazines and advertisements for perfume. It is a serif typeface with great contrast of stroke. The thinness of some strokes, however, makes it difficult to use in street signs and in small sizes of print.

To my mind, Bodoni is slightly overbearing for an everyday street sign, reflected in its high scores for evaluation and potency. The personality of Bodoni came over as performer (Hyndman, 2016) and medium for activity (Doyle *et al*., 2010).

This style of typographical research at least has possibilities for street sign research in that it tries to represent the views of readers on typefaces via the filter of various schemes for labelling their subjective responses. The main constraint on its usefulness for street signs research is its reliance on print typefaces. Indeed many typefaces used on printed documents are not appropriate for street sign use because of the different reading conditions (Gray, 1960); what makes a typeface readable in a book does not make it legible five feet above our heads or beneath our feet.

Connotations of Different Sign Functions

Let us now combine the insights from this approach with the opinions of various commentators and my own subjective judgments as a person with English as a first writing system and as a local street user on a selection of signs. The reaction is to the sign as a whole, not just the letters: 'We seldom react to letterforms alone but to legends in their entirety – letter-style, content, colour, material, size and position' (Kinneir, 1980: 14). Note: the letter forms used in the text here only approximate those in the signs, which are often unique individual designs.

Naming Signs

As we saw in Chapter 6, naming signs carry out several function, in particular asserting ownership and location.

Places to respect

Institutions that see themselves as an important and respected part of the local or national scene project their identity through the cross-media indexical name signs they display, whether universities (Figure 7.2), town halls, hospitals or the like.

Universities

Figure 7.2 University name signs (Newcastle and York)

The *University of Newcastle upon Tyne* is an older sign still featuring the university's former name. The letters are applied gold serif capitals raised from the brick surface so that the shadows come into play: an elegant, academic and traditional appearance.

Modern English universities, however, want to seem forward-looking and lively without forsaking the grand tradition of learning. One way of achieving these fairly contradictory goals is to state their name in two typefaces – an insight I owe to Paul Seedhouse. Part of the name has staid serif letters, say <University> as in *Newcastle University*, or all-capitals as in <University> in *The University of York*. These convey the seriousness and status of the university through the Roman serif letters or capitals, amplified by the coat of arms in the Newcastle sign.

The other part of the university name looks freer and more modern, whether the sans serif broad strokes of <**Newcastle** > or the joined-up sloping script letters of <*of York*>. These imply modernity and informality through sans serif letters or cursive semi-calligraphic letters. While seen here in naming signs, they form part of cross-media design policies that extend from the university letterhead to the direction signs on campus; that is to say, they control the writer with a careful design brief.

The signs are centred, either within a two-column display as in *Newcastle University*, or across the building façade as at York, although this leads to an awkward placement of < U > on a building column. The gold and silver letters and the workmanship proclaim quality. The old and new Newcastle University signs coexist at the same moment of time; quality street signs remain with us until there is a decision to remove them.

Churches

Figure 7.3 Church signs (*Baptist Church*, Colchester; *St Andrew's*, Newcastle)

Churches too are torn between wanting to seem ancient and respectable as well as modern and caring (Figure 7.3).

– *Baptist Church* has all-capitals with markedly thin and thick strokes, similar to Bodoni, and painted a cool blue – dignity and simplicity. The personality is leader and idealist (Hyndman, 2016), beautiful and potent (Doyle *et al.*, 2010).
– *St Andrew's* suggests its historic past through the Old English Blackletter Gothic <𝔗𝔥𝔢 𝔒𝔩𝔡𝔢𝔰𝔱 𝔠𝔥𝔲𝔯𝔠𝔥>. (In England, *gothic* refers to sans serif letter styles related to the traditional German Fraktur script, in North America to sans serif letter styles in general.) Old English letter styles are not found in historic 17th century street signs, on the evidence of collections such as Heal (1957) and Larwood and Hotten (1866). But nowadays they assert the antiquity of a building, like the fake archaism <ye> for <the> *Ye Olde Marquis* (Figure 2.23). According to Dawson (2013: 351), they occur mostly in street signs for tattoo parlours and pubs like *The Bull* (Figure 7.5); that is to say, they are not expected on a genuine 13th century building like St Andrews Church.

At the top of the notice is a barely legible light serif letter style for < **The Parish Church of St Andrew** >; in most church signs, this would be the dominant header for the rest of the sign, as in *St Peters* (Figure 5.4). The body of the notice <**REGULAR SERVICES**> is in a heavy sans serif letter style, standing out in red and black. At the bottom is an invitation <*ALL WELCOME*> in italic, informal all-capitals, also in red.

This notice uses several different letter styles in an eye-catching way, similar to exuberant Victorian posters advertising music halls. The letters on this one sign probably belong to all of Shaikh's (2006) groups from traditional to plain and to all of Brumberger's (2003) groups from elegant to friendly. The aim seems to be to project antiquity, practicality and friendliness at the same time. Whether you find this mixture lively and exciting or incoherent and aggressive seems a matter of taste.

Banks

Banks too want to project seriousness and responsibility at the same time as contemporary relevance (Figure 7.4).

– *Barclay and Co^Y* asserts dignity and endurance through its serif capitals, ornamental stone frame, abbreviations in superscript small capitals and the ageing appearance of the weathered letters and stone; the abbreviation *Co^Y* rather than *Co.* is now rarely seen. The modern *Barclays* sign adds an < s > and an eagle, its historic logo since the 17th century. The blue letters appear modern because of their almost even stroke contrast with flare serifs.
– *Lloyds Bank* has standard sans serif metal letters apart from the bent cross-bar of < A >, which presumably lends it individuality. Its respectability is asserted by the older stone portico that surrounds it – the modern Lloyds Bank name was only revived in 2009. Traditional banks like their names to be in imposing individual capital letters displayed in the fascia or high zones – quality, elegance and potency.

Figure 7.4 Bank signs (*Barclay & Co*[Y], *Lloyds Bank*, Newcastle; *Barclays*, *Metro*, Colchester)

– *Metro Bank*, however, shows a new face to banking, both literally – it was founded in 2010 – and figuratively – its website proclaims 'We do banking differently' (https://www.metrobankonline.co.uk/). Its dramatic, heavy, slightly sloping, sans serif letters and its jagged, interrupted < M > are similar in effect to chains like *Greggs* (Figure 3.15), suggesting modern dynamism rather than respectability.

Pubs

Perhaps the signs that most people associate with English streets are those hanging from public houses in the high vertical zone. Even by 1419, it was necessary to restrict their projections to 7 feet in length (Larwood & Hotten, 1866: 6). By the 1760s, projecting street signs were so numerous and led to so many accidents that they were banned altogether. A handful of pub signs that span the whole street still survive in England, for example *The Magpie* in Suffolk.

The Roman sign for a drinking place was a bush or vine, as described in Chapter 2. Hanging pub signs feature icons with or without the pub name. Pub names were chosen: to honour patrons like the *Ye Olde Marquis* (of Granby) (Figure 2.23); to flatter the gentry like the *Percy Arms* (Figure 3.8); to commemorate historical events like *The Royal Oak*, in which Charles II hid from the Roundheads (although alternative folk explanations trace it to the oaks used for building the navy); to commemorate famous racehorses, like *The Flying Fox* in Colchester; and for many other reasons. The imaginative stories behind pub names are spelled out in guides such as Jack (2009).

Syntactically, pub names often consist of:

- a definite article and a proper name, *The George* (Figure 2.12);
- a proper name modifying one of a small possible group of head nouns, *The Percy Arms* (Figure 3.8), *Harry's Bar*, *The Queen's Head* (in 1990s signs this often featured Freddie Mercury);
- two coordinated nouns, *The Slug and Lettuce* and *The Dog and Pheasant* (Figure 3.6).

Some include the article as part of the sign, like *Ye Olde Marquis* (Figure 2.23). According to the pub trade journal *The Morning Advertiser* (2017), the *Red Lion* is the most popular pub name in England.

In the early 18th century, before houses were consistently named or numbered, addresses were often stated in relation to street signs. London booksellers included 'John Walter, at the HOMER'S HEAD, Charing Cross', 'William Sandby, at the SHIP, Without Temple Bar' and 'Thomas Longman, at the SHIP & BLACK SWAN in Paternoster Row' (Heal, 1957: 31–34) – the ship still appears on Longman Pearson book covers. The custom of giving directions by pubs persists in England to this day.

Figure 7.5 Pub signs (*The Strawberry*, Newcastle; *Rosie's Bar*, SS; *The Bull*, Colchester; *Trent House*, LPR)

Hanging signs are the default for pubs (Figure 7.5).

– *The Strawberry* sign proclaims itself a long-established football pub in three icons: a strawberry based on the historical use of the site for strawberry fields; a black and white striped Newcastle United shirt; and a blue star for Newcastle Brown Ale, formerly brewed close by.

– *Rosie's Bar* is another sign for a football pub with a picture of Rosie and a text in gold serif capital letters.

– *Trent House* uses a wall-mounted sign for a youth- and university-oriented pub to assert its 'world-famous' identity through white-outlined capital letters, with a header in the centre and an icon of a disc.

– *The Bull* is a blackboard headed in gold blackletter on a genuinely old pub, highlighting issues with reusing blackboards any older teacher will sympathise with. It incidentally demonstrates the use of a common street sign initialism <B.O.G.O.F.>, fortunately spelled out above it *Buy one, get one free*.

These signs show a continuity from the mediaeval iconic hanging signs and the use of raised gilt letters; they are effectively claiming to be in the great English sign tradition. But they also assert loyalty to a particular subculture, whether football fans, traditional pub-goers, students or some other group (Moss, 1993). The aim is not primarily to seek respect or to attract passing trade so much as to maintain the loyalty of regulars who affiliate with a particular group, whether united by sport, age, sexuality or other factors. Further examples of pub signs are *Ye Olde Marquis* (Figure 2.23), *Dog & Pheasant* (Figure 3.6) and *The Percy Arms* (Figure 3.8).

Places to eat

Restaurants and cafés display their names on fascia boards, often with ancillary informing notices in the eye-level zone giving menus and opening times.

Figure 7.6 Restaurant signs (*Pizza Express*, Colchester; *Da Mimmos*, LPR; *Buffet King*, SS)

— *Pizza Express*: a curved sign displaying a cross-media brand name using ornate art nouveau style capitals, with dramatic white raised letters on a black background, a cross-media sign seen on most English High Streets.

— *Da Mimmos*: a unique sign in an italic cursive style with letters shaded in white against a vibrant red; the telephone number, however, is in sans serif, including a < 1 > substitute for the usual sans serif < I >.

— *Buffet King*: a hanging sign in Chinatown that suggests the exotic through its purple background, its gold frame and its unusual letter forms, combining the cursive <*Lau's*> , the eccentric script letters of <**Buffet King**> and the sans serif all-capitals of <**RESTAURANT**>, all outlined or shaded in white.

Further restaurant signs are seen in Figure 2.16 and elsewhere, while Chapter 8 looks in more depth at occasions where the letter style imitates another script.

Restaurant signs try to look lively, welcoming and individual, the opposite of the corporate respectability of signs for banks and universities. This is not necessarily the same as the promotion of ethnic food; there is no particular reason why pizza should be promoted through art nouveau letters or pasta through italic cursive letters. But they look dramatic and distinctive against their contrasting backgrounds, large enough to read high on the wall. It is not respect or age that are suggested so much as uniqueness and liveliness.

Places to buy things

While large retail organisations with many branches have an overall cross-media policy for their image, local businesses can assert themselves through unique street signs.

Figure 7.7 'Old School Vernacular' shops (*Colchester Pet Stores, A One Shoe Repairs*, Colchester)

 - *Colchester Pet Stores* uses light green serif letters, almost contacting each other, out-lined in black: the header <COLCHESTER / PET STORES> is on two lines, filled out to the right by texts in small letters, detailing items for sale in italics, and phone number in sans serif. The shop front cascades with items for sale and their descriptions.
 - *A One Shoe Repairs* similarly has its name in word-initial caps and fills its windows with lists and photos of its services.

Colchester Pet Stores somehow looks more authentic than *A One Shoe Repairs*, per-haps because of the latter's modern sans serif letter style with tilted < **e** >, perhaps because truly 'traditional' shops would not put the word *traditional* on their signs.

Trinch and Snajdor (2017) christened the style of these two signs Old School Vernacular. In pre-gentrification neighbourhoods, shops enumerate the things they have for sale in as many words as they can fit into their shop fronts, as opposed to dis-creet gentrified signs with as few words as possible. Traditional small businesses express their personalities as wholes, not just through their fascias but through their lists and their goods spilling over onto the frontage zone outside.

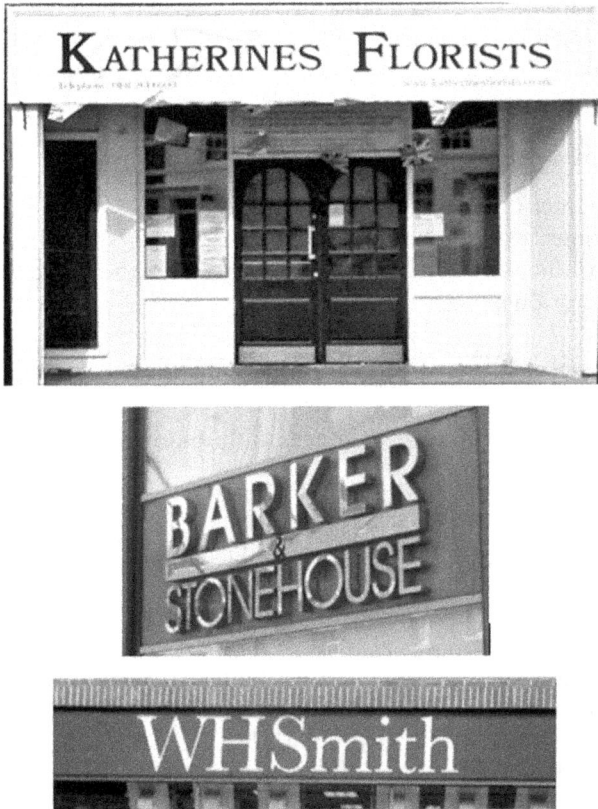

Figure 7.8 Shop signs (*WHSmith*, Colchester; *Katherines Florists, Barker & Stonehouse*, LPR)

The letters of *Katherines Florists* are from the Times New Roman family of type-faces (Figure 7.8). Hence they appear academic, direct and formal: floristry is a serious business concerned with weddings and funerals. The *WHSmith* cross-media sign, seen also in Figure 2.1, expresses its national brand through painted serif letters against a dramatic blue background, using lower case letters but no word spaces. The furniture shops owned by Barker & Stonehouse have main signs of large, sans serif, silver letters with a broad even stroke contrast, exploiting the ability of metal to act as a mirror.

These shop signs suggest the businesses are stable, informed and high on evaluation, with overtones of quality provided by the lettering and material. The signs are not so much directly selling things to the passer-by as stating their own solid virtues.

In England, Old School Vernacular signs like *Colchester Pet Stores* are traditional in a slightly quaint manner, although now rare. They suggest that the area has never abandoned its traditional community for the sake of gentrification.

The opposite to Old School Vernacular is gentrified signs that state a name without saying what can be bought there (Trinch & Snajdor, 2017), like *WHSmith*, sometimes through all lower case letters and a cryptic name like *next* (Figure 4.4). Minimalist discreet signs convey modernity and quality in *next* (Figure 4.4) and *artcafé* (Figure 4.9). Wit is not the prerogative of gentrified signs; fish and chip shops too have a tradition of punning names like *Ron's Plaice*, *Fryer Tucks* and *A Salt 'N' Battered* (Cook, 2004b).

Controlling Signs

As seen in Chapter 6, the variation in most controlling signs is limited by national and local regulations, extending down to the actual letter styles involved. A possible defence to some traffic violation charges is to argue that the signage was incorrect in some respect of location or size.

Warning signs

Presumably warning signs have to appear authoritative or threatening (Figure 7.9).

- *Wet Paint* is the universal warning sign, attesting here to the many writing scripts used by students at Newcastle University; it is crudely mounted underfoot on a step with tape and held down by bits of brick. The all-capital letters are printer produced, the English version in Arial Black. Other *Wet Paint* signs can be seen in Figures 4.1 and 3.10, all notable for their rough impact.
- *Pyrotechnic Detection Dogs* is also in Arial sans serif all-capitals. This variant on 'Beware of the dog' signs was on an empty building opposite the then central police station in Newcastle.
- *Danger of Death* is notable for its dramatic body icon with the text in sans serif all-capitals, on a yellow background.
- *Warning Troops* has sans serif all-capitals for the headings and cap-initial lower case for subheadings with some scary icons in yellow backgrounded black triangles.

Figure 7.9 Warning signs (*Warning Troops*, *Danger of Death*, Colchester; *Wet Paint*, *Pyrotechnic Detection Dogs*, Newcastle)

The preference for warning signs is for sans serif 'plain' letters, mostly centred, and for all-capitals, with few punctuation marks. They borrow conventions like the triangle from traffic signs and have adopted yellow as a warning colour for its high visibility. They are then 'potent doers'. Their temporary, 'amateurish' air and their icons add to their forcefulness, partly aimed at those who cannot read; other examples are *Watch yer heed!* (Figure 6.1), *Thieves will be prosecuted!* (Figure 6.4) and the parking signs in Figure 6.10.

Information Lists

As well as giving their names, business premises provide their visitors with details of their services in ancillary informing signs.

Figure 7.10 List-like information signs (*Opening times*, *Ice Creams*, LPR)

Figure 7.10 presents some ancillary signs with list-like structures.

– *Opening times* is a typical opening hours sign with a list of phrases separated by line-breaks, unpunctuated except for the from-to dash and numerical stops in <7.30am – 5.00pm> and with limited use of capitals for the start of phrases or lines <Closed> and days of the week. The header <**Opening times**> is signalled by greater point size and boldness.
– *Ice Creams* is a typical hand-drawn menu list in multi-coloured chalks on a half-cleaned blackboard in all-capitals. The word *sarnie* for *sandwich* is first attested in the *Dialect Dictionary* (Partridge, 1961), although it now seems in colloquial use across the country.

In addition, *Pillar box* (Figure 1.4) shows the standard arrangement on the Royal Mail pillar box: sans serif letters in left-centred lines with the collection times emphasised in bold.

The differences of information lists from other street signs are the left-aligned, line-by-line layout, the use of headers, and punctuation by line-breaks, commas, colour, etc. These signs are notable for their use of colour, whether the bright brown background of *Opening times* or the multicoloured chalks of *Ice Creams*; the presentation of straight information in tabular form is aided by use of colour, as seen in Excel. Their materials, chalk and paper, also suggest their temporariness: 'do not expect this information to be true next week'. They are indexed to the moment rather than signs for perpetuity.

Commemorating Signs

Figure 7.11 Commemorative signs (*David Frew Pain*, Blakeney (edited for contrast); *A Fallen Soldier*, Colchester; *Lying-in Hospital*, Newcastle)

The commemorating signs in Figure 7.11 have different types of owner:

- *David Frew Pain*: a memorial bench plaque, usually subscribed by friends and family, a small metal plaque with engraved serif capital letters;
- *A Fallen Soldier*: a small ceramic plaque sponsored by North Primary School in Colchester, with raised serif capital letters and a red poppy;
- *Lying-in Hospital*: an official 'blue plaque' commemorating the original use of the building, now owned by the BBC, in raised white serif letters, the header in all-capitals, the sub-header in sentence-initial lower case without punctuation.

Other commemorating signs are seen in *Town Hall* (Figure 4.2), *Earl Grey Memorial* (Figure 4.2) and *Erected 1844* (Figure 4.1).

All of these commemorating signs are designed to be seen by passers-by on foot, with text centred within their plaques. They are three-dimensional signs made of metal or stone with raised or recessed letters, asserting their permanence. The letters are formal and biased towards capitals: potent, traditional, assertive, direct, in the terms of typographic evaluation.

Informal Signs

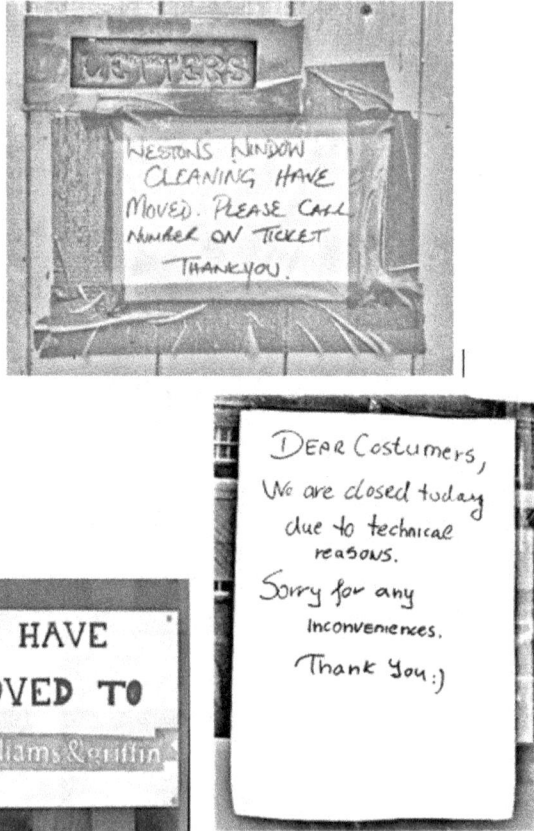

Figure 7.12 Informal shop notices (*Westons Window Cleaning*, Blakeney; *We have moved*, *Dear Costumers*, Colchester)

Figure 7.12 shows different styles of 'amateur' unique notices, hand-drawn with various kinds of pen or marker.

- *We have moved* has slab serif (square-ended) capitals with counters almost filled in, the first line left-aligned, the second centred, with a version of the Williams & Griffin logo below. It is bravely attempting to make an ordinary announcement more conspicuous; it is certainly more characterful.

- *Westons Window Cleaning* is done with a fibre tip, the combination of italic and non-italic capitals and small capitals making it lively, although not immediately legible, contrasting with the fat ornamental capitals on the metal letter box flap.
- *Dear Costumers* is a typical temporary closing notice in felt-tip in semi-joined-up handwriting, very legible, with sentence-initial capitals.

The connotations of these informal notices are personal and individual but the signs in themselves do not express particular identities. Except for *We have Moved*, the individuality of these signs appears accidental rather than intentional, with the writers doubtless concentrating on how to get their message across.

Novelty and Play in Signs

One of the strengths of street signs is their element of play. The conventions of print language are deliberately broken to create connotations of novelty, humour and inventiveness, contributing to strong individuality or indeed eccentricity.

Substituted letter forms

Figure 7.13 Alternatives to letters (*Have you read the signs?, Read¥ $tead¥ No%*, Colchester; *Chopstix*, Cambridge)

- *Have you read the signs?* exploits both the homophones *no* and *know* and the round red traffic sign to represent a capital < O >, using condensed Gill Sans capitals.
- *Chopstix* is a further example of the alternative letter forms discussed in Chapter 2, where icons of appropriately shaped objects substitute for letters, here chopsticks for <cks> in a noodle bar, embedded in faux Oriental lettering. Figure 2.26 includes a tick for < V > and a cut-throat razor for < C >; other examples are given in Cook (2004b).

— *Read¥ $tead¥ No%* advertises a bureau de change, substituting currency symbols for letters < €/E ¥/Y $/S >, only the < % > having its usual meaning.

The street user has to invest effort in interpreting the street sign, gaining a mild cognitive reward for puzzle solving, and an appreciation of the wit of the owners of the sign, thus making the sign more memorable.

Novel spellings

Many street signs contain unintentional spelling mistakes, such as *costumers* for *customers* in Figure 7.12 and <Guienea Fowl> in *Fresh Pheasants* (Figure 4.14), whether typos or errors; a sample can be found in Cook (2004b). Novel spellings, however, deliberately use non-standard spelling, mostly overriding the 'orthographic regularities' of English described in Chapter 2 by having sound-letter correspondences that are inappropriate for a particular position in the word.

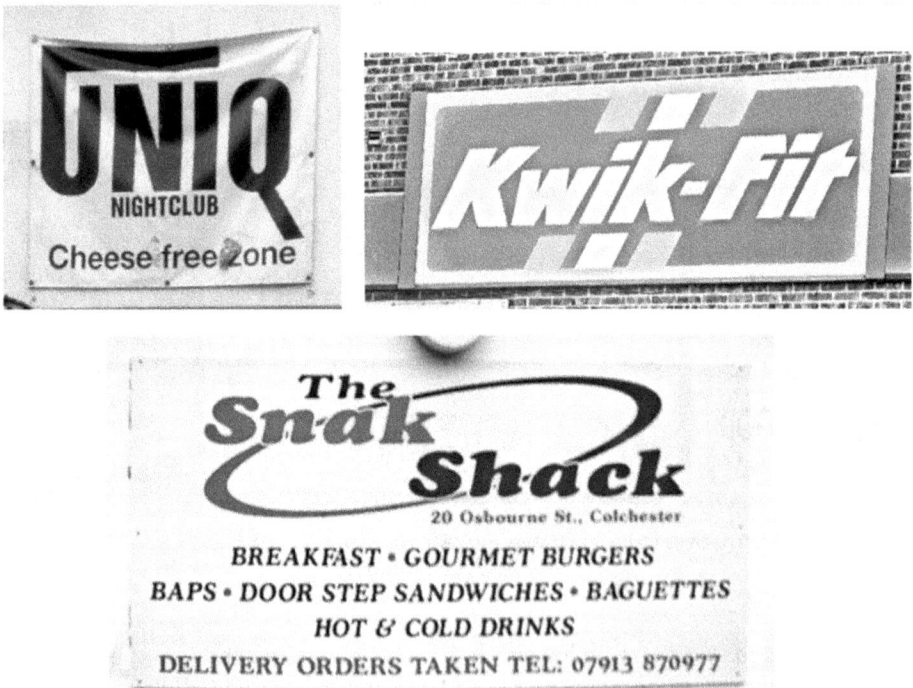

Figure 7.14 Novel spellings (*Uniq*, Newcastle; *Kwik-Fit*, *Snak Shack*, Colchester)

The signs in Figure 7.14 exploit correspondences that appear novel in writing but in fact correspond to standard spoken forms once orthographic regularities are set aside.

– *Kwik-Fit* uses < kw > for < qu > and final < k > rather than < ck > with italic letters. Colchester also has *Kwik Spar* and *Kwick Dry* and children play a game called *Kwick Cricket*; Newcastle businesses include *Kwik Flow*, *Kwik Tan* and *Kwik Kutz*.
– *Uniq* truncates < que > to < q >, which is indeed a possible correspondence for /k/, but not in the final position in the word (apart from a few exceptions like *Iraq*). It uses heavy sans serif letters with an eccentric < u > and < q > in a cross-media logo.
– *Snak Shack* has final < k > rather than < ck >, in italic all-capitals apart from the name itself and the serif address.

The orthographic choice between < c > and < k > for /k/ depends on the following vowel, *call* versus *kill*, and that between < k > and < ck > on initial versus final position, *kit* versus *tick*. The deliberate substitution of < k > for < c > was described by Louise Pound in the 1920s, although *Ku Klux Klan* shows that it existed as early as the 1860s.

All in all, there is no mistaking the kall of 'k' over our kountry, our kurious kontemporary kraving for it, and its konspicuous use in the klever koinages of kommerce. (Pound, 1926)

The read-aloud program in Microsoft Word in fact has no problem with this paragraph. The tradition lives on in the *Kwik-e-mart* and *Krusty the Clown* on *The Simpsons*. Apparently as a spin-off from *Ku Klux Klan*, the substitution of < k > for < c / q > became a political statement in Spain in the 2010s (Screti, 2015). So the novel spellings of street signs are not random deviations but exploit traditional loopholes in the English letter/sound correspondence system to create identities for businesses. Indeed such names are a matter of course in genres where a unique identity has to be created for copyright or patent purposes, like drugs such as *Vioxx*, pop groups *The Beatles* or racehorses *Cute Cait*. Hence this naming practice is not so much street language as a general resource of the English spelling system, there to be exploited when needed.

Novel non-standard forms from texting, etc.

The connotations of street signs also draw on other spellings that exist around the fringes of the standard print system, some in specific genres, some showing particular features of people's speech, etc.

Figure 7.15 Other novelties (*Wotz on*, Colchester; *Mark lvz Liz*, South Shields; *Salt 'n' Pepper*, *Ironed-4-U*, Newcastle)

The street signs in Figure 7.15 represent different styles of novel spelling.

- *Wotz on* is a colourful pub blackboard. <WOTZ> is a conventional version of <what's>, on the lines of <woz> for <was>, perfectly acceptable when read aloud; < o > is indeed a normal letter/sound correspondence for /ɒ/, but not in a group of words following /w/, *what*, *swan*, *watch*, *was*, etc. These are based on the 'eye-dialect' literary tradition in which alternative spellings correspond more closely to how words are pronounced than the standard spelling (Cook, 2004b). Eye-dialect is used in novels to suggest that a character speaks a dialect without actually representing any deviation from standard speech, common since at least Charles Dickens.
- *Mark lvz Liz 4EVA* is typical of traditional graffiti on walls, as discussed in Chapter 3. As well as < 4 > for <for> and < z > for < s >, it has the round cursive < ∈ > and < a > for <er> in <eva>, common in text messaging and vaguely suggesting rap music; it is in all-capitals.
- *Salt 'n' Pepper.* This striking sign has letters in gold capitals with the apostrophes being salt and pepper cellars, and italic sans serif all-capitals. Its art nouveau

typeface is Arnold Bolkin, a favourite of kebab shops for its exotic appearance. < 'n' > corresponds to the usual reduced syllabic /n/ pronunciation of *and* in speech, familiar from *Rock 'n' Roll* or, as some Chinese restaurants have it, *Wok 'n Roll*. Two apostrophes of omission < 'n' > are perhaps more accurate than one < 'n >.

− *Ironed-4-U* uses novel spellings associated with text messaging and social media, in which numbers and letter names are correspondences rather than letters, <4 U> for *for you* /fə: ju:/ etc. More examples can be found in Cook (2004b). In a sense, the English writing system harbours an embryonic syllabic writing system like Japanese katakana, limited to 10 digits and 26 letter names.

Novel punctuation

Punctuation marks may also create novel names for businesses, etc. as graphic symbols unrelated to their meaning-based uses.

Figure 7.16 Novel punctuation (all, Newcastle)

Pop group names like *Motörhead*, product names like *Yahoo!* and businesses like *Accenture* depend on unorthodox use of punctuation and diacritics. The fascia signs from Newcastle use a colon in three different ways: in <sk:n> as a substitute for the letter < i >, in <all:sports> as a word divider, and in <b:eats> as a kind of pun to show that both music and food are available. All are lower case sans serif to imply modernity.

Overall these novel spellings are cross-media choices for a business, although their appearance on a shop front doubtless forms one motive for inventing them. However, novelty is far from a sign of quality. Novel spellings can be witty and youth oriented but they may also seem slovenly: in other words these novelty signs exude cheapness and matiness rather than quality. You cannot imagine a Michelin-starred restaurant called *Kaff 4 U*.

Conclusion

This chapter combines insights from earlier chapters to show the additional connotative meanings of street signs. Unlike the anonymity and neutrality of books, street signs have attitude.

One purpose of street signs is to establish and reinforce the appropriate functional relationship between the owner and the target street user. Traffic signs speaking with the voice of authority, university buildings displaying education and culture, banks showing their lasting worth and the like need to seem respectable and firm in their forms and materials. Shops encouraging people to buy and pubs getting them to drink need to suggest the unique values of their wares with exciting letter shapes and particular appeals to subcultures. Amateur notices warning you of dangers, bargains and attractions need to convey urgency and temporariness through materials, colours and letter styles. In a sense, much of this may be accidental; obviously a temporary notice will be on a blackboard or a post-it, a permanent building name on stone. But much may be the result of the skill of writers in exploiting these features.

This chapter also stressed the need to move street signs research away from the subjective judgment of experts of one discipline or another to data-based research based on the signs themselves and their meaning for street sign users. We have mostly relied here on the characteristics of the street signs themselves and the intuitions of native speakers or experts. But other approaches could be more objective. The big data analysis of billions of words led to the availability of computer translation: similar work with millions of signs might yield useful results. Controlled experimentation using eye-tracking techniques (Cook *et al.*, in preparation), already extensively used by supermarkets and others for assessing the placement of products, etc., rather than academic research, looks promising.

The application of typographic research to street signs in the first part of the chapter after the fact yielded rather little, mostly because the letter styles of street signs are not necessarily best considered in terms of typographic typefaces. Although books like Dawson (2013) rely on typefaces for discussing street signs, the letters of many street signs are one-off creations or come from lettering traditions other than print. Print typefaces are most used for the cross-media signs designed for large businesses and for the unique 'amateur' street signs produced on desktop computers. But this does not mean that research techniques such as the semantic differential cannot be employed in the future to establish more firmly what people make of the connotations of street signs.

8   Street Signs in Other Languages

This chapter is concerned with street signs in England that use languages other than English. While cities such as Quebec have tight controls about the languages used in public display, in England there is no overt regulation of which language may be used in street signs. The only mention of English is with regard to the No Smoking signs decreed by the *Smoke-free (Premises and Enforcement) Regulations* (2006). The other three countries of the United Kingdom nevertheless have signs in their respective languages, ever a focus for political controversy and protest. Nothing better demonstrates the low status of the indigenous languages of the UK such as Welsh and Scottish Gaelic or of the widely spoken minority languages such as Urdu or Polish as their virtual absence from street signs in England apart from a few small areas.

Figure 8.1 Signs in languages or scripts other than English (*Entrance*/入口, SS; *Civic Centre, Ma Provence*, Newcastle)

The main reasons for multilingual signs on English streets include:

- the need for local people who speak other languages to communicate with each other, as in *Entrance*/入口;
- the need for local governments to provide access to their services for local residents in their own language, as in *Civic Centre*;
- the perception that a 'foreign' language is exotic and attractive, as in *Ma Provence*.

Important as the tourist industry is in England, few signs are addressed to tourists in their own languages.

The choice of when to use another language on a sign and which language to use depends on many factors and is usually in the hands of the owner rather than the licensor.

Figure 8.1 displays different sides of multilingualism in street signs. Gaiser and Matras (2016) counted 51 languages and 16 scripts on street signs in Manchester. Some have similar scripts to English apart from accents, like the French of *Ma Provence*. English speakers can attempt to read anything written in the roman alphabet using letter-to-sound correspondences, with greater or lesser success. Witness the confidence with which TV anchors pronounce the names of foreign politicians like *Mateusz Morawiecki* and places like *Guangzhou*, the ease with which Microsoft Word reads any text aloud or the pronounceable invented languages of Middle Earth in *The Lord of the Rings*.

The NCL corpus includes signs in the roman alphabet scripts used in Spanish, Italian and French. The Newcastle signs in the general corpus add Irish Gaelic and Polish signs. It becomes more problematic for the English speaking street user when the script involves multiple diacritics, like Polish < ń ł ą >, or has letter clusters that do not conform to English orthographic regularities, like *niedziele* (Sunday) in *Zapraszamy* (Figure 8.7).

Multilingual signs that English speakers cannot process through letter/sound correspondences are a different case, whether phonologically based like Arabic in *Civic Centre* or character based like Chinese in *Entrance*/入口. *Civic Centre* displays six non-roman scripts in use in Newcastle; the general corpus for Newcastle also includes Japanese, Thai, Persian and Korean. So far as the English speaking reader is concerned, these signs are unreadable and unpronounceable.

A further dimension to a writing system is direction, as outlined in Chapter 2; the Arabic text below the arrow in *Civic Centre*, for instance, is read from right-to-left rather than the English left-to-right. Texts with multiple directions like *Civic Centre* pose a particular problem in signs, here solved by left-aligning the texts regardless of writing system. Multilingual signs with different scripts have to ensure that the connotations of the letter styles are equivalent; Qiu *et al.* (2018) have proposed an elaborate methodology for matching them.

However, a Halal sign in Arabic (Figure 8.8) does not necessarily establish the first language of the street user, as the sign is read by many Muslims who are not Arabic speakers. Nor is a mother tongue the same as a nationality or an ethnic group. Speaking

French does not mean you are French; being Jewish does not mean that your first language is Hebrew.

Atmospheric Use of Other Languages

People choose other languages for street signs for their prestige and their exotic air, not because they are spoken locally – 'atmospheric' multilingualism (Cook, 2013a). The languages on signs evoke particular national stereotypes – the elegance of France, the engineering excellence of Germany or the exotic mystery of China. In other countries, it is often 'display' or 'vogue' English that creates this atmosphere, famously in the shops, T-shirts and advertisements of Japan.

Name signs in status foreign languages

The modern language with the most prestige in England is undoubtedly French. The 300-odd years during which French was the language of the occupying power have left their mark on English society. Until recently, French has been the most taught language in schools; laws and royal mottos still make use of Norman French; students with Norman-looking names are statistically more likely to be admitted to Oxford and Cambridge universities (Clark & Cummins, 2013); and English books tend not to translate French quotations as the reader is expected to understand them.

Figure 8.2 Shop and café signs in other languages (*JoJo Maman Bébé*, *Schuh*, Colchester; *Les Petits Choux*, LPR; *moda in pelle*, Newcastle)

Figure 8.2 presents some fascia board signs in languages other than English. These need to be large enough and simple enough to be read by pedestrians from the pavement and by drivers from passing cars.

JoJo Maman Bébé, translatable as French for 'Little rascal Mummy baby', is a general sign for a chain of mother and baby shops that started in London 'inspired by French nautical style', according to their website; the sign uses heavy sans serif letters, its modernity reinforced by the high x-height. The serif all-capitals and typographical ornaments of *Les Petits Choux*, meaning 'little darlings/cabbages/small pastry buns', suggest French elegance and style. *Ma Provence* (Figure 8.1) uses the Chancery style to similar effect. It is a good example of a business name that makes sufficient sense to the English speaker without translation while being readable and pronounceable.

Italian also has prestige value in England, as in *moda in pelle*, 'fashion in leather', a chain started in Leeds 'combining British sophistication with Italian quality', according to their website, projected through the lack of capitals and the tight spacing of the letters. German occurs in *Schuh* ('shoe'), a chain of shoe shops that started in Edinburgh; the sign is in a lower case, sans serif with a distinctive < s >.

The non-English names here are general signs used for multiple shops, with only *Les Petits Choux* being a local individual sign. The display of other languages on these signs is a cross-media choice made by a business, not one for the writer or author of the sign to decide. They believe that foreign names make their customers feel they are buying something special, a strategy called 'foreign branding' in marketing. For instance, when German customers were informed that the brands *Häagen-Dasz* and *Milford* were not Scandinavian and British but American and German respectively, they said they would not pay so much for them (Aichner *et al.*, 2017).

Foreign name signs rarely display an English translation, since this would undermine the sophistication they attribute to their potential customers. The short length of Leazes Park Road has restaurant names invoking Spanish *El CoTo* (Figure 8.4), Turkish *red mezze* (Figure 3.1), French *Les Petits Choux* (Figure 8.2) and Italian *Da Mimmo's* (Figure 7.6). The choice of language projects the identity of the business onto the street sign.

Figure 8.3 Other non-English signs (*fáiLte*, *Cellar d'Or*, *Coctelleria*, Newcastle)

Some shops and restaurants decorate their windows and walls with foreign texts that are clearly not aimed at native speakers (Figure 8.3). *Coctelleria pasticceria spremute* ('cocktails pastry juice', Italian) is a sign on a bar outside the Tyneside Cinema. *FáiLte* is the ubiquitous welcome sign for Irish pubs in England. Many shops and brands use tags of other languages, such as Japanese in the clothes shop Superdry, founded in Cheltenham. The gratuitous use of a prestige language in ancillary signs compliments street users on how cosmopolitan they are. An entertaining variant is the French code-switching in posters advertising Stella Artois, *C'est cidre, not cider,* although it is actually brewed in Zonhoven, a Flemish speaking part of Belgium.

Some Montreal businesses 'wink' at their customers by wittily combining two languages to get round the bilingual language regulations. For instance, a shoe shop is named *Chouchou*, 'sweetie-pie' in French (Lamarre, 2014) – a cross-linguistic pun. Bilingual winking in England is more of a sales ploy. *The Cellar d'Or* combines English *cellar* (*cellier* in French is typically a pantry and *cave* is the usual translation of 'cellar') with French *d'or* ('golden'), alias *door*, in cursive imitation handwriting. Such signs assume their potential customers appreciate the wit in punning across languages. In Quebec, this subverts the highly regulated bilingual situation (Lamarre, 2014). The other punning language in England is usually French, which has few actual speakers but is familiar to most English people from school.

Typographical mimicry

The term *writing system mimicry* is defined as:

The mapping of (real or imagined) design features and/or graphemes of a mimicked writing system onto a base writing system, so that the base writing system somewhat resembles the mimicked writing system while retaining legibility. (Sutherland, 2015: 150)

This adds another dimension to the connotations of letter forms discussed in Chapter 7, in some ways the equivalent to a foreign accent in the spoken language (Seargeant, 2012).

The signs for restaurants and shops in Figure 8.4 are large enough to be seen from a distance, whether on fascia boards or glass windows or hanging in the high zone.

(1) Actual mimicry of script

Typographical mimicry involves imitating the script used in another language, say by hanging the word *Bollywood* from the line as in Devanagari script (Sutherland, 2015). Some characteristics of *Albatta* make it look like an Arabic letter, including the thickness of the vertical strokes, a < b > that resembles the Arabic letter *ta* < ط >, and the drops of coffee that resemble Arabic dots. Sutherland (2015) describes several London signs mimicking Arabic by trying to make Roman letters look exotic in this way. The *Tyneside Irish Centre* uses distinctive letter forms such as < τ > and < ᵭ > from the early Irish script familiar from the *Book of Kells*, in a sense closer to the real thing than mimicry.

Figure 8.4 Typographical mimicry in restaurant and shop signs (*El Coto*, LPR; *Albatta* (edited for visibility), *Faveloso*, Colchester; *Wing Hong Chinese Supermarket*, SS; *Tyneside Irish Centre*, Newcastle)

(2) Stylised 'orientalism'

Wing Hong is typical of impressionistic faux Chinese lettering, alias 'chop suey' lettering (Sutherland, 2015). The main resemblance to Chinese characters is the imitation brush strokes, seen also in *Choi Lee Fut* (Figure 8.9). Here and in *Hot Pot House* (Figure 8.10) the < O > appears to be written with a clockwise Chinese ductus ('flow of writing') rather than in a counter-clockwise English fashion. This generic 'oriental' writing signifies Chinese to non-Chinese audiences.

(3) Letter styles

Certain letter styles in restaurant signs go with particular identities in a fairly arbitrary way, more a matter of association with the other culture than of mimicry. *El CoTo* has elegant roman capital letters, with ornamental capitals < R > and < A >, and a dot inside the counter of the < ⊙ >, also found in *moda in pelle* (Figure 8.2), suggesting traditional elegance. Italian restaurants often use cursive italic scripts, like *faveloso*. Some restaurant signs have single non-initial capital letters, as in <EL coTo> (Figure 8.4) and <fáiLte> (Figure 8.3), and use the word for *restaurant* in the appropriate language, *ristorante* (*faveloso*) or *restaurante* (*El Coto*), close enough to English not to need translation.

These names and letter styles are chosen to attract custom by appearing foreign and authentic. But this may be misguided. Research in the United States into the effects of signs in other languages on the perception of a restaurant's personality and the authenticity of its food showed that Mexican and Korean signs did not have the desired effect (Magnini *et al.*, 2011): while English speakers indeed found English signs more down-to-earth and contemporary than bilingual ones, Korean speakers saw Korean script signs as less family oriented, honest, up-to-date, secure, successful and good looking. Neither group felt that the non-English signs vouched for the authenticity of the food.

Latin on the street

Latin continues to have considerable standing in England as the historic language of education and religion and as the model on which traditional grammar teaching was based. It was still, for example, a university entrance requirement for arts degrees when I was an undergraduate. Latin quotations crop up in the speeches of Etonian politicians; Boris Johnson indeed claims that it should be taught in school.

Figure 8.5 Signs in Latin (*Platform 1*, Newcastle)

Platform 1 is not strictly a street sign but a station sign from Wallsend – the eastern end of the 2nd century Hadrian's Wall in Newcastle. An art project by Michael Pinsky in 2003 translated the station signs and advertisements into Latin, even *No Smoking/ Noli fumare*. These signs commemorate the Roman connection and occupation while implicitly advertising the local Roman museums and remains. *Platform 1* uses a version of the geometric sans serif Futura rather than classic roman capitals. A more straight-forward use of Latin in serif all-capitals is found in the modern street name sign *Via Romana Urbis* (Figure 5.3). Latin has then a marginal use in street signs for asserting and advertising the history of an area.

War memorials and Latin

The most visible use of Latin in the street is in the war memorials found in almost every town and village of England, typically erected after World War I with funds from local subscription rather than local or national government. They now form a focal point for ceremonies of remembrance.

Figure 8.6 War Memorials: *Dulce et decorum* (The Winged Victory, Boer War Memorial, 1908, Thomas Macklin), *Non sibi sed* (The Response, WWI Memorial, 1923, William Goscombe John), Newcastle

— *Dulce et decorum est pro patria mori* ('It is sweet and proper to die for one's coun-try', Horace) is a 1908 memorial commemorating the Boer War (1899–1902), in tall sans serif recessed letters cast in bronze, now barely legible. It is unusual in that it names only one soldier (War Memorials Register, 2020) and predates the two World Wars that most memorials commemorate.
— *Non sibi sed patriae* ('Not for oneself but for one's country', Cicero, shortened) is on a nearby World War I (1914–1918) memorial to the Northumberland Fusiliers called *The Response*. It has fat raised letters in granite with rounded serifs and raised dots as word separators, like some Roman inscriptions.

Perhaps no language other than Latin or English would be deemed suitable for a war memorial. Mottos of schools, universities, football clubs and so on similarly use Latin, although the Royal Family's tend to be in French like *Dieu et mon droit*, the other status language through conquest. The choice of Latin for these signs was a matter for their owners, usually committees of local dignitaries and politicians. Most war memorials draw on classical themes, such as the statue of Victory looming above *Dulce et Decorum*, as much as on Christian symbols and crosses (Figure 1.5). Latin was also used alongside English in overseas war memorials to British WWI soldiers in Belgium to avoid deciding between the two local languages (Quinlan, 2005: 111).

The texts of war memorials often consist of lists of the dead on one side, most famously the 58,320 names on the US Vietnam Veterans Memorial in Washington, DC. In England, inscriptions usually consist of snippets from Latin sources, as in Figure 8.6, or from English poems, such as *Lest we forget* (Kipling), *We will remember them* (Binyon) and *Here was a royal fellowship of death* (Shakespeare), or the single word *Remember* (Figure 1.5).

As the inscriptions are usually at low-level or eye-level and are aimed at pedestrians, the letters are medium size. All-capitals dominate war memorials, like the sans serifs of *Dulce et decorum* and the serifs of the *Welcome* plaque on the pavement of Eldon Square (Figure 3.9). Only two of the hundreds of memorial inscriptions in the comprehensive catalogue *British War Memorials* (Quinlan, 2005) and only one in Abousnnouga and Machin (2013) are in lower case, apart from quotations. Letter styles on war memorials are highly conservative (Gurrey, 2009), cutting them off from 20th century typography, or even the Headstone Standard Alphabet specifically designed for war cemeteries (Turner, 2015). Indeed the style of their statues of soldiers and classical feminine symbols has more in common with the Pre-Raphaelite art of the 19th century than with their contemporary British sculptors such as Henry Moore, Barbara Hepworth or Jacob Epstein.

The impression of permanence and traditional respectability that war memorials project is built out of the use of Latin, the formal lettering, the quality of materials such as stone or cast metal and the skilled execution by specialised craftsmen such as stonemasons. The choice of material sometimes militates against their legibility, as in the black raised letters of *War Memorial* (Figure 1.11); like other commemorative signs, it is their existence in a prominent location in the street space that is important, not their legibility. The verbal text is, however, a small part of their complex constructions and symbolism, described in detail in Abousnnouga and Machin (2013). Indeed this is perhaps the only type of sign where the typical street user does not need to understand the text, only to respect it.

Community Bilingualism

This chapter can only deal with some aspects of community bilingualism; others are covered in great detail in recent books such as Pütz and Mundt (2019) and Lou (2016). The closest to the current analysis is the scheme in Amos (2016), which uses categories such as materiality, locus and context frame similar to those here. This book does not cover the geolocation of bilingual street signs used in much linguistics landscape research, say Soukup (2020), only the sign-relevant geometry of street space. To reiterate Chapter 1, it is not intended as a direct contribution to linguistic landscapes research or the other disciplines it draws on such as typography so much as an interdisciplinary field of street sign research.

In England, traffic signs for drivers and pedestrians are in English, with the exception of multilingual 'Drive on the left' signs in German and French near ferry ports. Such multilingual traffic signs are inherently dangerous as drivers slow down while reading them and so cause pile-ups with the vehicles behind (Jamson *et al.*, 2005).

Building names, street names and service signs are also in English, with rare exceptions. Commemorative signs, clocks, etc. are in English or Latin. The *Civic Centre* sign (Figure 8.1) shows the city council dealing with the multilingualism of its residents, although such signs are still comparatively rare; Newcastle University similarly uses some of its students' languages in *Wet Paint* (Figure 7.9). But the domain of bilingual signs is primarily shops and restaurants.

Signs in one locally spoken language

Monolingual signs in other languages are primarily for street users who speak a language that is used locally, in effect excluding speakers of other languages.

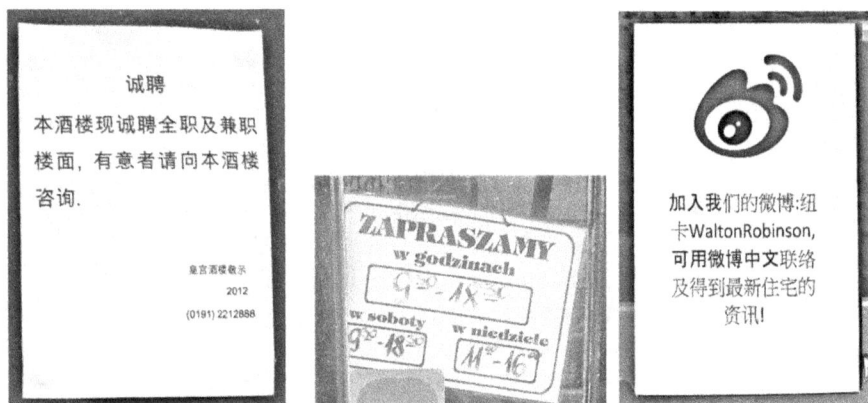

Figure 8.7 Monolingual signs in other languages (*Job ad* (Chinese), SS; *Zapraszamy* (Polish 'Opening hours'), Newcastle; *Walton Robinson*, LPZ)

These monolingual signs are computer-printed sheets to be read by pedestrians at eye-level at a close distance; hence they use simple layout, a single letter style and small letters. The *Job ad* sign from Chinatown is a minimal paper notice aimed at Chinese speaking workers. In effect, a job sign in Chinese tactfully prevents non-Chinese speakers from applying. One club on Stowell Street tells members to ring the bell to enter after 1am – only in Chinese. *Zapraszamy* gives the opening hours of a Polish shop, on a hanging reversible card in a letter style with notably varying stroke contrast, filled in with handwritten letters and a distinctive < 1 >. Both are informal functional notices, authored and written by speakers of Chinese and Polish for their peers. Monolingual informal signs in other languages are sparse in England, except in Chinatowns.

The flat-letting agency sign *Walton Robinson* is a functional computer-printed notice aimed at Chinese students. However, it is written by outsiders for people inside the community, not so much for the local long-term Chinese residents as for the ever-shifting student population of Newcastle and Northumbria universities; the sign is located effectively on the border between their two campuses in Percy Street. This use of street signs to attract people in their own language by English speaking businesses is surprisingly rare.

Signs in two languages

Notices in parallel languages

Figure 8.8 Notices in two languages (*Air-conditioned* (simplified Chinese characters), *No Smoking* (traditional Chinese characters), SS; *Halal*, LPZ; *Wędliny*, Newcastle)

The pedestrian-oriented eye-level signs in Figure 8.8 differ in how the two texts relate to each other.

– *Air-conditioned* is a parallel sign for both Chinese and English speaking users, an informal computer-printed sheet in unobtrusive sans serif.

- *Wędliny* lists the Polish food available in the shop, in large white-outlined, red, sans serif capitals; English speakers are given a translation in smaller black capitals.
- *No Smoking* presents the compulsory controlling sign in two languages with the Chinese text on top.
- *Halal* is a familiar restaurant notice with Arabic above English, addressed to Muslim readers, in Newcastle not necessarily native speakers of Arabic.

English is the less prominent language in all these signs.

Signs of organisations

Figure 8.9 Chinese organisation signs (*Chinese Methodist Church* (truncated), Newcastle; *Cheung & Co*, *Choi Lee Fut*, SS)

Chinese is used for many of the name signs for Chinese organisations in Newcastle Chinatown, mostly accompanied by an English version.

- *Cheung & Co* is the standard brass plate for a registered business address, with information duplicated in English and Chinese, engraved on metal and filled in with black.

- *The Chinese Methodist Church* sign conveys the church name and times of services in alternating lines of English and Chinese in blue, red or black sans serif letters.
- *Choi Lee Fut* is dramatically gold on black, the English text being italic all-capitals in brush lettering.

These name signs seem sober, plain and straightforward, conveying respectability and dignity in their letters and their solid materials. They are displayed in the eye-level or high-level zones associated with building or business names, as opposed to the fascia-level of restaurant signs.

Restaurant signs

Restaurant signs with texts in English and another language are sometimes translations of each other, sometimes less straightforward.

Figure 8.10 Bilingual restaurant signs in two languages (*Palace Garden, Hot Pot House,* SS; *Heihei, Al Basha, Authentic Thai,* Newcastle)

At the core of Chinatown, Stowell Street abounds in bilingual English/Chinese name signs, amounting to 64% of the SS corpus, higher than the 52% recorded in the densest streets in Liverpool (Amos, 2016). *Palace Garden* has vertical columns of

English and Chinese, the English version being in all-capitals as lower case letters do not work in columns (see Chapter 2). *Al Basha* has Arabic script below the English version. Since these are both illuminated signs, they are difficult to read in daylight. The restaurant sign *Heihei* in vertical Chinese columns and horizontal English lower case has two Chinese columns that are vertical mirror images of each other, a witty touch for the Chinese reader.

Hot Pot House has a header in all-capitals in a brush letter style, a sub-header in sans serif <Authentic Chinese Cuisine>, phrases of English in a fat cursive italic script <Value for Money> and names of dishes in Chinese characters, against a dramatic red background shading to yellow. While it is undeniably attention catching, the overall effect of multiple letter styles and lurid colouring may be over the top for English readers, particularly when the dishes are only listed in Chinese. The side-by-side bilingual messages of *Authentic Thai* are written in a script typeface called Rage Italic on a frosted glass background, a pillar making the English version less legible. These signs are intended for speakers of both languages, as well as adding atmosphere to the premises and the neighbourhood. Most are in semi-permanent painted materials and have a lively feel for colour.

Much research has taken the text of the dominant language to be bigger, above the other text, and on the left. Thus *Air-conditioned* (Figure 8.8) and *Entrance* (Figure 8.1) are Chinese dominant in that the Chinese text is above the English one, whereas *No Smoking* (Figure 8.8) and *Al Basha* (Figure 8.10) are English dominant because English is on top. In the SS sample of Chinese/English bilingual signs, 55% have Chinese on top, 45% English; in other words, Chinatown signs are not dominated by one language, even simple controlling signs like Chinese-on-top *Entrance*/入口 (Figure 8.1) versus English-on-top *Push*/推 (Figure 2.24).

Side-by-side bilingual texts are also common. *Authentic Thai* (Figure 8.10) has Thai script on the left, English on the right; *Palace Garden* (Figure 8.10) has vertical Chinese to the left of vertical English; in *Mangos* (Figure 4.9), the English name is flanked on both sides by the Chinese name. On many restaurant signs, the centre of the sign is important, say in *faveloso* (Figure 8.4) and *Mangos* (Figure 4.9).

To my eye, the top and left of signs are indeed more prominent, but this is probably because I learnt English as a first writing system with its left-to-right top-to-bottom directions. It would be dangerous to ascribe the same reaction to users of different writing systems without more objective support, say from eye-tracking data. Chinese and English speaking people, for example, remember logos differently; Cantonese speakers are governed by shape, English speakers by sound, reflecting the biases in their respective writing systems (Tavassoli & Han, 2002). In particular, salience takes different forms in Japanese, English and Chinese writing systems (Backhaus, 2007: 103). As seen in Chapter 3, the layout of commercial signs by designers is influenced by other factors, such as the Ogilvy Formula and the Visual Hierarchy.

The issue is complicated by typographic mimicry. In *Al Basha*, for example, the text in Arabic script comes below the large version in English script, hence it should appear less prominent. But the English name is written in faux Arabic script, so that

Arabic culture dominates the whole sign. Establishing dominance from position has to be modulated by other factors in the sign, particularly the connotations of the letter style.

Translation equivalences

When there are texts in two or more languages on a sign, they do not necessarily have the same meaning. Backhaus (2007: 90–101) distinguishes between homophonic texts, mixed texts and polyphonic texts.

– *Homophonic texts* are 'complete translations or transliterations of each other' (Backhaus, 2007: 91). The texts in the control sign *Entrance*/入口 (Figure 8.1), for example, mean the same in both languages. Homophonic bilingual signs are often informal eye-level control signs for pedestrians, like *Entrance*/入口 (Figure 8.1), *Push*/推 (Figure 2.24) or the multilingual *Wet Paint* (Figure 7.9), rather than official direction signs or traffic signs. Some council-owned signs such as *Civic Centre* (Figure 8.1) also duplicate information in different languages.

   Yet the *Planning Notice* (Figure 3.1) displayed by the city council in Stowell Street has no Chinese text, nor do the collection times on the *Pillar box* (Figure 1.4).
– *Mixed texts* in which there are interpolated elements of the other language. For instance, *Walton Robinson* (Figure 8.7) was called monolingual above but the name of the letting agency is actually in English and needs no translation.
– *Polyphonic texts* that differ in the two languages. *Hot Pot House* (Figure 8.10) uses English only for the name and the prices, with names of dishes given in Chinese; it thus gives more information in one language than the other, called by Reh (2004) 'fragmentary multilingualism'.

Many restaurants in Chinatown take this to an extreme by supplying alternative rather than complementary names. The *Palace Garden* (Figure 8.10) is called 'Palace Big Restaurant' in Chinese, while *The Mandarin* (Figure 2.4) translates as 'Han Palace'. Malinowski *et al.* (2013) describe a business called *King Tsin*/厚德福 in Berkeley where the name effectively covers two separate businesses. Even the bilingual street name sign *Stowell Street* (Figure 5.3) is deceptive in that the Chinese text simply means 'Chinatown'. The texts are not so much complementary as contradictory; different names are supplied in the two languages.

Neighbourhood identity and Chinatown

To some extent, neighbourhoods deliberately project distinct identities through their street signs. At one level, this is the regulation of street signs by the local authority and the requirements for local conservation areas like Leazes Park Road (LPZ) (Newcastle City Council, 2000). At another level, some neighbourhoods and estates have local policies on street name signs and the like, say the tight control in estates like Hampstead Garden Suburb in London.

The five Chinatowns in England promote an ethnic neighbourhood identity. They are the chief areas with bilingual street name signs in England, apart from the Bengali/English street signs around Bethnal Green in London (Sutherland, 2015). The Chinese language has a particular status within Newcastle; while Urdu speakers outnumber Chinese speakers ten to one in the city, there is no equivalent area to Chinatown with such a concentration of Urdu signs.

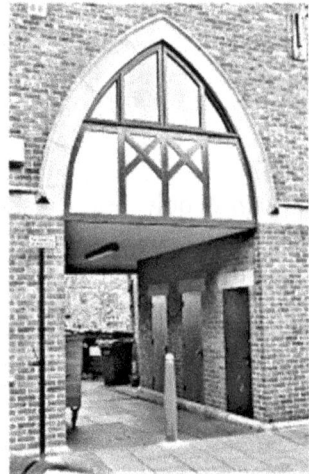

Figure 8.11 Signs for neighbourhood identity in Chinatown (*Litter bin, Lantern, Mandarin roof, Pillar box, Bollard*, SS; *Stone lion, Archway inscription*, Newcastle)

The objects in Figure 8.11 go beyond the usual bounds of street signs to create atmosphere. Stowell Street, for example, is pervaded by the 'lucky' Chinese colour red. So everyday street furniture is coloured in red and gold, such as the *Litter bin*, the *Lantern*, the *Bollard* and the timbered arch above it. Red characters, letters and backgrounds are used in restaurant signs like *Palace Garden* (Figure 8.10) and *Mangos* (Figure 4.9). Lou (2016: 47) also remarks on the traditional use of symmetry in Chinese fascia signs, for example the repetition of the same texts in English and Chinese to the left and right of the main name in *Mangos* (Figure 4.9). These features alone make Chinatown stand out from the relative drabness of English streets like Leazes Park Road. Even the *Pillar box* has been chosen for its exotic qualities, sometimes taken to be Chinese but in fact a replica of the historic 1866 Penfold design.

The *Mandarin* entrance shows an ornamental porch roof in green Chinese roof tiles. The buildings in Newcastle Chinatown are conversions rather than specially built, unlike those in Washington, DC, and so such Chinese architectural features are additions. The *Stone Lion* ('Shíshī') and the *Archway inscription* are part of the traditional Chinese arch ('paifang'). Ceremonial archways form entrances to many Chinatowns, often the joint responsibility of the local Chinese association and the local council, and part-funded by organisations or twin cities in China. In Newcastle, the archway serves as a focus for the celebration of the Chinese Spring Festival. Stowell Street thus looks Chinese to the non-Chinese street user, even though it bears little resemblance to modern Chinese cities apart from the script.

Chinatowns in England mostly coalesced about 50 years ago within a rundown area, rather than developing out of earlier Chinese enclaves, say the early Chinese community in Limehouse in London, the scene of many early 20th century English detective stories, versus its modern home in Soho. The first Chinese restaurants in Newcastle crystallised around the Wing Hong supermarket (Figure 8.4) when it moved to Stowell Street in 1978.

The chief indications of the Chinese community in Newcastle Chinatown are the monolingual Chinese notices (Figure 8.7) and the informal bilingual controlling signs (Figure 8.8). Its presence is also signalled by the signs for Chinese-related organisations seen in Figure 8.9, such as the North East Chinese Association, accountants like Cheung & Co and the Kung Fu club Choi Lee Fut. Other similar organisations are located within a mile or so of Chinatown proper, such as the Chinese Methodist Church (Figure 8.9) and Mascot House sheltered Chinese accommodation. Chinese organisations and signs are not therefore confined to Chinatown proper.

Few of the Chinese community live in the handful of streets that make up Chinatown. Rather, it acts as a centre to go to for social and business activities. As in Manchester (Barabantseva, 2016), Chinatown restaurants are frequented by Chinese workers from take-aways outside the city centre on days when they are closed and by young Chinese students on pre-university and degree courses. Nor is the area exclusively Chinese: the Tyneside Irish Centre (Figure 8.4) is beside the Chinese arch; Rosie's, the football pub (Figure 7.5), is on the opposite street corner. Non-Chinese enterprises rarely display names or informing signs in Chinese, perhaps because chain stores and restaurants are not present in this area. Newcastle Chinatown uses Chinese to promote local Chinese businesses, unlike the Chinatown in Washington, DC, where non-Chinese businesses promote themselves through Chinese (Lou, 2016). Newcastle has not reached the point where the Chinese language has become 'a floating signifier that can be used to signify, or to sell not just things Chinese but anything at all' (Leeman & Modan, 2009: 353–354), although Manchester already has betting shops with Chinese signs (Gaiser & Matras, 2016).

Chinatowns partly function as theme parks to attract non-Chinese visitors; people come there to be intrigued by the differences – the selling power of atmosphere – similar to Carnaby Street or Soho in London or, indeed, Welsh tearooms in Patagonia (Coupland & Garrett, 2010).

> 'culture' itself is part and parcel of the new symbolic economy that produces 'abstract' goods – in this case ethnic food or the ethnic district itself as a branded ethnic space. (Hatziprokopiou & Montagna, 2012: 722)

The Chinese atmosphere created in Chinatown is a conservative, studied form of Chinese culture, often at odds with China today. It is traditional China projected to a Western audience. Starbucks in Hangzhou, for example, displays its name in the roman alphabet, Starbucks in Washington, DC in Chinese characters (Leeman & Modan, 2009). In particular, this masks the heterogeneity of the Chinese speaking community (Hatziprokopiou & Montagna, 2012); one label fits all, as in the very concept of Chinese food itself rather than Cantonese food, Shanghainese food, Sichuan food, etc. The Chinatown enclave reinforces the conservative image of a stereotype long past in the home country (Barabantseva, 2016). This may be changing, however: Manchester Chinatown Action Group, for instance, have aimed to transform the area:

> ... from stereotypical Chinatown to a multinational, cultural, business and residential area embracing the Far East, Southeast Asian and mainstream communities. (*Manchester Chinatown Partnership Charter*, cited in Barabantseva, 2016: 99)

From the evidence of street signs, English Chinatowns are not dominated by the processes of immigration and gentrification that drive other multilingual areas, to be discussed in Chapter 9. The 20 nationalities living or working in Rye Lane in South London, for instance, do not include Chinese or Japanese (Hall, 2015). The multilingual signs in Newcastle Chinatown suggest a hub of cultural centres and workplaces for diverse Chinese speakers living in a wide catchment area, combined with the commercial branding of an area for potential customers, rather than an immigrant enclave. To cite a parallel case in the Netherlands:

> Chinatown in Amsterdam today is *not* a migration hub, *not* an area where a large proportion of the Chinese community resides, *not* a space of marginalisation and certainly *not* a space where Chineseness is self-evident. (Rath *et al.*, 2018: 83)

Language and Community

The dilemma in defining a speech community is whether you specify a community in geographical terms and then look at the languages they use, or you specify a particular language and look for where its speakers live. Is the geographical neighbourhood of Chinatown the starting point or the Chinese speakers of Newcastle? Or are language communities not organised around where people live or work but virtual?

Multiple language communities

It might be that each language has a community of speakers without there being any all-inclusive community to which speakers of both languages belong.

> An individual's use of two languages supposes the existence of two different language communities; it does not suppose the existence of a bilingual community. (Mackey, 1972: 554)

The two languages are parallel lines that never meet, as separate as the fictional communities in *The City & the City* (Mieville, 2009). So signs like *Entrance*/入口 (Figure 8.1) serve the English speaking and Chinese speaking people that share the same doorway without doing more than literally brush shoulders. *Civic Centre* (Figure 8.1) is addressed separately to the multiple language communities of Newcastle. In much research, the languages in a sense are seen as competing for the signs in terms of prominence and location rather than being partners. In this view, a bilingual sign is in effect the combination of two monolingual signs, addressing two communities, not one.

Tagging communities with language labels furthermore blurs the differences within each community in language and social terms. Many Francophones in Newcastle, for example, are from Africa rather than from France. The Chinese community is particularly complex. One often-made division is between the Chinese 'restaurant' community and the 'professional' community of lawyers, university academics, etc. In addition, Newcastle has many young Chinese speakers attending the two universities, drawn from both mainland China and Taiwan; Newcastle University alone had 1800 Chinese students in 2019. Although Chinese speakers more or less share the same overall writing system, they do not necessarily share a spoken language: many of the Chinese in England speak Cantonese rather than Mandarin through immigration from Hong Kong. Nor is the Chinese writing system uniform, since the script divides into traditional characters, for example in *No Smoking* (Figure 8.8), mainly associated with Taiwan, used by some of the university students, and simplified characters, for example *Air-conditioned* (Figure 8.8), from mainland China, and indeed some special characters for writing colloquial Cantonese. The Chinese signs of Newcastle are addressed to interrelating communities separated by work, class and profession, by variety of Chinese, by spoken and written varieties of Chinese, and by age.

The multi-competence of the community

An alternative is a single community that uses more than one language, switching between them when necessary. The multi-competence approach to second language acquisition asserts that 'multi-competence concerns the total system for all languages (L1, L2, LN) in a single mind or community and their inter-relationships' (Cook, 2016b: 3). It treats the diverse languages of the community as a coherent whole rather than separately.

The emerging superdiversity of the modern city is not characterised by linguistic ghettos where only one or two languages are present but by the complex language relationships across the whole city. The shopkeepers of Rye Lane in London each speak four languages (Hall, 2015). Multi-competence is a constantly shifting dynamic rather than a static relationship between two languages within a defined area.

So the question in a sense is whether bilingual signs are two signs or one. That is to say, are they presenting two messages in parallel to two separate groups or a single message for a complex multi-competent group who use both languages? As always, the answer varies along the multi-competence continuum from separation to integration. At the separation end come the single language signs in languages other than English, which are bilingual only if the majority language is taken as the norm. This category includes atmospheric signs and typographic mimicry, which are not so much about the languages or scripts they feature as about the associations they have for speakers of English. At the other integration end are signs where the two languages work together. In between are code-switching signs where English acts as a matrix language into which parallel messages in other languages are slotted, mostly informing signs or street name signs.

Conclusion

This chapter has shown that the reason for having another language than English for a sign is more than showing the existence, location and status of a non-English speaking community. The choice is made at several levels, whether by a business owner deciding a name for a restaurant, an author writing the contents of a poster, or a writer deciding to use scripts that suggest other languages. Although unconstrained by official regulations, single individuals are seldom able to choose which language to use.

A status language may be chosen that is not spoken at all locally, as in Latin commemorating signs aimed at the English speaking community. Other status languages may be chosen that are not spoken widely in the area, with the aim of selling products to any street user, through individual signs like signs in French, and through the cumulative atmosphere built up by the Chinese signs in Chinatown. Bilingual signs may also be aimed at the multi-competent community made up of speakers of diverse first languages, catering for their everyday social needs or responding to the communications of local government. Some may act as rallying points for the identity of a local language group, who may well not live in the area but see it as a hub for their activities. Rarely does the use of another language simply show who lives in an area or visits it.

9   The Nature of Street Signs

This book has presented an approach to street sign research based on samples of English street signs, showing how the signs and their meanings can be described. On the one hand, this provides an overview that can be exploited, revised or challenged. On the other, it yields a descriptive apparatus that related disciplines like psychology and linguistic landscapes research can use for their own ends. This chapter summarises some broader issues about streets and about street signs research arising from this approach.

The Functions of Street Signs

Let us first revisit the five functions for street signs outlined in Chapter 1 in the light of our discussion, namely, controlling, naming, informing and selling, servicing, and commemorating (Box 1.1).

As discussed in Chapter 5, naming signs are both name-creating – 'I name this building *Percy House*' – and location-indexing – '*This* building is *Percy House*'. Naming thus in a sense brings into existence the objects that feature on the physical and mental maps of the city. Displaying a business name on a brass plate near the door of a registered office, for example, confers a legal status on a building. The performative naming of street and building signs is virtually independent of the need for the sign to be read.

Naming signs also assert identity, whether the stolid national identity of government-controlled traffic signs, the distinctive cultural identity of Chinatown, the neighbourhood identity of linked street names, the individual identity of pubs or the corporate identity of banks. These identities are conveyed through the letter styles, the choice of linguistic forms and features such as centring. Multiple identities are often merged within a single sign, say for the local Irish historical football pub.

Controlling signs activate the individual's mental map as a living process of movement – 'How do I get from A to B?' – converting the physical map into rolling mental GPS displays. Signs that control forms of behaviour other than movement are rare apart from *No Smoking* signs, although occasional signs discourage stealing or provide health messages.

The naming and controlling functions of signs have emerged here as an interlocked cognitive and political systematisation of the physical and mental space in which we live. Together they control the space of the city. The location system created by naming permits taxation, enlistment, health treatment and other processes of access and control. It enables the ownership of property, ultimately through the Land Registry, hence its importance for the World Bank (Farvacque-Vitkovic *et al.*, 2005). Control is both an abstract concept indexed to the position of the individual or property in space and the everyday practical control of acceptable behaviours.

One domain for informing and selling signs is restaurants, flower shops and the like that need to draw in customers through their cross-media choice of name, display of menus, notices of sales, choice of language, and so on. These are the most obviously manipulative of signs in that they present an image calculated to gain customers, whether traditional Old School, modern minimalism, the Ogilvy Formula or whatever. Hence they are innovative, individual street signs, hoping to stand out through unusual letter styles, eccentric spellings, striking display, humour and the like. In reverse, informing signs are the grave instructions and pronouncements of authorities telling street users what to do, conveying authority through their solemn formality and uniformity of design. Informing signs then are at both poles of individuality and impersonality, asserting two opposing types of identity.

Servicing signs reveal the access to service conduits, etc., salient for service providers such as utilities but almost invisible to unaddressed sign users. These are parasitic on the street in the sense that they are intended for the city organisation, not the average street user, and use the addressing system for their own purposes. While important for their operators, the content is need to know.

Commemorating signs remind people of their official history, directly through the inscriptions, plaques and statues that instruct them on their heritage, mostly erected by public subscription of local citizens or national charities. The names of Earl Grey, Alderman Fenwick and John Dobson still walk the streets of Newcastle 200 years after their times. These signs reflect a top-down selective view of history, usually dating from the period immediately after the events or people they commemorate and hence out of touch with later interpretations. Such signs have always been controversial, even war memorials; few seem to have been erected in the past 20 years and indeed many have been removed. They suggest dignity and solemnity through their letter forms and enduring material.

The set of functions introduced in the first chapter is thus useful as a broad overview. Some functions of street signs such as naming turn out to be more complex than anticipated, in both production and reception. The 11 functions of Kinneir (1980) go further: regulation, celebration, individualisation, orientation, information, intercession, admonition, direction, commemoration, identification and mystification, although none of the signs in the NCL sample represents intercession or mystification, save perhaps graffiti. The original five-way divide does need amplifying and qualifying to represent the dynamic complexity of the street, particularly for naming and controlling.

Characteristics of Street Signs

Let us bring together some of the distinctive characteristics of street signs that have emerged in the course of this book.

- *Street signs are embedded in a physical location.* Individual signs are part of a material environment, locked into their physical location in the street space so that moving them destroys or alters their meaning. At one level, the organisation of cities and towns is defined through the naming of streets, like *Piccadilly*, and the numbering of buildings, like *10 Downing Street*. At another level, any point on the street reveals signs that apply solely to one location and to one orientation of the street user.
- *Street signs embody unique relationships between the producer of the sign and the street user.* Unlike speech or printed text, the producers of the street sign are invisible, anonymous, genderless owners, authors and writers. The street users are equally anonymous, except as general groupings such as drivers, service workers, shop customers and the like. Any street sign is only relevant to a proportion of those who encounter it.
- *The meaning of street signs depends on more than words.* Street signs are more than the actual linguistic expressions they contain: the size, colour and form of the letters in a fascia sign say more about a restaurant than its actual name; the materials of a sign's background and of its letters announce its pretensions; the shape of a traffic sign conveys vital aspects of its meaning; pictures and icons are integral to many signs. A street sign combines different aspects of meaning to carry out its function for the owner and the street user.
- *Street signs are concrete and visible.* Light from the sun, from street lights or from other sources is necessary to their functioning and is exploited in various ways, such as shadows and on/off light sequences. Some letters are themselves three-dimensional and stand out from the background; architectural signs are embedded in buildings or exist in the round.
- *Some street signs are individual.* While general and cross-media signs are uniform across situations, unique individual signs are created for particular locations. Since the invention of the printing press, individuality and uniqueness have not applied to most books and texts, reproduced in many identical clones. Street signs can be individual and idiosyncratic, whether intentionally or otherwise.
- *Street signs are legally regulated.* Street signs are controlled by regulations, both local and national. Some apply to particular types, like traffic signs and no smoking signs. Others apply to all signs, chiefly concerning size. Some are spinoffs of legislation that is not directly about signs, say the requirements for businesses to have registered addresses or for buildings to be numbered.
- *Street signs have particular relationships to time.* Signs can keep their meaning for as long as they are legible; signs from different historical periods exist side by side, some still conveying a meaning, others little more than decoration. This has few parallels in other forms of language, save perhaps for the fossilised history embedded in the English spelling system.
- *Street signs have a language system of their own,* in grammar, letter styles, etc. In particular, they differ from other varieties of English in their use of capital letters, centring, minimal punctuation and other aspects touched on in this book. Their

language differs from that of printed texts such as books and newspapers, to some seen as deviating from the 'standard' language, to others as existing independently in their own right.

– *Street signs are decorative.* Ordinary street signs are also decorative (Kinneir, 1980): the very look of signs contributes to the identity and visual appeal of the places involved. Some aim to look good in themselves, such as commemorative signs; others are integral to the structures in which they find themselves and thus add to their overall appearance, such as the incised street names of Bath (Bartram, 1978b). A few are primarily artistic creations, like graffiti and text art.

These characteristics emphasise that street signs use multiple types of meaning, some unavailable to other forms of writing or speech. The total meaning of the street sign comes from its text, its forms, its location and its materials.

The Street Sign and the City: Immigration, Gentrification and Rurification

The street sign has a unique relationship to the material and social reality of the urban street. The material side has been stressed throughout the chapters on naming, material and control. To recap, signs are part of the physical framework of towns and cities and are located at unique points in their space; they are essential to the functioning of the street.

Cities are prime centres for immigration and gentrification. Certain streets have provided bases for successive waves of immigrant traders, like the Walworth Road in London (Hall, 2012) or Mount Dennis in Toronto (Zukin *et al.*, 2016). Street signs in the 2010s documented the arrival of Poles in England, as they did previously the political, religious or economic refugees from Uganda and Cyprus of the 1950s or the Huguenots of Colchester's Dutch Quarter, centuries earlier. Effectively ever since the Roman invasion, many city streets in England have been a superdiversity of different cultures.

The languages of street signs are a fallible guide to who lives in an area; street signs do more than meet the needs of local residents or express their identity. Immigrant-run shops, for example, often cater at first for fellow immigrants from outside the area but later sell all-comers an exotic atmosphere and culture, like Indian sweetshops and Turkish restaurants. From the signs in Newcastle streets, you could deduce the existence of a large French community keen on shopping and dining, groups of Irish who spend their time in pubs, and some Latin-speaking zombies who congregate around war memorials and cemeteries.

The gentrification of the street has similarities across the world. The intention is to attract outside visitors to art galleries, boutiques and cafés, the ABC of Zukin *et al.* (2016). Art galleries do not, however, seem as important to gentrification in England as artisan bakers and gin distillers. Urban regeneration frequently means rendering an area suitable for a more affluent middle-class group, not so much improving the status of the people who are already there. The original inhabitants move or are compulsorily relocated out of town to new estates, as with East Enders in London after World War II (Willmott & Young, 1957). Chapter 7 showed how street signs accompany gentrification, for example how traditional shop exteriors contrast with gentrified shops. Expressing quality through serif roman capitals, modernity through lower case sans serif letters, or exoticness through other scripts is more pervasive than gentrification.

A new wave of gentrification, however, involves building towers for the super-rich in the inner centres of cities, like Toronto, New York and London (Graham, 2016); vertical living is again a sign of wealth, not poverty. Indeed a sign of super-richness in London in the 21st century is how many basements you can excavate beneath your house. Verticality effectively removes the social activities and pedestrian movements of the ground-level street to the interiors of buildings, along with the signs that accompany them.

The alternative tendency to gentrification can be called 'rurification', or greening. In early 20th century England this emerged as the garden city concept embodied in Letchworth with regulation of street signs, and continued to some extent in new towns such as Milton Keynes in the 1960s. Now rurification is seen more as greening the streets through trees, living walls and roofs, exemplified in Singapore and by groups such as Create Streets (Boys Smith, 2016; Iovene *et al.*, 2019), who campaign for walkable streets of medium density with frequent trees and green spaces, or by the creation of green urban pathways like the High Line in New York (Hynes, 2020). It will be interesting to see how green ideas affect future street signs, particularly in terms of materials, say the moss graffiti now being developed (Baley, 2020).

Street Signs Research

The study of writing starts from the description of the written symbols through which it communicates. Street signs research needs a solid descriptive infrastructure that includes all relevant aspects of the sign, paralleling the disciplines of phonetics and phonology in the spoken language.

Such a discipline needs to be based on an adequate vocabulary. In the absence of an agreed shared terminology, this book has filled in gaps with terms borrowed from other disciplines, for example the basic schema of street space in Chapter 1, important for any individual sign. But street signs research needs to make these terms its own. This book has, for instance, preferred the terms letter style over typeface, and letter over grapheme, but these may need more precision within street signs research.

Much of what has come up here is, indeed, relevant to all written language, not just street signs. The limitations of printed texts have blinkered our vision of written language, such as its purposes, material properties and indexicality; printed language is an unusually decontextualised and standardised form of writing. Onscreen written language will also reveal further depths unavailable if it is put in the straitjacket of printed text.

A study of street signs that is not assisted by typography, signwriting, psychology, architecture and other related areas is impoverished. A minimal account of any sign involves setting it in its regulatory context, describing the meaning of its layout and letter forms, and putting it and its users in their physical and social worlds. If nothing more, these disciplines can prevent unnecessary duplication of effort. There is no need, for example, to propose new ways of analysing letters or layout for street signs, when parallel schemes already exist in calligraphy, marketing or typography that could be built on by extending, correcting or refuting.

A theme running through this book has been the need to base accounts of street signs on empirical research. Reporting our own views on which letter style conveys most emotion or is most legible, what a sign means to a street user, etc., without empirical support, amounts to no more than one person's judgment. It may well be equivalent to the intuition of the native speaker employed in other areas of linguistics or to the judgment of the experienced expert but, as we have seen, experts and ordinary street users often disagree. Empirical evidence comes both from the actual sign, which needs to be presented and described as accurately and relevantly as possible, and from capturing the street sign user's perception and understanding of the signs through questionnaires, semantic differential tests, legibility tests, eye-tracking measures or whatever is appropriate.

The researchers' faith in their own judgments as native speakers has in effect coloured their analysis of signs. But reading and writing are taught, not acquired naturally like speech. Everybody carries on their backs the burden of how they have been taught. It was many years, for instance, before I realised that what English teachers called my 'defective' capital < $\mathcal{G}$ > was a German form I had acquired while living in Switzerland as a child. During this book, I have indeed ventured to express opinions, like all writers in this area, but these should be taken as unconfirmed except when supported by the signs themselves or the behaviour of street users. The rationale for displaying so many original street signs here is to allow readers to make their own judgments. This cannot, however, replace the street user's full experience of the location and indexicality of each sign. So open your door, walk down your street and see what the street signs now say to you.

References

ABBYY Flexicapture (2009) *A Guide to Creating Machine Readable Forms*. London: ABBYY. See https://www.abbyy.com/media/4673/abbyy-flexicapture-80-form-creation-guide.pdf.

Abercrombie, D. (1949) What is a letter? *Lingua* 2, 54–63.

Abousnnouga, G. and Machin, D. (2013) *The Language of War Memorials*. London: Bloomsbury.

Agarwal, A. (2012) Which fonts should you use for saving printer ink? *digital inspiration*, 29 January. See https://www.labnol.org/internet/fonts-for-saving-printer-ink/12603/.

Aichner, T., Forza, C. and Trentin, A. (2017) The country-of-origin lie: Impact of foreign branding on customers' willingness to buy and willingness to pay when the product's actual origin is disclosed. *International Review of Retail, Distribution and Consumer Research* 27 (1), 43–60.

Albrow, K.H. (1972) *The English Writing System: Notes towards a Description*. London: Longman for the Schools Council.

Amos, H.W. (2016) Chinatown by numbers: Defining an ethnic space by empirical linguistic landscape. *Linguistic Landscape* 2 (2), 127–156.

Apostrophe Protection Society, The (2020) See http://www.apostrophe.org.uk/page9.html.

Arditi, A. and Cho, J. (2007) Letter case and text legibility in normal and low vision. *Vision Research* 47 (19), 2499–2505.

Aristotle (4th century BCE) *De Interpretatione* 16a. Cited in Harris, R. (2000) *Rethinking Writing*. London: Athlone Press.

Augé, M. (1995) *Non-Places: Introduction to an Anthropology of Supermodernity* (J. Howe, trans.). London: Verso.

Backhaus, P. (2007) *Linguistic Landscapes: A Comparative Study of Urban Multilingualism in Tokyo*. Clevedon: Multilingual Matters.

Backhaus, P. (2013) The Japanese traffic light blues: Stop on red, go on what? *The Japan Times*, 25 February. See http://www.japantimes.co.jp/life/2013/02/25/language/the-japanese-traffic-light-blues-stop-on-red-go-on-what/#.WKgv5Tjm614.

Baines, P. and Dixon, C. (2002) *Signs: Lettering in the Environment*. London: Lawrence King.

Baird, J.A. and Taylor, C. (2016) Ancient graffiti. In J.I. Ross (ed.) *The Routledge Handbook of Graffiti and Street Art* (pp. 17–28). Abingdon: Routledge.

Baley, A. (2020) What is moss graffiti? How to make moss graffiti. *Gardening KnowHow*, 8 October. See https://www.gardeningknowhow.com/ornamental/foliage/moss/making-moss-graffiti.htm.

Banksy (2005) *Wall and Piece*. London: Century.

Barabantseva, E. (2016) Seeing beyond an 'ethnic enclave': The time/space of Manchester Chinatown. *Identities* 23 (1), 99–115. doi:10.1080/1070289X.2015.1016522.

Barthes, R. (1997) Semiology and the urban. In N. Leach (ed.) *Rethinking Architecture: A Reader in Cultural Theory* (pp. 166–172). London: Routledge.

Bartram, A. (1976) *Lettering on Architecture*. New York: Watson-Guptill.

Bartram, A. (1978a) *Fascia: Fascia Lettering in the British Isles*. London: Lund Humphries.

Bartram, A. (1978b) *Street: Street Name Lettering in the British Isles*. London: Lund Humphries.

Bartram, D. (1982) Perception of semantic quality in type: Difference between designers and non-designers. *Information Design Journal* 3 (1), 38–50.

Bayraktar, M., Say, B. and Akman, V. (1998) An analysis of English punctuation: The special case of the comma. *International Journal of Corpus Linguistics* 3 (1), 33–57.

BBC (2012) Waterstone's drops name apostrophe. *BBC News*, 12 January. See https://www.bbc.co.uk/news/entertainment-arts-16529653.

BBC (2017) Meet the 'grammar vigilante' of Bristol. *BBC News*, 3 April. See https://www.bbc.co.uk/news/av/uk-39459831/meet-the-grammar-vigilante-of-bristol.

Beech, D., Harrison, C. and Hill, W. (2009) *Art and Text*. London: Black Dog.

Beier, S. (2012) *Reading Letters: Designing for Legibility*. Amsterdam: BIS.

Ben-Rafael, E., Shohamy, E., Amara, M.H. and Trumper-Hecht, N. (2006) Linguistic landscape as symbolic construction of the public space: The case of Israel. In D. Gorter (ed.) *Linguistic Landscape: A New Approach to Multilingualism* (pp. 7–30). Clevedon: Multilingual Matters.

Bernard, M., Mills, M., Peterson, M. and Storrer, K. (2001) A comparison of popular online fonts: Which is best and when? *Usability News* 3 (2). See http://www.pasotti.org/tbook/download/Usability_News%20.pdf.

Binet, L. (2012) *HHhH*. London: Harvey Secker.

Blommaert, J. (2013) *Ethnography, Superdiversity and Linguistic Landscapes: Chronicles of Complexity*. Bristol: Multilingual Matters.

Bloomfield, L. (1926) A set of postulates for the science of language. *Language* 2, 153–164. Reprinted in Joos, M. (ed.) (1957) *Readings in Linguistics I*. Chicago, IL: University of Chicago Press.

Bloomfield, L. (1933) *Language*. New York: Holt.

Boys Smith, N. (2016) *Heart in the Right Street*. London: Create Streets.

Bringhurst, R. (2005) *The Elements of Typographic Style, Version 3.1*. Vancouver: Hartley & Marks.

Bristol Legible City (2019) See https://www.bristollegiblecity.info/portfolio-items/public-art-projects/.

Brooks, G. (2015) *Dictionary of the British English Spelling System*. Cambridge: Openbook.

Brown, F.C. (1921) *Letters and Lettering*. Boston, MA: Bates & Guild.

Brumberger, E.R. (2003) The rhetoric of typography: The persona of typeface and text. *Technical Communication* 50 (2), 205–223.

Carney, E. (1994) *A Survey of English Spelling*. London: Routledge.

Carter, S. (1995) *Twentieth Century Type Designers*. London: Lund Humphries.

Catich, E.M. (1968) *The Origin of the Serif: Brush Writing and Roman Letters*. Davenport, IA: Catfish Press.

Chadwick, P. (2018) Splashes of colour and a new Guardian masthead divide readers. *Guardian*, 6 May. See https://www.theguardian.com/commentisfree/ 2018/may/06/colour-guardian-masthead-opinion-tabloid-redesign.

Champion, M. (2015) *Medieval Graffiti*. London: Ebury Press.

Changizi, M. and Shimojo, S. (2005) Character complexity and redundancy in writing systems over human history. *Proceedings of the Royal Society B* 272, 267–275.

Chaucer, G. (1473) *The Canterbury Tales*. London: Caxton.

Christie's (2020) *Sold Lots*. See https://www.christies.com/lotfinder/paintings/christopher-wool-apocalypse-now-5739095-details.aspx?from=searchresults&intObjectID=5739095.

City of London (2021) *Street Naming and Numbering Advice Note*. https://www.cityoflondon.gov.uk/assets/Services-Environment/street-naming-and-numbering-advice-note-2021-feb.pdf.

City of London (2021) *Modern Architecture*. See https://www.cityoflondon.gov.uk/things-to-do/architecture/modern-architecture.

City of London (2021) *Our Role in London*. See https://www.cityoflondon.gov.uk/about-us/about-the-city-of-london-corporation/our-role-in-london.

City of Los Angeles (2014) *Complete Streets Design Guide*. See https://planning.lacity.org/documents/policy/CompleteStreetDesignGuide.pdf.

Clark, G. and Cummins, N. (2013) Surnames and social mobility: England 1230–2012. Economic History Working Paper No. 181. London: London School of Economics and Political Science.

Clayton, E. (2014) *The Golden Thread*. London: Aldine Books.

Coates, R. (2009) A strictly Millian approach to the definition of the proper name. *Mind & Language* 24, 433–444.

Companies (Trading Disclosures) Regulations, The (2008) See http://www.legislation.gov.uk/uksi/2008/495/contents/made.

Cook, V.J. (2004a) *The English Writing System*. London: Hodder.

Cook, V.J. (2004b) *Accomodating Brocolli in the Cemetary*. London: Profile. [Note: Slightly updated versions of much of this are available online at *English Spelling Topics*. See http://www.viviancook.uk/EnglishSpellingSystem.htm.]

Cook, V.J. (2010) Prolegomena to second language learning. In P. Seedhouse, S. Walsh and C. Jenks (eds) *Conceptualising Language Learning* (pp. 6–22). Basingstoke: Palgrave MacMillan.

Cook, V.J. (2013a) The language of the street. *Applied Linguistics Review* 4 (1), 43–81.

Cook, V.J. (2013b) Standard punctuation and the punctuation of the street. In M. Pawlak and L. Aronin (eds) *Essential Topics in Applied Linguistics and Multilingualism* (pp. 267–290). Cham: Springer International.

Cook, V.J. (2015) Meaning and material in the language of the street. *Social Semiotics* 25, 181–109.

Cook, V.J. (2016a) Background to the English writing system. In V.J. Cook and D. Ryan (eds) *The Routledge Handbook of the English Writing System* (pp. 5–24). Abingdon: Routledge.

Cook, V.J. (2016b) Premises of multi-competence. In V.J. Cook and W. Li (eds) *The Cambridge Handbook of Linguistic Multi-competence* (pp. 1–25). Cambridge: Cambridge University Press.

Cook, V.J. (2017) Handmade: Review of Elena Pagliarini *et al.*, 'Children's first handwriting productions show a rhythmic structure'. *Nature Scientific Reports* 7, 5516. doi:10.1038/s41598-017-05105-6. *Inference* 3 (3). See http://inference-review.com/article/handmade.

Cook, V.J. (2018) The signs of an English street. *English Today* 34 (3), 27–29.

Cook, V.J. (2020a) *The Greengrocer's Apostrophe*. See http://www.viviancook.uk/Punctuation/ApostGrocers.htm.

Cook, V.J. (2020b) *English Spelling Statistics*. See http://www.viviancook.uk/SpellStats/Index.html.

Cook, V.J. (forthcoming) Language in multi-competence and translanguaging. In J. MacSwan (ed.) *Language(s): Multilingualism and Its Consequences*. Bristol: Multilingual Matters.

Cook, V.J. (2021, unpublished) A thousand words are worth more than a picture.

Cook, V.J, Alenzi, O., Almutradi, F. and Alqadi, H. (in preparation) The interpretation of bilingual street signs using eye-tracking.

Coulmas, F. (2003) *Writing Systems*. Cambridge: Cambridge University Press.

Coupland, N. and Garrett, P. (2010) Linguistic landscapes, discursive frames and metacultural performance: The case of Welsh Patagonia. *International Journal of the Sociology of Language* 205, 7–36.

Criminal Damage Act (1971) See https://www.legislation.gov.uk/ukpga/1971/48/section/1.

Crosby, A. and Seale, K. (2018) On Carrington Road: Street numbers as metonyms of the urban. *Visual Communication* 17 (4), 433–450.

Dalton Maag (2020) *BBC Reith*. See https://www.daltonmaag.com/work/bbc-reith.

Dawson, P. (2013) *The Field Guide to Typography*. London: Thames & Hudson.

DCLG (2007) *Outdoor Advertisements and Signs: A Guide for Advertisers*. London: Department for Communities and Local Government. See http://www.communities.gov.uk/documents/planningand-building/pdf/326679.pdf.

Dehaene, S. (2009) *Reading in the Brain: The New Science of How We Read*. New York: Penguin.

Department for Education (2013) *National Curriculum in England: Primary Curriculum*. See https://www.gov.uk/government/publications/national-curriculum-in-england-primary-curriculum.

Department for Transport (2004) *Traffic Signs Manual*.[1] *Chapter 5: Traffic Signs*. London: The Stationery Office.

Department for Transport (2007) *UK Manual for Streets*. London: Thomas Telford.

Department for Transport (2013) *Traffic Signs Manual. Chapter 7: The Design of Traffic Signs* (4th edn). London: The Stationery Office.

Department for Transport (2015) *Consultation on the Draft Traffic Signs Regulations and General Directions 2015*. https://assets.publishing.service.gov.uk/government/uploads/system/uploads/attachment_data/file/371570/response.pdf.

Department for Transport (in preparation) *Traffic Signs Manual. Chapter 6: Illumination of Street Signs*. London: The Stationery Office.

Department of the Environment, Transport and the Regions (2007) *Guidance on the Use of Tactile Paving Surfaces*. See https://www.gov.uk/government/publications/guidance-on-the-use-of-tactile-paving-surfaces.

Department of Transport (1993) *Circular Roads 3/93*. See http://webarchive.nationalarchives.gov.uk/20100304070241/http://www.dft.gov.uk/pgr/roads/tpm/tal/circulars/ular393streetnameplatesa4055.pdf.

de Roover, R. (1946) The three golden balls of the pawnbrokers. *Bulletin of the Business Historical Society* 20 (4), 117–124.

de Saussure, F. (1976 [1916]) *Cours de Linguistique Générale*. Paris: Payot. (Critical edn: De Mauro, T. (1976).)

Development Management Procedure (England) Order 2010 (SI 2184) (2010) See http://www.legislation.gov.uk/uksi/2010/2184/made.

Dobson, T. and Dobson, S.C. (2017) Tip of the icon: Examining socially symbolic indexical signage. *Dialectic* 1 (1). See https://quod.lib.umich.edu/d/dialectic/14932326.0001.106/—tip-of-the-icon-examining-socially-symbolic-indexical?rgn=main;view=fulltext.

Doyle, J.R. and Bottomley, P.A. (2010) Norms for Osgood's affective meaning (evaluation, potency, activity): Ratings of logos, colors, products and services, names, and typefaces. See http://ssrn.com/abstract=1640198.

Dray, S. (2010) Ideological struggles on signage in Jamaica. In A. Jaworski and C. Thurlow (eds) *Semiotic Landscapes: Language, Image, Space* (pp. 102–122). London: Continuum.

Dyson, M.C. (2014) Applying psychological theory to typography: Is how we perceive letterforms special? In D. Machin (ed.) *Visual Communication* (pp. 215–242). Berlin: De Gruyter Mouton. See http://centaur.reading.ac.uk/38641/.

English Heritage (1999) *Graffiti on Historic Buildings and Monuments – Methods of Removal and Prevention*. See https://historicengland.org.uk/images-books/publications/graffiti-on-historic-buildings-and-monuments/.

Evetts, L.C. (1938) *Roman Lettering*. London: Pitman.

Farvacque-Vitkovic, C., Godin, L., Leroux, H., Verdet, F. and Chavez, R. (2005) *Street Addressing and the Management of Cities*. Washington, DC: World Bank.

Filika, R., Purdy, K., Gale, A. and Gerrett, D. (2004) Drug name confusion: Evaluating the effectiveness of capital ('Tall Man') letters using eye movement data. *Social Science & Medicine* 59, 2597–2601.

Finkel, R.J. (2015) *History of the Arrow*. New York: American Printing History Association. See https://printinghistory.org/arrow/.

Fiset, D., Blais, C., Ethier-Majcher, C., Arguin, M., Bub, D. and Gosselin, F. (2008) Features for identification of uppercase and lowercase letters. *Psychological Science* 19 (11), 1161–1168.

Frith, U. (1985) Beneath the surface of developmental dyslexia. In K.E. Patterson, J.C. Marshall and M. Coltheart (eds) *Surface Dyslexia* (pp. 301–330). Mahwah, NJ: Lawrence Erlbaum.

Fuller, G. (2002) The arrow – directional semiotics: Wayfinding in transit. *Social Semiotics* 12 (3), 231–244.

Gaiser, L. and Matras, Y. (2016) *The Spatial Construction of Civic Identities: A Study of Manchester's Linguistic Landscapes*. Manchester: University of Manchester.

Garrioch, D. (1994) House names, shop signs and social organisation in Western European cities. *Urban History* 21 (1), 20–48.

Geoplace (2021) Bringing location to life. See https://www.geoplace.co.uk/.

Giles, H. (1970) Evaluative reactions to accents. *Educational Review* 22, 211–227.

Gill, E. (1931) *An Essay on Typography*. London: Lund Humphries.

Goffman, E. (1963) *Behavior in Public Spaces*. New York: Free Press.

Gombrich, E.H. (1999) Pictorial instructions. In E.H. Gombrich, *The Uses of Images* (pp. 226–239). London: Phaidon.

Gorter, D. (2019) Methods and techniques for linguistic landscape research: About definitions, core issues and technological innovations. In M. Pütz and N. Mundt (eds) *Expanding the Linguistic Landscape: Linguistic Diversity, Multimodality and the Use of Space as a Semiotic Resource* (pp. 38–57). Bristol: Multilingual Matters.

Graham, S. (2016) *Vertical: The City from Satellites to Bunkers.* London: Vortex.

Gray, N. (1960) *Lettering on Buildings.* London: Architectural Press.

Gregory, R. (2020) *Signwriter.* See https://www.signpainting.co.uk/books/.

Gunraj, D.N., Drumm-Hewitt, A.M., Dashow, E.M., Upadhyay, S.S.N. and Klin, C.M. (2016) Texting insincerely: The role of the period in text messaging. *Computers in Human Behaviour* 55B, 67–107.

Gurrey, C. (2009) Towards the verbal-visual object: Looking for progress in inscriptional lettering. *Sculpture Journal* 18 (2), 89–99.

Hall, S.M. (2012) *City, Street and Citizen: The Measure of the Ordinary.* London: Routledge.

Hall, S.M. (2015) Super-diverse street: A 'trans-ethnography' across migrant localities. *Ethnic and Racial Studies* 8 (1), 22–37.

Halliday, M.A.K. (1967) *Grammar, Society and the Noun: An Inaugural Lecture.* London: University College.

Halliday, M.A.K. and Mattheisen, C. (2013) *An Introduction to Functional Grammar.* London: Hodder.

Haslam, A. (2011) *Lettering: A Reference Manual of Techniques.* London: Lawrence King.

Hatziprokopiou, P. and Montagna, N. (2012) Contested Chinatown: Chinese migrants' incorporation and the urban space in London and Milan. *Ethnicities* 12 (6), 706. doi:10.1177/1468796811434909.

Heal, A. (1957) *Sign Boards of Old London Shops.* London: Portman Books.

Heritage England (2019) *Leazes Conservation Zone.* See https://historicengland.org.uk/listing/the-list/list-entry/1024832.

Highway Code (1999) *The Highway Code.* London: Stationery Office.

Hill, W. (2010) *The Complete Typographer.* London: Thames & Hudson.

HM Land Registry (2020) See https://www.gov.uk/government/organisations/land-registry.

Howet, G. (1983) *Size of Letters Required for Visibility as a Function of Viewing Distance and Observer Visual Acuity.* Technical Note 1180. Washington, DC: National Bureau of Standards.

Hyndman, K. (2016) *Why Fonts Matter.* London: Virgin Books.

Hynes, S.K. (2020) *The Story behind the High Line.* New York: Center for Active Design. See https://centerforactivedesign.org/highlinehistory.

Iovene, M., Boys Smith, N. and Illushka Seresinhe, C. (2019) *Of Streets and Squares: Which Public Places do People Want to Be in and Why?* London: Create Streets.

Jack, A. (2009) *The Old Dog and Duck: The Secret Meanings of Pub Names.* London: Penguin.

Jackson, D. (1981) *The Story of Writing.* London: Studio Vista.

Jackson, D. (2002–2011) *The Saint John's Bible.* See http://www.saintjohnsbible.org/. (Reproduced 2012.)

Jacobs, J. (1961) *The Death and Life of Great American Cities.* New York: Random House.

Jamson, S.L., Tate, F.N. and Jamson, A.H. (2005) Evaluating the effects of bilingual traffic signs on driver performance and safety. *Ergonomics* 48 (15), 1734–1748.

JCDecaux (2019) *The Morris Column: An Historical and Mythical Advertising Support.* See https://www.jcdecaux.com/blog/morris-column-historical-and-mythical-advertising-support.

Jenkins, S. (1975) *Landlords to London.* London: Constable.

Johnston, E. (1906) *Writing and Illuminating and Lettering.* London: Pitman.

Joos, M. (ed.) (1957) *Readings in Linguistics I.* Chicago, IL: University of Chicago Press.

Kallen, J.L. (2010) Changing landscapes: Language, space, and policy in the Dublin linguistics landscape. In A. Jaworski and C. Thurlow (eds) *Semiotic Landscapes: Language, Image, Space* (pp. 41–58). London: Continuum.

Kastl, A.J. and Child, I.L. (1968) Emotional meanings of four typographical varieties. *Journal of Applied Psychology* 52 (6), 440–446.

Kerswill, P. (1994) *Dialects Converging: Rural Speech in Urban Norway.* Oxford: Oxford University Press.

Kindersley, D. and Cardozo, L.L. (1990) *Letters Slate Cut.* Cambridge: Cardozo-Kindersley Editions.

Kinneir, J. (1980) *Words and Buildings*. London: Architectural Press.

Koopman, A. (2016) Names of dwellings. In C. Hough (ed.) *The Oxford Handbook of Names and Naming* (pp. 636–644). Oxford: Oxford University Press.

Kotkin, J. (2016) *The Human City: Urbanisation for the Rest of Us*. Chicago, IL: Agate.

Kramer, R. (2016) Straight from the underground: New York City's legal graffiti writing culture. In J.I. Ross (ed.) *The Routledge Handbook of Graffiti and Street Art* (pp. 113–123). Abingdon: Routledge.

Kress, G. and van Leeuwen, T. (1996) *Reading Images: The Grammar of Visual Design*. London: Routledge.

Labov, W. (1966) *The Social Stratification of English in New York City*. Washington, DC: Center for Applied Linguistics.

Lamarre, P. (2014) Bilingual winks and bilingual wordplay in Montreal's linguistic landscape. *International Journal of the Sociology of Language* 228, 131–151.

Landry, R. and Bourhis, R.Y. (1997) Linguistic landscape and ethnolinguistic vitality: An empirical study. *Journal of Language and Social Psychology* 16, 23–49.

Larwood, J. and Hotten, J.C. (1866) *The History of Signboards*. London: Hotten.

Leech, G.N. (1966) *English in Advertising*. London: Longman.

Leeman, J. and Modan, G. (2009) Commodified language in Chinatown: Contextualized approach to linguistic landscape. *Journal of Sociolinguistics* 13 (3), 332–362.

Levinson, S.C. (1996) Relativity in spatial conception and description. In J.J. Gumperz and S.C. Levinson (eds) *Rethinking Linguistic Relativity* (pp. 177–202). Cambridge: Cambridge University Press.

Levy, D.M. (2001) *Scrolling Forward: Making Sense of Documents in the Digital Age*. New York: Arcade.

Lewery, A.J. (1989) *Signwritten Art*. Newton Abbot: David & Charles.

Lou, J.J. (2016) *The Linguistic Landscape of Chinatown: A Sociolinguistic Ethnography*. Bristol: Multilingual Matters.

Lupton, E. (2004) *Thinking with Type: A Critical Guide for Designers, Writers, Editors & Students*. Princeton, NJ: Princeton Architectural Press.

Lynch, K. (1960) *The Image of the City*. Cambridge, MA: MIT Press.

Mackey, W.F. (1972), The description of bilingualism. In J.A. Fishman (ed.) *Readings in the Sociology of Language* (pp. 554–584). The Hague: Mouton.

Magnini, V.P., Miller, T. and Kim, B.-C. (2011) The psychological effects of foreign-language restaurant signs on potential diners. *Journal of Hospitality and Tourism Research* 35, 24–44.

Malinowski, D., *et al.* (2013) What's in a name? Reading Berkeley's bilingual signs. *Berkeleyside*, 17 April. See https://www.berkeleyside.com/2013/04/17/whats-in-a-name-reading-berkeleys-bilingual-signs.

Marquis, D. (1927) *Archy and Mehitabel*. New York: Doubleday.

Mask, D. (2020) *The Address Book*. London: Profile.

McCaskill, M.K. (1998) *Grammar, Punctuation, and Capitalization: A Handbook for Technical Writers and Editors*. SP-7084. Hampton, VA: NASA. See https://www.rose-hulman.edu/class/ee/HTML/ECE340/PDFs/grammar_NASA.pdf.

McPharlin, P. (1942) *Roman Numerals, Typographic Leaves and Pointing Hands. Some Notes on their Origin, History and Contemporary Use*. See https://babel.hathitrust.org/cgi/pt?id=uc1.b4200870;view=1up;seq=14.

Meletis, D. (2019) The grapheme as a universal basic unit of writing. *Writing Systems Research* 11 (1), 26–49.

Mieville, C. (2009) *The City & the City*. London: Macmillan.

Miles, J. (2001) *Owl's Hoot: How People Name their Houses*. London: John Murray.

Ministry of Transport Roads Dept. Mem. No. 297 (1929).

Morning Advertiser (2017) The Morning Advertiser's top 50 most popular pub names. *The Morning Advertiser*, 23 October. See https://www.morningadvertiser.co.uk/Article/2017/10/23/Most-popular-pub-names-in-the-UK-2017.

Mosley, J. (2007) The Nymph and the Grot, an update. *Typefoundry*, 6 January. See http://typefoundry.blogspot.co.uk/search?q=nymph+and+grot.

Moss, K., with and Morris, D. (1993) *Pubwatching*. Stroud: Allen Sutton.

Multilingual Typesetting (2016) See http://multilingualtypesetting.co.uk/blog/chinese-typesetting/.

Nedeljković, U., Novaković, D. and Pinćjer, I. (2017) Detecting universal structure and effects of typefaces. *Tehnički vjesnik* 24 (2), 557–564.

Nesbitt, A. (1957) *The History and Technique of Lettering*. Meneola, NY: Dover.

Newcastle City Council (2000) *Leazes Conservation Area Character Statement*. See http://www.newcastle.gov.uk/wwwfileroot/legacy/regen/plantrans/conservation/Leazes_CA_CS.pdf.

Newcastle City Council (2021) *Statistics and Intelligence*. See https://www.newcastle.gov.uk/our-city/statistics-and-intelligence.

Noon, J. (1995) *Pollen*. Manchester: Ringpull.

Norman, D. (2002) *The Design of Everyday Things*. New York: Basic Books.

Nunberg, G. (1990) *Linguistics of Punctuation*. Stanford, CA: Centre for the Study of Language and Information.

NY Design (2013) *Street Design Manual*. New York: Department of Transportation. See https://www1.nyc.gov/html/dot/html/pedestrians/streetdesignmanual.shtml#download.

Nyström, S. (2016) Names and meaning. In C. Hough (ed.) *The Oxford Handbook of Names and Naming* (pp. 39–51). Oxford: Oxford University Press.

OED (2015) *Oxford English Dictionary Online*. Oxford: Oxford University Press. See www.oed.com.

Ogilvy, D. (1983) *Ogilvy on Advertising*. London: Pan Books.

Osgood, C.E., Suci, G.J. and Tannenbaum, P.H. (1957) *The Measurement of Meaning*. Urbana, IL: University of Illinois Press.

O'Toole, M. (1994) *The Language of Displayed Art*. London: Routledge.

Pagliarini, E., Scocchia, L., Vernice, M., Zoppello, M., Balottin, U., Bouamama, S., Guasti, M.T. and Stucchi, N. (2017) Children's first handwriting productions show a rhythmic structure. *Nature Scientific Reports* 7, 5516. doi:10.1038/s41598-017-05105-6.

Parkes, M.B. (1992) *Pause and Effect: An Introduction to the History of Punctuation in the West*. Aldershot: Scholar Press.

Partridge, E. (1961) *A Dictionary of Slang and Unconventional English*. London: Routledge.

Patrick, P. (2001) The speech community. In J.K. Chambers, P. Trudgill and N. Schilling-Estes (eds) *Handbook of Language Variation and Change* (pp. 573–602). Oxford: Blackwell.

Pearce, M. (2017) The linguistic landscape of North East England. In S. Hancil and J.C. Beal (eds) *Perspectives on Northern Englishes* (pp. 61–81). Berlin: Mouton De Gruyter.

Pearlman, A. (2018) *Restaurant Menus and the Art of Persuasion*. Chicago, IL: Agate.

Peirce, C.S. (1906) Prolegomena to an apology for pragmaticism. *The Monist* XVI (4), 492–546.

Pennycook, A. (2009) Linguistic landscapes and the transgressive semiotics of graffiti. In E. Shohamy and D. Gorter (eds) *Linguistic Landscapes: Expanding the Scenery* (pp. 302–311). Abingdon: Routledge.

Perfetti, C.A. (1999) Comprehending written language: A blueprint of the reader. In C. Brown and P. Hagoort (eds) *The Neurocognition of Language* (pp. 167–210). Oxford: Oxford University Press.

Petrucci, A. (1993) *Public Lettering: Script, Power and Culture*. Chicago, IL: University of Chicago Press.

PMG (2015) *The Ogilvy Formula: What Does it Mean for Print Advertising?* See http://www.pmg-pm.co.uk/2015/10/the-ogilvy-formula-what-does-it-mean-for-print-advertising/.

Poole, A. (2008) Which are more legible: Serif or sans serif typefaces? See http://alexpoole.info/blog/which-are-more-legible-serif-or-sans-serif-typefaces/.

Pound, L. (1926) The Kraze for K. *American Speech* 1 (1), 43–44.

Primus, B. (2004) A featural analysis of the modern Roman alphabet. *Written Language & Literacy* 7 (2), 235–274.

Public Health Act 1925 S.17–19 (1925) See http://www.legislation.gov.uk/ukpga/Geo5/15-16/71.

Pütz, M. and Mundt, N. (eds) (2019) *Expanding the Linguistic Landscape: Linguistic Diversity, Multimodality and the Use of Space as a Semiotic Resource*. Bristol: Multilingual Matters.

Qiu, Q., Watanabe, S. and Omura, K. (2018) Affective font selection: The hybrid of Japanese and Latin typefaces. *International Journal of Affective Engineering* 17 (2), 89–98.

Quinlan, M. (2005) *British War Memorials*. Hertford: Authors Online.

Raos, V. (2018) Bilingual street signs policy in EU member states: A comparison. *Journal of Multilingual and Multicultural Development* 39 (10), 895–911.

Rath, J., Bodaar, A., Wagemaakers, T. and Wu, P.Y. (2018) Chinatown 2.0: The difficult flowering of an ethnically themed shopping area. *Journal of Ethnic and Migration Studies* 44 (1), 81–98.

Reh, M. (2004) Multilingual writing: A reader-oriented typology – with examples from Lira Municipality (Uganda). *International Journal of the Sociology of Language* 170, 1–41.

Rhys-Taylor, A. (2013) The essences of multi-culture: A sensory exploration of an inner-city street market. *Identities* 20 (4), 393–406.

RNIB (2019) *The Little Known Language of our Pavements.* See https://www.rnib.org.uk/rnibconnect/welfare-and-money/tom-scott-tactile-paving.

Roberts, J. (2005) *Guide to Scripts Used in English Writing up to 1500.* London: British Library.

Room, A. (1992) *The Street Names of England.* Stamford: Paul Watkins.

Rose-Redwood, R.S. (2008) Indexing the great ledger of the community: Urban house numbering, city directories, and the production of spatial legibility. *Journal of Historical Geography* 34, 286–310.

Ross, J.I. (ed.) (2016) *The Routledge Handbook of Graffiti and Street Art.* Abingdon: Routledge.

Royal Mail Guidelines (2019) *User Guide: Machine Readable Letters & Large Letters.* London. Royal Mail. See https://www.royalmailtechnical.com/rmt_docs/User_Guides_2019/Machine_Readable_Letters_and_Large_Letters_20190827.pdf.

Ryan, D. (2016) Modern theories of English spelling. In V.J. Cook and D. Ryan (eds) *The Routledge Handbook of the English Writing System* (pp. 41–64). Abingdon: Routledge.

Saenger, P. (1997) *Space between Words.* Stanford, CA: Stanford University Press.

Sanocki, T. (1992) Effect of font and letter-specific experience on the perceptual processing of letters. *American Journal of Psychology* 105 (3), 435–458.

Schmitt, H. (2018) *Language in the Public Space: An Introduction to the Linguistic Landscape.* ISBN 978-1-9829-2542-0.

Scholfield, P. (2016) Modernization and standardization since the sixteenth century. In V.J. Cook and D. Ryan (eds) *The Routledge Handbook of the English Writing System* (pp. 143–162). Abingdon: Routledge.

Scollon, R. and Scollon, S. (2003) *Discourses in Place: Language in the Material World.* Abingdon: Routledge.

Screti, F. (2015) The ideological appropriation of the letter <k> in the Spanish linguistic landscape. *Social Semiotics* 25, 200–208.

Seargeant, P. (2012) Between script and language: The ambiguous ascription of 'English' in the linguistic landscape. In C. Hélot, M. Barni, R. Janssens and C. Bagna (eds) Linguistic Landscapes, Multilingualism and Social Change (pp. 187–200). Frankfurt: Peter Lang.

Sebba, M. (2010) Discourses in transit. In A. Jaworski and C. Thurlow (eds) *Semiotic Landscapes: Language, Image, Space* (pp. 59–76). London: Continuum.

Seidenberg, M.S. (1992) Beyond orthographic depth in reading: Equitable division of labour. In R. Frost and L. Katz (eds) *Orthography, Phonology, Morphology and Meaning* (pp. 85–118). Amsterdam: Elsevier.

Shaikh, A.D., Chaparro, B.S. and Fox, D. (2006) Perception of fonts: Perceived personality traits and uses. *Usability News* 8 (1). See doi:10.1142/9789814759540_0013.

Sheedy, J.E., Subbaram, M.V., Zimmerman, A.B. and Hayes, J.R. (2005) Legibility and the letter superiority effect. *Human Factors: The Journal of the Human Factors and Ergonomics Society* 47 (4), 797–815.

Sherman, W.H. (2005) Toward a history of the manicule. FOR/2005/04/001. See http://www.livesandletters.ac.uk/.

Signs.com (2017) Signage 10.1. *Signs.com*, 14 September. See https://www.signs.com/blog/aqueous-coatings-signage-101/.

Simmel, G. (1997) In D. Fisby and M. Featherstone (eds) *Simmel on Culture.* London: Sage.

Smeijers, F. (2011) *Counterpunch: Making Type in the Sixteenth Century, Designing Typefaces Now* (2nd edn). London: Hyphen Press.

Smoke-free (Premises and Enforcement) Regulations, The (2006) See http://www.legislation.gov.uk/uksi/2006/3368/contents/made.

Soukup, B. (2020) Survey area selection in Variationist Linguistic Landscape Study (VaLLS): A report from Vienna, Austria. *Linguistic Landscape* 6 (1), 52–79.

Spolsky, B. (2009) Prolegomena to a sociolinguistic theory of public signage. In E. Shohamy and D. Gorter (eds) *Linguistic Landscapes: Expanding the Scenery* (pp. 25–39). Abingdon: Routledge.

Stinson, L. (2016) The overlooked beauty of London's manhole covers. *Wired*, 23 March. See https://www.wired.com/2016/03/overlooked-beauty-londons-manhole-covers/.

Streetwise (2013) *Wayfinding – What's Out There? A Survey of 186 Cities and Towns*. Edinburgh: Streetwise. See http://www.streetwisesystems.com/WayfindingReport.pdf.

Stroud, C. and Mpendukana, S. (2009) Towards a material ethnography of linguistic landscape: Multilingualism, mobility, and space in a South African township. *Journal of Sociolinguistics* 13, 363–386.

Sutherland, P. (2015) Writing system mimicry in the linguistic landscape. *SOAS Working Papers in Linguistics* 17, 147–167.

Tannenbaum, P.H., Jacobson, H.K. and Norris, E.L. (1964) An experimental investigation of typeface connotations. *Journalism Quarterly* 41, 65–73.

Tantner, A. (2015) *House Numbers*. London: Reaktion Books.

Tavassoli, N.T. and Han, J.K. (2002) Auditory and visual brand identifiers in Chinese and English. *Journal of International Marketing* 10 (2), 13–29.

Thangaraj, J. (2004) Fascinating fonts: Is the power of typography a marketing myth? *Prism* 2. See https://www.prismjournal.org/uploads/1/2/5/6/125661607/v2-no1-c3.pdf.

Tinker, M. (1963) *Legibility of Print*. Ames, IA: Iowa State University Press.

Todd, L. (1995) *The Cassell Guide to Punctuation*. London: Cassell.

Tonkiss, F. (2005) *Space, the City and Social Theory*. Cambridge: Polity Press.

Towns Improvement Clauses Act (1847) See https://www.legislation.gov.uk/ukpga/Vict/10-11/34.

Traffic Signs Regulations and General Directions (2016) See http://legislation.data.gov.uk/uksi/2002/3113/made/data.htm?wrap=true.

Trask, R.L. (1997) *The Penguin Guide to Punctuation*. Harmondsworth: Penguin.

Treiman, R. and Kessler, B. (2014) *How Children Learn to Write Words*. Oxford: Oxford University Press.

Trinch, S. and Snajdr, E. (2017) What the signs say: Gentrification and the disappearance of capitalism without distinction in Brooklyn. *Journal of Sociolinguistics* 21 (1), 64–89.

Truss, L. (2004) *Eats Shoots and Leaves*. London: Profile.

Tschichold, J. (1998 [1928]) *The New Typography* (R. McLean, trans.). Berkeley, CA: University of California Press.

Tuan, Y.-F. (1991) Language and the making of place: A narrative-descriptive approach. *Annals of the Association of American Geographers* 81 (4), 684–696.

Turner, S.V. (2015) The poetics of permanence? Inscriptions, memory and memorials of the First World War in Britain. *Sculpture Journal* 24 (1), 73–96.

Tversky, B., Kugelmass, S. and Winter, A. (1991) Cross-cultural and developmental trends in graphic productions. *Cognitive Psychology* 23, 515–557.

Uebele, A. (2007) *Signage Systems & Information Graphics*. London: Thames & Hudson.

Unwin, S. (2009) *Analysing Architecture*. Abingdon: Routledge.

Vachek, J. (1973) *Written Language: General Problems and Problems of English*. The Hague: Mouton.

Van Leeuwen, T. (2006) Towards a semiotics of typography. *Information Design Journal* 14 (2), 139–155.

Velasco, C., Hyndman, S. and Spence, C. (2018) The role of typeface curvilinearity on taste experience and perception. *International Journal of Gastronomy and Food Science* 11, 63–74.

Venezky, R.L. (1970) *The Structure of English Orthography*. The Hague: Mouton.

Venturi, R., Brown, D.S. and Izenour, S. (1977) *Learning from Las Vegas* (revised edn). Cambridge, MA: MIT Press.

Vienna Convention on Road Signs and Signals (1968) Paris: UNESCO. See http://www.unece.org/fileadmin/DAM/trans/conventn/signalse.pdf.

Vink (2015) *Lighting for Signs and Display*. Bilston: Vink Lighting Solutions. See https://www.vinklighting.com/.

Waclawek, A. (2011) *Graffiti and Street Art*. London: Thames & Hudson.

Walker, P. (2008) Font tuning: A review and new experimental evidence. *Visual Cognition* 16 (8), 1022–1058.

Walker, S. (2001) *Typography in Everyday Life*. Harlow: Longman.

Waller, R.H.W. (1990) Typography and discourse. In R. Barr, M.L. Kamil, P.B. Mosenthal and P.D. Pearson (eds) *Handbook of Reading Research, Vol II* (pp. 341–380). New York: Longman.

Wallop, H. (2016) If it had a lovely, posh name, it might have been different: Do street names matter? *The Guardian*. See https://www.theguardian.com/society/2016/oct/22/street-names-matter-property-values.

Warde, B. (1932) 'The Crystal Goblet'. (Originally published as by P. Beaujon.) See https://veryinteractive.net/content/2-library/52-the-crystal-goblet/warde-thecrystalgoblet.pdf.

War Memorials Register (2020) *Capt. E.B. Eagar*. See https://www.iwm.org.uk/memorials/item/memorial/34429.

WHO (World Health Organisation) (2016) *Tobacco Packaging and Labelling*. See https://apps.who.int/iris/bitstream/handle/10665/204198/Fact_Sheet_TFI_2014_EN_15309.pdf?sequence=1&isAllowed=y.

Willmott, M. and Young, P. (1957) *Family and Kinship in East London*. London: Routledge.

Worboys Report (1963) *Traffic Signs for All-purpose Roads, Implemented as Traffic Signs Regulations and General Directions* (TSRGD).

Wrights of Lymm (2020) *Decorating*. See https://www.stonehouses.co.uk/specialist-decorating.html.

Yang, S.S. (2012) Eye movements on restaurant menus: A revisitation on gaze motion and consumer scanpaths. *International Journal of Hospitality Management* 31 (3), 1021–1029.

Yule, V. and Yasuko, I. (2016) Spelling reform. In V.J. Cook and D. Ryan (eds) *The Routledge Handbook of the English Writing System* (pp. 413–428). Abingdon: Routledge.

Zandvoort, R.W. (1957) *A Handbook of English Grammar*. London: Longman.

Ziegler, E., Schmitz, U. and Uslucan, H.H. (2019) Attitudes towards visual multilingualism in the linguistic landscape of the Ruhr. In M. Pütz and N. Mundt (eds) *Expanding the Linguistic Landscape: Linguistic Diversity, Multimodality and the Use of Space as a Semiotic Resource* (pp. 264–299). Bristol: Multilingual Matters.

Ziminski, A. (2020) *The Stone Mason: A History of Building Britain*. London: John Murray.

Zukin, S., Kasintz, P. and Chen, X. (2016) *Global Cities, Local Streets*. London: Routledge.

Note

(1) This publication consists of 'chapters' that appeared in different years, with one still in preparation.

Index

For Product Safety Concerns and Information please contact our EU Authorised
Representative:

Easy Access System Europe

Mustamäe tee 50

10621 Tallinn

Estonia

gpsr.requests@easproject.com

www.ingramcontent.com/pod-product-compliance
Lightning Source LLC
Chambersburg PA
CBHW081434270326
41932CB00019B/3200